ACCESS FOR ALL
Building Inclusive Financial Systems

CGAP

CONSULTATIVE GROUP TO ASSIST THE POOR

BRIGIT HELMS

CAPTURING 10 YEARS OF CGAP EXPERIENCE

ISBN	0-8213-6360-3
ISBN-13	978-0-8213-6360-7
e-ISBN	0-8213-6361-1
e-ISBN-13	978-0-8213-6361-4
DOI	10.1596/978-0-8213-6360-7

Library of Congress Cataloging-in-Publication Data

Helms, Brigit.
  Access for all: building inclusive financial systems / Brigit Helms
      p. cm.
   Includes bibliographical references and index.
   ISBN-13: 978-0-8213-6360-7
   ISBN-10: 0-8213-6360-3
   1.Microfinance–Developing countries. 2. Credit–Developing countries. 3. Financial–institutions–Developing countries. 4. Financial services industry–Developing countries. 5. Poor–Developing countries. 6. Microfinance–Government policy–Developing countries.
   I. Title

   HG178 33.D44H45 2006
   332.109172'4–dc22

                                                                        2005057738

Contents

Foreword   v

Acknowledgments   vii

The Consultative Group to Assist the Poor   ix

Key Principles of Microfinance   xi

Chapter 1. Introduction   1

Chapter 2. Poor and Low-Income Clients   17

Chapter 3. Financial Service Providers: The Micro Level   35

Chapter 4. Financial Infrastructure: The Meso Level   59

Chapter 5. Governments: The Macro Level   75

Chapter 6. Funders   93

Chapter 7. Cross-Cutting Challenges   113

Chapter 8. Conclusion   139

Afterword   145

Recommended Reading and Web Sites   147

References   151

Index   163

Foreword

Access for All is more than a slogan. For 10 years, the world's largest aid agencies have worked together under the banner of the Consultative Group to Assist the Poor (CGAP), committing people, money, and countless hours to building more inclusive financial systems—systems that work for the poor.

The efforts of this consortium and its many partners—networks, funders, microfinance institutions—are unprecedented. Through publications, training, and advocacy, the CGAP family has helped build near-universal consensus around the fundamentals of an inclusive financial system: from regulation and supervision at the policy level, to financial reporting and disclosure at the institutional level, to fairly priced products at the client level.

Together we have built this consensus around solid research, practical operational tools, and a persistent public information effort. All have contributed to the *professionalization* of microfinance, once considered a marginal, even charitable, activity by financiers. In the process, we have helped push microfinance beyond the conference rooms of aid agencies, to the boardrooms of commercial bankers and policymakers.

The CGAP Key Principles of Microfinance—which call for, among other things, more enlightened policies from donor countries—have been endorsed and championed by the Group of Eight industrial nations as well as governments throughout the developing world. Queen Rania of Jordan has made them the foundation of her work as chairperson of CGAP's microfinance initiative for the Arab world.

Worldwide, "best practice" microfinance is becoming standard practice. Almost 600 microfinance institutions now report to the Microfinance Information eXchange (MIX), the CGAP-created portal that has become "the Bloomberg of microfinance" to give a no-nonsense picture of transparency, sustainability, and growth in the microfinance sector. Indeed, mainstream rating agencies themselves are now including microfinance institutions in their reviews.

In the area of aid effectiveness, CGAP members have consented to peer reviews and made unprecedented efforts and difficult decisions to improve their support of financial-sector development: pooling funds to ensure best practice, agreeing on common reporting formats, and building and applying consensus on best practice at both the headquarters and field level.

The picture so far is breathtaking. Where small, heavily subsidized microcredit schemes used to be the norm, hundreds of profitable microfinance providers of all institutional shapes and forms are now offering a wide range of financial services—money transfers, deposit services, and insurance—to ever-larger numbers of poor people in their communities. In a sure sign that microfinance is going mainstream, domestic and international commercial banks are now entering the fray, motivated by the excellent performance of poor clients and the promise of new information and delivery technologies to reduce cost and risk.

Examples abound. In Kenya, Equity Bank is opening 18,000 accounts of poor people each month. K-Rep bank, which began as a small nongovernmental organization, is today a fully converted commercial bank—among the fastest growing in the country. India's ICICI Bank, through partnerships with microfinance institutions and nongovernmental organizations, has added 1.2 million microfinance clients in the past three years. In Mexico, Compartamos has grown from a donor-supported institution to a licensed financial institution serving more than 400,000 clients and regularly tapping the local bond markets.

Strong institutions follow from sound practices, solid standards, and committed leaders. But that is not the whole picture. In the foreground are as many as 3 billion people who still lack access to basic financial services, from loans to finance a microenterprise or a medical emergency, to safe places to save, to reliable ways to transfer money within and across borders.

As we mark a decade of service to the microfinance industry, we at CGAP remain steadfast in our commitment to dramatically expand access to financial services. That is the theme of this book, which draws on and captures 10 years of experience shared by CGAP staff and their partners. In this text, you will find the reasons why this expansion is important, the challenges to making it happen, and the many hopeful signs that it is possible, and even within reach.

Much more than a compendium of CGAP's learning and experiences over the past decade, *Access for All* opens a new chapter in our ongoing work. We invite you to join us.

Elizabeth Littlefield
Chief Executive Officer and Director
Consultative Group to Assist the Poor

Acknowledgments

This book reflects the collective experience of CGAP, an organization that works to ensure poor people have access to financial services that can help improve their lives. The ideas captured here emerged from CGAP in the course of the past decade, but they also reflect an ongoing discussion in the wider microfinance community.

CGAP's work and its place in building inclusive financial systems are made possible by the cumulative work and commitment of our 31 member donors. Their support has lent CGAP the opportunity to learn and pass on that learning to the broader community. Many of the ideas and examples in *Access for All* are also drawn from their experience. Several of them also helped by reviewing this book, in particular Kate McKee of the U.S. Agency for International Development, Nimal Fernando of the Asian Development Bank, and Frank deGiovanni of the Ford Foundation, who deserves my thanks for reviewing the whole book over his summer vacation.

Access for All draws on the original research and thinking of some remarkable individuals at CGAP. I would like to thank Elizabeth Littlefield, Bob Christen, Syed Hashemi, Martin Holtmann, Jennifer Isern, Alexia Latortue, Tim Lyman, Xavier Reille, Rich Rosenberg, and Ousa Sananikone. In writing this book my special thanks are due to the unflagging research and support of Jasmina Glisovic-Mezieres and Hannah Siedek. Their tireless curiosity was critical to this effort.

A host of other experts gave generously of their time to review *Access for All.* My thanks to Monique Cohen, Kathryn Imboden, David Porteous, Stuart Rutherford, Beth Rhyne, Alex Silva, and Graham Wright for their expert advice on individual chapters. In addition, I would like to thank Jeanette Thomas and Maggie Duggan for their comments, and my family for putting up with me throughout.

While I take full responsibility for any errors, omissions, and distortions, this book really is the work of all the CGAP staff. These past nearly 10 years at CGAP have been the most rewarding of my professional life, thanks to them.

The Consultative Group to Assist the Poor

M ore than 3 billion poor people seek access to basic financial services essential to managing their precarious lives. At CGAP, we work in developing countries to build financial systems that are inclusive, systems that serve the entire population and not just a tiny minority. Why? Because we have seen the cascading power of microfinance. We have seen how access to loans and deposit services has empowered millions of people to work their way out of poverty.

For many of the world's poor, microfinance works. But to reach the billions more people who could benefit from financial services, we need to provide access on a much more ambitious scale. We need to convince commercial banks and other financial and nonfinancial institutions that poor and low-income clients represent a viable business proposition.

We work toward a world in which microfinance is no longer viewed as a marginal or niche sector—a world where poor people are considered valued clients of their country's financial system, where an array of financial institutions provide poor people with permanent access to the varied financial services they need. We believe microfinance is an integral part of a competitive and diverse financial system that fosters innovation and growth in all segments of society.

CGAP is a global resource center for microfinance standards, operational tools, training, and advisory services. Its 31 members—including bilateral, multilateral, and private donors—are committed to building more inclusive financial systems for the poor.

Key Principles
of Microfinance

CGAP is a consortium of 31 public and private development agencies working together to expand access to financial services for the poor, referred to as microfinance. These principles were developed and endorsed by CGAP and its 31 member donors, and further endorsed by the Group of Eight leaders at the G8 Summit on 10 June 2004 (Sea Island, Georgia, USA).

1. **Poor people need a variety of financial services, not just loans.** In addition to credit, they want savings, insurance, and money transfer services.

2. **Microfinance is a powerful tool to fight poverty.** Poor households use financial services to raise income, build their assets, and cushion themselves against external shocks.

3. **Microfinance means building financial systems that serve the poor.** Microfinance will reach its full potential only if it is integrated into a country's mainstream financial system.

4. **Microfinance can pay for itself, and must do so if it is to reach very large numbers of poor people.** Unless microfinance providers charge enough to cover their costs, they will always be limited by the scarce and uncertain supply of subsidies from governments and donors.

5. **Microfinance is about building permanent local financial institutions** that can attract domestic deposits, recycle them into loans, and provide other financial services.

6. **Microcredit is not always the answer.** Other kinds of support may work better for people who are so destitute that they are without income or means of repayment.

7. **Interest rate ceilings hurt poor people by making it harder for them to get credit.** Making many small loans costs more than making a few large ones. Interest rate ceilings prevent microfinance institutions from covering their costs, and thereby choke off the supply of credit for poor people.

8. **The job of government is to enable financial services, not to provide them directly.** Governments can almost never do a good job of lending, but they can set a supporting policy environment.

9. **Donor funds should complement private capital, not compete with it.** Donor subsides should be temporary start-up support designed to get an institution to the point where it can tap private funding sources, such as deposits.

10. **The key bottleneck is the shortage of strong institutions and managers.** Donors should focus their support on building capacity.

11. **Microfinance works best when it measures—and discloses—its performance.** Reporting not only helps stakeholders judge costs and benefits, but it also improves performance. MFIs need to produce accurate and comparable reporting on financial perfomance (e.g., loan repayment and cost recovery) as well as social performance (e.g., number and poverty level of clients being served).

Chapter 1
Introduction

Make poverty history. This rallying cry is galvanizing world leaders and public opinion in developed countries in an unprecedented way. A new era has dawned when dinner table conversation from Seattle to Stuttgart to Sydney regularly turns to how to address poverty through equitable trade, debt relief, and increased aid flows. These big-picture issues are indeed crucial for reducing poverty in the long term. But for the 3 billion people living on less than $2 per day, access to even basic financial services can be a critical ingredient in alleviating poverty.

Most people in the developing world—that is, the majority of the world's population—do not have access to formal financial services. Very few benefit from a savings account, loan, or convenient way to transfer money. Those who do manage to, say, open a bank account, are often faced with sub-optimal services.

Why should we care? *Because the lack of access to financial services prevents poor and low-income people from making everyday decisions that most people around those dinner tables take for granted.* How to pay for a child's schooling—or even schoolbooks—next year? Where to get the cash to bury a loved one? How to send money from the capital city back to family living in a remote rural area? Where will the funds come from to fix the leaky roof? How to acquire inventory for a business?

Financial services for the poor, often referred to as microfinance, cannot solve all the problems caused by poverty. But they can help put resources and power into the hands of poor and low-income people themselves, letting them make those everyday decisions and chart their own paths out of poverty. The potential is enormous, and so is the challenge.

Meeting this challenge is the topic of this book. It is also the main focus of the Consultative Group to Assist the Poor (CGAP), a multidonor consortium dedicated to advancing microfinance.[1] CGAP envisions a world in which poor people everywhere enjoy permanent access to a range of financial services that are delivered by different financial service providers through a variety of convenient delivery channels. It is a world where poor and low-income people in

---

[1.] For more about CGAP, visit www.cgap.org.

developing countries are not viewed as marginal but, rather, as central and legitimate clients of their countries' financial systems.

In other words, this vision is about *inclusive financial systems,* which are the only way to reach large numbers of poor and low-income people. To get there, diverse approaches are needed—a one-size-fits-all solution will not work. Diverse channels are needed to get diverse financial services into the hands of a diverse range of people who are currently excluded. Making this vision a reality entails breaking down the walls—real and imaginary—that currently separate microfinance from the much broader world of financial systems.

A Brief History of Microfinance[2]

Over the past 10 years or so, microfinance has rapidly evolved and expanded from the relatively narrow field of microenterprise credit to the more comprehensive concept of microfinance (which includes a range of financial services for poor people, including savings, money transfers, and insurance) to the enormous challenge of building inclusive financial systems (see figure 1.1).

The ideas and aspirations behind microfinance are not new. Small, informal savings and credit groups have operated for centuries across the world, from Ghana to Mexico to India and beyond. In Europe, as early as the 15th century, the Catholic Church founded pawn shops as an alternative to usurious moneylenders. These pawn shops spread throughout the urban areas in Europe throughout the 15th century. Formal credit and savings institutions for the poor have also been around for generations, offering financial services for customers who were traditionally neglected by commercial banks. The Irish Loan Fund system, started in the early 1700s, is an early (and long-lived) example. By the 1840s, this system had about 300 funds throughout Ireland.

In the 1800s, Europe saw the emergence of larger and more formal savings and credit institutions that focused primarily on the rural and urban poor. The financial cooperative was developed in Germany. It aimed to help the rural population break from their dependence on moneylenders and to improve their welfare. The movement emerged in France in 1865 and Quebec in 1900. Many of today's financial cooperatives in Africa, Latin America, and Asia find their roots in this European movement. Another early example is the Indonesian People's Credit Banks (BPRs) that opened in 1895 and became the largest microfinance system in Indonesia, with close to 9,000 branches.

In the early 1900s, variations on the savings and credit theme began to appear in rural Latin America and elsewhere. These rural finance interventions aimed to modernize the agricultural sector, mobilize "idle" savings, increase investment through credit, and reduce oppressive feudal relations that were enforced through indebtedness. In most cases, these new banks for the poor

---

[2.] This section draws on Zeller, "Promoting Institutional Innovation in Microfinance: Replicating Best Practices Is Not Enough"; Wenner, *Lessons Learned in Rural Finance, The Experience of the Inter-American Development Bank;* Cunningham, "Microfinance: Flavour of the Month or Practical Development Alternative"; Hollis, *Women and Microcredit in History: Gender in the Irish Loan Funds;* and Lhériau, *Precis de réglementation de la microfinance.*

FIGURE 1.1 The History of Microfinance

Since the beginning of time...
Informal savings and credit groups have operated for centuries across the developing world.

Middle Ages
In Europe an Italian monk created the first official **pawn shop** in 1462 to counter usury practices. In 1515 Pope Leon X authorized pawn shops to charge interest to cover their operating costs.

1700s
Jonathan Swift initiates the **Irish Loan Fund System**, which provides small loans to poor farmers who have no collateral. At its peak, it is lending to 20 percent of all Irish households annually.

1800s
The concept of **the financial cooperative** is developed by Friedrich Wilhelm Raiffeisen and his supporters in Germany. From 1865, the cooperative movement expands rapidly within Germany and other countries in Europe, North America, and eventually developing countries.

Early 1900s
Adaptations of these models begin to appear in parts of **rural Latin America**.

1950–1970
Efforts to expand access to agricultural credit use **state-owned development finance institutions**, or farmers' cooperatives, to channel concessional loans and on-lend to customers at below-market interest rates. These development banks lose most or all of their capital because their subsidized lending rates cannot cover their costs, including the cost of massive default.

Early 1970s
Experimental programs extend tiny loans to groups of poor women to invest in micro-businesses, and **microcredit** is born. Early pioneers include Grameen Bank in Bangladesh; ACCION International, which started out in Latin America; and the Self-Employed Women's Association Bank in India.

1980s
Microcredit programs throughout the world improve on original methodologies. Microlenders, such as Bank Rakayat Indonesia, defy conventional wisdom about financing the poor. **Cost-recovery interest rates and high repayment** permit them to achieve long-term sustainability and reach large numbers of clients.

Early 1990s
The term "microcredit" begins to be replaced by "**microfinance**," which includes not only credit, but also savings and other services, such as insurance and money transfers.

Today
The borders between traditional microfinance and the larger financial system are starting to blur. In some countries, banks and other commercial actors are entering microfinance. Increasing emphasis is placed on building entire financial systems that work for the poor.

were not owned by the poor themselves, as they had been in Europe, but by government agencies or private banks. Over the years, these institutions became inefficient and, at times, corrupt.

Between the 1950s and 1970s, governments and donors focused on providing agricultural credit to small and marginalized farmers in hopes of raising productivity and incomes. These efforts to expand access to agricultural credit used state-owned development finance institutions, or farmers' cooperatives in some cases, to make loans to customers at below-market interest rates. These subsidized schemes were rarely successful. Rural development banks were unable to cover their costs with subsidized interest rates. Customers had poor repayment discipline, because they saw their loans as gifts from the government. Consequently, these institutions' capital base eroded and, in some cases, disappeared. Worst of all, these funds did not always reach the poor. Instead, they often ended up in the hands of more influential and better-off farmers.

Meanwhile, the 1970s saw the birth of microcredit. Programs in Bangladesh, Brazil, and a few other countries began lending to poor women entrepreneurs. Early microenterprise credit was based on solidarity group lending in which every member of a group guaranteed the repayment of all members. Examples of early pioneers include Grameen Bank in Bangladesh, which started out as an experiment by Prof. Muhammad Yunus; ACCION International, which began in Latin America and then spread to the United States and Africa; and the Self-Employed Women's Association Bank in India, which is a bank owned by a women's trade union. These institutions continue to thrive today and have inspired countless others to replicate their success.

In the 1980s, microcredit programs throughout the world improved on the original methodologies and defied conventional wisdom about financing for the poor. First, well-managed programs showed that poor people, especially women, paid their loans more reliably than better-off people with loans from commercial banks. Second, they demonstrated that poor people are willing and able to pay interest rates that allow microfinance institutions (MFIs) to cover their costs. MFIs that cover their costs can become viable businesses that attract deposits, commercial loans, and investment capital. They can reach huge numbers of poor clients without being limited by a scarce and uncertain supply of subsidized funds from governments and donor agencies. Bank Rakayat Indonesia (BRI) is a dramatic example of what can happen when MFIs focus on collecting loans and covering costs. BRI's village-level branch system now serves more than 30 million low-income savers and borrowers.

The 1990s saw growing enthusiasm among international development agencies and networks for promoting microfinance as a strategy to alleviate poverty. Microfinance blossomed in many countries where multiple MFIs serve the needs of microentrepreneurs and poor households. These gains, however, tended to concentrate in urban and densely populated rural areas.

In the early 1990s, the term "microfinance" rather than "microcredit" began to be used to refer to a range of financial services for the poor, including credit, savings, insurance, and money transfers.

To reach ever larger numbers of poor clients, MFIs and their networks increasingly began to pursue a strategy of commercialization, thus transforming themselves into for-profit corporations that could attract more capital and become more permanent features of the financial system. An emphasis on creating and growing strong institutions (as opposed to channeling credit to specific groups) is a core element of this recent history.

Microfinance Today

Microfinance has achieved astonishing accomplishments over the past 30 years. It has demonstrated that poor people are viable customers, created a number of strong institutions focusing on poor people's finance, and begun to attract the interest of private investors. But despite these achievements, there is still a long way to go to extend access to all who need financial services. Specifically, three major challenges define the frontier of financial services for the poor:

1. Scaling up quality financial services to serve large numbers of people (scale);
2. Reaching increasingly poorer and more remote people (depth); and
3. Lowering costs to both clients and financial service providers (cost).

The question is: How do we overcome these challenges? The answer: By making financial services for the poor a part of every country's mainstream financial system.

Just as the term microcredit gave way to microfinance in the 1990s, many people now advocate moving away from the term microfinance. These people argue that meeting the frontier challenges means many different kinds of financial service providers—not just specialized ones—should recognize that poor and low-income clients are a viable business proposition. They believe the prefix "micro" conjures up an image of something small or marginal. But today's microfinance should not be marginalized or relegated to a narrow space within the financial system. The potential market, which is the majority of people in the developing world, is simply too enormous.

The good news is that this integration into the larger financial system is beginning (although progress is uneven across regions and countries). The borders between traditional microfinance and the larger financial system are starting to blur. Many specialized MFIs are working at the grassroots level and continue to achieve greater scale. Commercial banks and other formal financial institutions increasingly move down-market to reach larger numbers of ever poorer and more remote clients. As these different institutions start to meet in the middle, they hold out the promise of serving more and more people.

Unfortunately, no comprehensive database tracks the size of the current or potential market for financial services among poor and low-income clients. To begin to grasp the extent of the market, CGAP recently surveyed a broad range of financial institutions that aim to reach clients below the radar screen of traditional commercial banks.[3] These institutions—state-owned agricultural, development, and postal banks; member-owned savings and loan institutions; other savings banks; low-capital community and/or rural banks; and specialized MFIs

---

[3] Christen, Rosenberg, and Jayadeva, "Financial Institutions with a 'Double Bottom Line'."

of all kinds—share the common characteristic of a "double bottom line." They aim to serve poorer markets, but they also aim to cover their costs and even turn a profit. The CGAP research revealed a surprising 750 million savings and loan accounts collectively.

The seemingly large number of existing accounts does not indicate that the job is done and that financial systems already work for the poor. On the contrary, adjusted for inactive accounts and for people with multiple accounts, the 750 million accounts may translate into (at most) 500 million active clients, who constitute only a fraction of the potential market of 3 billion poor people. Also, the quality of services in some of these institutions is not high when it comes to truly meeting the needs of poor and low-income clients. Access is not only about having a bank account. It is also about the convenience and safety of the account and whether these services are fairly priced, meet the needs of customers, and are offered by a solid institution that will be around over the long haul to help its customers manage their financial lives. Many of these institutions fall short of providing quality financial access for all, but they represent a huge potential opportunity to reach large numbers of poor clients.

As shown in figure 1.2 and table 1.1, a large number of accounts are highly concentrated, both geographically and in the types of financial institutions that offer them. State-owned banks, including postal banks, account for nearly three-quarters of all accounts. Meanwhile, 84 percent of all accounts are in Asia and more than half of these are in two countries alone—China and India.

Generally, MFIs, financial cooperatives, and rural banks are the institutions that have been most deliberate about serving poor and low-income clients with high-quality, accessible financial services. Table 1.2 reviews the global landscape, with an emphasis on these more specialized institutions.

FIGURE 1.2 Accounts by Region

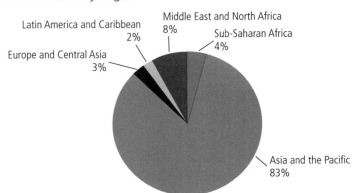

Source: Christen, Rosenberg, and Jayadeva, "Financial Institutions with a 'Double Bottom Line.'"

TABLE 1.1 Combined Loans and Savings Accounts (in thousands)[a]

	MFIs	Co-ops and credit unions	Rural banks	State/agricultural/development banks	Postal banks	Total	Percent of total	Account per hundred people
Asia and the Pacific[b]	107,255	14,579	17,677	140,752	277,388	557,651	83	17
Middle East and North Africa	1,422	11	not available	30,712	16,525	48,670	8	13
Sub-Saharan Africa	6,246	5,940	1,117	634	12,854	26,791	4	4
Europe and Central Asia	495	5,692	not available	28	11,503	17,718	3	5
Latin America and Caribbean	5,156	8,620	162	81	179	14,198	2	3
Total	120,574	34,842	18,956	172,207	318,449	665,028	100	13

Source: Christen, Rosenberg, and Jayadeva, "Financial Institutions with a 'Double Bottom Line,'" Occasional Paper No. 8, CGAP, July 2004.

[a] These figures do not include (non-postal) savings banks because the number of accounts was not available. The researchers assume that non-postal savings banks would add 150 million, bringing the total number of all alternate finance institution accounts to well over 750 million.

[b] China and India are included: China = 156,924; India = 187,812.

TABLE 1.2 The Global Landscape of Microfinance

Region
Asia

General Characteristics of the Microfinance Sector	Trends

• The microfinance sector in Asia has a strong social orientation.
• There is more emphasis on finance in densely populated rural areas.
• Except for a few institutions, there is a focus on enterprise credit (as opposed to multiple financial services).
• The two Asian giants, China and India, have little sustainable microfinance relative to their population sizes—mostly because of extensive historic government involvement in the financial sector.
• Bangladesh and Indonesia are the giants from the microfinance perspective. But each has taken a completely different approach:
  – Bangladesh's 24.6 million microfinance clients generally receive microcredit from large NGOs and other traditional MFIs that prioritize their social mission.[a]
  – Indonesia's microfinance sector is led by BRI, the largest MFI in world history. BRI is an affiliate of a reformed state bank, recently partially privatized, that operates on a more commercial basis.[b]
	• Recently, India has started to take off, with a few commercial banks joining traditional community-based self-help groups to offer financial services to poor clients.

Asia in Numbers

	Financial cooperatives	NGOs	Banks and NBFIs	All institutions
No. of borrowers (thousands)	11.2	96.0	248.3	119.3
Gross loan portfolio (million $)	2.3	12.7	59.0	29.9
Loan balance per borrower as % GNI per capita	28.9	17.1	91.6	48.5
Deposit per saver as % GNI per capita	6.1	25.0	34.0	25.6
Return on assets	8.9	-4.5	1.0	-0.7
Costs per borrower ($)	37.9	32.0	75.0	50.0

Note: All figures in tables are averages; BRI = Bank Rakayat Indonesia; ECA = Eastern Europe and Central Asia; GNI = gross national income; MFI = microfinance institution; NBFIs = nonbank financial institutions; NGO = nongovernmental organization. These tables are based on available data from a subset of institutions that have reported their information to one or more of several existing databases and do not represent the performance of the entire microfinance sector in each region. The tables include data on institutional averages in developing countries. Data also come from an interview with Adrian Gonzalez, research analyst, CGAP/The MIX, based on MFIs reporting data for 2003 to *Microbanking Bulletin* (MBB)-11, Microcredit Summit Campaign Report 2004 (for number if borrowers only), and Mix Market.

[a] Credit and Development Forum, 19, 23, 248; email interview with Iftekhar Hossain, consultant.

[b] Robinson, "The Future of Commercial Microfinance Industry in Asia," 3.

TABLE 1.2 The Global Landscape of Microfinance—*continued*

Region

 Latin America

General Characteristics of the Microfinance Sector	Trends
• Of all regions, Latin America has the longest tradition of commercially viable microfinance. • Most microfinance clients in the region obtain services from regulated financial institutions. • Competition tends to be fierce in some countries, especially in urban areas. • In some countries, interest rates have declined dramatically as a result of that competition; for instance, in Bolivia interest rates plummeted from an average of 50 percent in the mid-1990s to around 21 percent in 2004.[c]	• While most financial institutions focus more on microcredit, leading institutions are increasingly offering a variety of financial services to their clients, including savings and management of international and domestic funds transfers. • Despite market penetration and a variety of services offered in some countries, there are enormous opportunities in larger countries where little microfinance is happening (for example, Mexico and Brazil), in secondary cities, and in rural areas.

Latin America and the Caribbean in Numbers

	Financial cooperatives	NGOs	Banks and NBFIs	All institutions
No. of borrowers (thousands)	12.6	17.0	36.0	21.0
Gross loan portfolio (million $)	35.2	10.1	36.9	22.1
Loan balance per borrower as % GNI per capita	72.2	47.3	71.7	58.4
Deposit per saver as % GNI per capita	30.9	55.3	213.4	129.3
Return on assets	-0.3	-1.0	1.4	-0.1
Costs per borrower ($)	156.2	150.3	224.7	176.1

Note: All figures in tables are averages; BRI = Bank Rakayat Indonesia; ECA = Eastern Europe and Central Asia; GNI = gross national income; MFI = microfinance institution; NBFIs = nonbank financial institutions; NGO = nongovernmental organization. These tables are based on available data from a subset of institutions that have reported their information to one or more of several existing databases and do not represent the performance of the entire microfinance sector in each region. The tables include data on institutional averages in developing countries. Data also come from an interview with Adrian Gonzalez, research analyst, CGAP/The MIX, based on MFIs reporting data for 2003 to *Microbanking Bulletin* (MBB)-11, Microcredit Summit Campaign Report 2004 (for number if borrowers only), and Mix Market.

[c] Gonzalez-Vega and Ibarnegaray, *Las Microfinanzas en el Desarrollo del Sistema Financiero de Bolivia*, 92.

TABLE 1.2 The Global Landscape of Microfinance—*continued*

Region
Sub-Saharan Africa

General Characteristics of the Microfinance Sector	Trends
• Overall, microfinance in Africa is under-developed and faces higher operating costs than in other regions. In most African countries, a very small minority of the population have bank accounts. Even in the most developed economy, South Africa, half the adult population is still "unbanked," and the vast majority of the self-employed are unbanked in two of the other leading economies, Kenya and Nigeria, where only 11 percent and 10 percent, respectively, have bank accounts.[d] • Financial cooperatives are the dominant model in French-speaking Africa, reaching several hundred thousand clients. • English-speaking Africa (outside South Africa) and Portuguese-speaking countries also have large numbers of financial cooperatives, but specialized microfinance NGOs are more prominent in those parts of the continent than in others.	• Recently, banks have begun to enter the market. Examples include Equity Bank in Kenya and Teba Bank in South Africa.

Sub-Saharan Africa in Numbers				
	Financial cooperatives	NGOs	Banks and NBFIs	All institutions
No. of borrowers (thousands)	11.6	17.9	24.3	17.4
Gross loan portfolio (million $)	4.3	2.3	4.5	3.7
Loan balance per borrower as % GNI per capita	144.6	59.9	140.1	115.9
Deposit per saver as % GNI per capita	32.7	25.0	85.6	49.8
Return on assets	-1.6	-16.8	-3.9	-7.3
Costs per borrower ($)	136.9	256.1	346.3	237.7

Note: All figures in tables are averages; BRI = Bank Rakayat Indonesia; ECA = Eastern Europe and Central Asia; GNI = gross national income; MFI = microfinance institution; NBFIs = nonbank financial institutions; NGO = nongovernmental organization. These tables are based on available data from a subset of institutions that have reported their information to one or more of several existing databases and do not represent the performance of the entire microfinance sector in each region. The tables include data on institutional averages in developing countries. Data also come from an interview with Adrian Gonzalez, research analyst, CGAP/The MIX, based on MFIs reporting data for 2003 to *Microbanking Bulletin* (MBB)-11, Microcredit Summit Campaign Report 2004 (for number if borrowers only), and Mix Market.

[d] Oxford Analytica, "South Africa: Banking the 'unbanked' proves viable" and "Africa: Low banking penetration constrains growth."

TABLE 1.2 The Global Landscape of Microfinance—*continued*

Region

 Eastern Europe and Central Asia

General Characteristics of the Microfinance Sector	Trends
• Eastern Europe and Central Asia is a newcomer to microfinance and is dominated by NGOs and other institutions that focus primarily on loans (although there are a few notable exceptions, such as the ProCredit Banks in several countries, which offer a variety of services). • Microfinance has developed differently in this region than in the rest of the world. For instance, higher income and education levels partly explain the larger loans offered in the region. And interestingly, institutions have rapidly achieved financial self-sufficiency when compared with other regions.	• The main threats to future viability are high costs and moving from donor dependence to linking to financial systems. • Microfinance in the region still has a significant opportunity to expand to reach poorer and more remote clients.[e]

Eastern Europe and Central Asia in Numbers

	Financial cooperatives	NGOs	Banks and NBFIs	All institutions
No. of borrowers (thousands)	0.7	5.2	5.1	4.8
Gross loan portfolio (million $)	1.3	4.2	12.4	7.0
Loan balance per borrower as % GNI per capita	52.8	77.6	264.6	144.3
Deposit per saver as % GNI per capita	87.2	not available	92.9	89.6
Return on assets	-0.2	-0.1	1.9	0.6
Costs per borrower ($)	392.6	263.7	362.0	309.8

Note: All figures in tables are averages; BRI = Bank Rakayat Indonesia; ECA = Eastern Europe and Central Asia; GNI = gross national income; MFI = microfinance institution; NBFIs = nonbank financial institutions; NGO = nongovernmental organization. These tables are based on available data from a subset of institutions that have reported their information to one or more of several existing databases and do not represent the performance of the entire microfinance sector in each region. The tables include data on institutional averages in developing countries. Data also come from an interview with Adrian Gonzalez, research analyst, CGAP/The MIX, based on MFIs reporting data for 2003 to *Microbanking Bulletin* (MBB)-11, Microcredit Summit Campaign Report 2004 (for number if borrowers only), and Mix Market.

[e] MIX, "Benchmarking Microfinance in Eastern Europe and Central Asia."

TABLE 1.2 The Global Landscape of Microfinance—*continued*

Region
Middle East and North Africa

General Characteristics of the Microfinance Sector	Trends
• 70 percent of MFIs in the Middle East and North Africa are NGOs and donor dependent. • Microfinance is largely perceived as charity and not part of an inclusive financial system. • Nonetheless, commercial banks from the region (especially Egypt) are starting to move down-market and develop services for the poor.	• Microfinance is growing fast, with an annual average growth rate of 50 percent, although much of that growth is happening in two countries—Morocco, where two MFIs reach more than 300,000 clients,[f] and Egypt, where commercial banks are downscaling.

Middle East and North Africa in Numbers

	Financial cooperatives	NGOs	Banks and NBFIs	All institutions
No. of borrowers (thousands)	1.6	29.6	4.7	22.7
Gross loan portfolio (million $)	n.a.	6.9	2.1	6.1
Loan balance per borrower as % GNI per capita	n.a.	17.4	35.7	20.6
Deposit per saver as % GNI per capita	n.a.	2.4	0.8	2.1
Return on assets	n.a.	85.9	258.4	116.4

Note: All figures in tables are averages; BRI = Bank Rakayat Indonesia; ECA = Eastern Europe and Central Asia; GNI = gross national income; MFI = microfinance institution; NBFIs = nonbank financial institutions; NGO = nongovernmental organization. These tables are based on available data from a subset of institutions that have reported their information to one or more of several existing databases and do not represent the performance of the entire microfinance sector in each region. The tables include data on institutional averages in developing countries. Data also come from an interview with Adrian Gonzalez, research analyst, CGAP/The MIX, based on MFIs reporting data for 2003 to *Microbanking Bulletin* (MBB)-11, Microcredit Summit Campaign Report 2004 (for number if borrowers only), and Mix Market.

n.a. = not available.

[f] www.mixmarket.org.

Individual countries within regions show strongly divergent growth patterns. Emerging market countries, such as India, Brazil, and South Africa, will probably be fertile testing grounds for new methods to reach large numbers of poor people. They each have extensive financial and nonfinancial infrastructure and more advanced technology options. Private investors are anxiously competing to enter the market. Examples include the ICICI Bank, which is opening more than 2,000 rural Internet kiosks that will provide limited financial services throughout India, and the Caixa Bank, which is extending financial service franchises to nearly 14,000 lottery kiosks, supermarkets, and local vendors in Brazil.[4] Some people working on microfinance believe that these countries will "leapfrog" the traditional trajectory of microfinance and use a more commercial approach to skip straight to massive scale, thus affecting the lives of millions (perhaps hundreds of millions) of poor and low-income people.

Conversely, more classic microfinance countries like Bolivia, Uganda, and Bangladesh are likely to witness another type of growth. Microfinance already thrives in these countries, with market saturation for some types of financial services among certain market segments. But significant pockets of the population are left unserved, for instance, the remote rural areas of Bolivia and Uganda. These countries might not grow at such a spectacular pace as the "leapfrog" countries, but their history of innovation suggests they may develop new ways to serve very poor clients and remote rural areas.

Still other countries are at the beginning of the learning and growth curve. These countries (particularly postconflict countries), which include some countries in Africa and the Middle East, for instance, will benefit from advances elsewhere. These countries have the unique opportunity to start from scratch and may be able to avoid the mistakes made elsewhere. Many have weak governments, fragile financial systems, and limited infrastructure, such as roads and telecommunications networks. The challenge will be to harness the lessons, energy, and expertise from more rapidly growing economies to help make financial systems work for the poor majority in these fledgling countries.

Inclusive Financial Systems Framework

The G8 endorsed CGAP's *Key Principles of Microfinance* at its 2004 Sea Island, Georgia, USA, meeting. This book translates those principles into a framework for an inclusive financial system. That framework recognizes that the massive number of excluded people will gain access only if financial services for the poor are integrated into all three levels of the financial system: micro, meso, and macro (see figure 1.3). Ultimately, integration into the financial system could open financial markets to the majority of people living in developing countries, including poorer and more geographically remote clients than are currently reached.

---

4. ICICI Bank to deliver kiosk-based ebanking to rural India, June 2005, available at: www.finextra. com; Littlefield and Rosenberg, "Microfinance and the Poor: Breaking Down the Walls between Microfinance and Formal Finance"; and Ivatury, *Using Electronic Payments to Build Inclusive Financial Systems.*

FIGURE 1.3 An Inclusive Financial System

Clients. Poor and low-income clients are at the center of the financial system. Their demand for financial services drives the actions of those at all the other levels.

Micro. The backbone of financial systems remains retail financial service providers that offer services directly to poor and low-income clients. These micro-level service providers run the gamut from informal moneylenders or savings clubs to commercial banks and encompass everything in-between.

Meso. This level includes the basic financial infrastructure and the range of services required to reduce transactions costs, increase outreach, build skills, and foster transparency among financial service providers. It includes a wide range of players and activities, such as auditors, rating agencies, professional networks, trade associations, credit bureaus, transfer and payments systems, information technology, technical service providers, and trainers. These entities can transcend national boundaries and include regional or global organizations.

Macro. An appropriate legislative and policy framework is necessary to allow sustainable microfinance to flourish. Central banks, ministries of finance, and other national government entities constitute the primary macro-level participants.

Although up to now microfinance has depended heavily on international donor funding, the focus of financial systems that work for the poor is on building domestic markets, where numerous strong and viable financial service providers compete for the business of poor and low-income clients. These financial service providers would ideally obtain financing from domestic funding sources, such as deposits from the public or investments via the capital markets. While many have succeeded in tapping into domestic sources, there has been and will likely continue to be a role for international funding to expand access to financial services. In fact, international funding can be helpful at all levels of the financial system—micro, meso, and macro—to jump-start and accelerate the process of building domestic systems.

This Book

This book lays out what we at CGAP and others in the development field have learned over the past 10 years about building inclusive financial systems. It is not a technical handbook. It is not a chronicle of the history of microfinance. Instead, it pulls together disparate sources of information to describe for the general reader where the microfinance field finds itself now, as well as the opportunities and challenges ahead.

This book explains the practical implications of a fairly murky concept—inclusive financial systems—by making a comprehensive argument about what we know now, what we need to find out, and where we need to go for further information.

Chapter 2 begins with a discussion of the clients who are at the center of it all. It asks (and partially answers) the questions: Who are microfinance clients? What financial services do they want? And what is the impact of financial services on their lives?

Chapters 3, 4, and 5 examine the micro, meso, and macro levels of the financial system in turn. Each chapter offers an overview of the diverse actors at each level, including information on what works, what does not work, and where more learning is needed. These chapters describe promising models and practices, with cautionary notes on where things might go wrong.

Chapter 6 analyzes the respective roles of international and domestic funding sources. It highlights how important it is that each funder identify its relative strengths and then stick to those funding activities in which it has a comparative advantage.

These six chapters offer key insights into how to address the frontier challenges of scale, depth, and costs. Chapter 7 examines five issues that also contribute to pushing the financial frontier—problems for which solutions seem particularly evasive or opportunities that are exciting but not quite within reach. These frontier issues are optimizing technology, leveraging remittances and other transfers, reaching farmers and other remote rural clients, measuring social performance, and protecting poor consumers. Tackling these and other core challenges described throughout this book will ultimately result in inclusive financial systems that deliver on the promise of access for all.

Finally, chapter 8 sums up what we've learned and points to the challenges that await.

Chapter 2

Poor and Low-Income Clients

For a financial system to be truly inclusive, it should meet the needs of everyone who can fruitfully use financial services, including the poor. Poor people in developing countries, like everyone else, need access to a wide range of financial services that are convenient, flexible, and reasonably priced. This simple observation has transformed the thinking and practice of microfinance over the past decade. A better understanding of client (and potential client) demand has driven the shift from microcredit to microfinance and, most recently, to inclusive financial systems.

In the past, two features characterized microfinance: (1) a focus on microenterprise credit (small loans to meet working capital needs of entrepreneurs); and (2) an approach to delivering credit that was largely supply driven. As a result, a fairly narrow range of credit services attracted an equally narrow range of clients. Today, there is a growing recognition that not all poor people are necessarily entrepreneurs, but all poor people do need and use a variety of financial services. The challenge is to understand and meet this demand among increasingly poor and remote populations.

Recognizing the diversity of people who are excluded from financial services (not just microentrepreneurs) has enormous implications for building inclusive financial systems. Farmers may need credit for agricultural inputs but also a safe place to save the proceeds of the harvest to use when lean times arise. Pensioners need a reliable system for receiving their payments. Factory workers need help managing from paycheck to paycheck. In short, these diverse clients require diverse financial services. These services range from emergency or mortgage loans to consumer credit, deposit services of all kinds, methods for transferring funds, and insurance.

This chapter addresses the following questions: Who are the clients? How poor are they really? What financial services do poor clients want and how do they use them? And, what is the impact of financial services on the lives of poor people?

Characteristics of Microfinance Clients

There are two ways to think about the first question "Who are the clients?" First, potential clients extend far beyond microentrepreneurs, encompassing anyone excluded from formal financial services—sometimes referred to as the "unbanked." These potential clients include, for example, farmers, factory workers, and pensioners, as well as others. They range from the very poor to the vulnerable non-poor. Although little is known about this universe of potential clients, the number of excluded households is certainly enormous, even in developed countries. For instance, in the United States, where the financial system is well developed, it is estimated that more than 50 million people do not have bank accounts.[1]

More information exists on *current* microfinance clients. Typical microfinance clients are self-employed, often home-based entrepreneurs. In rural areas, they are small farmers and others engaged in small income-generating activities, such as food processing and petty trade. In urban areas, the population reached is often more diverse and includes not only street vendors but also shopkeepers, service providers, artisans, and so on. In some cases, regional differences in clientele prevail. In Latin America and East Africa, the focus of traditional microfinance is primarily on urban or near-urban entrepreneurs, mostly traders. In South Asia, many programs focus on rural women just starting income-earning opportunities. See box 2.1 for the stories of three microfinance clients.

Much debate has raged in recent years over the poverty level of microfinance clients relative to standard poverty measurements like the poverty line or those living on less than $1 to $2 per day. This debate has taken various forms. First, there is the moral question about reaching the poorest—shouldn't microfinance be viewed as a poverty-alleviating activity targeted at the very poorest? Many South Asian practitioners and several international nongovernmental organizations (NGOs) take this approach. The second dimension is a question of public policy. Because donor subsidies play a large role in funding microfinance, shouldn't authorities demand that public funds go to those most in need? See box 2.2 for a discussion of the specific case of the U.S. Agency for International Development.

Most current microfinance clients seem to fall around or just below the poverty line (see figure 2.1). The destitute, or those households making up the poorest 10 percent of households, are not generally microcredit clients, but neither are the better-off. Most clients fall into the "moderate poor" category (those in the top 50 percent of households below the poverty line). However, some extreme-poor households participate, as well as the vulnerable non-poor (those just above the poverty line at risk of falling below it). The extreme poor are defined as those households in the bottom 10 to 50 percent of households below the poverty line, and the vulnerable non-poor are those above the poverty line but at risk of slipping into poverty.[2]

[1.] Anft, "A New Way to Curb Poverty," 8.
[2.] Sebstad and Cohen, *Microfinance, Risk Management, and Poverty*, 4.

BOX 2.1 Prudence in Kenya, Amina in Bangladesh, and Marcelino in Colombia

Microfinance clients come in different shapes and sizes, but they have one thing in common: they all need a range of financial services to help them organize their financial lives, accumulate assets, protect themselves from adversity, and take advantage of opportunities. Here are a few typical stories.

Prudence is a market trader in Karatina, Kenya, who belongs to several informal savings groups or "merry-go-rounds," as they are called in Kenya. She uses the different merry-go-rounds for different purposes: one has a monthly payout that she uses to pay for her grandchildren's school fees (she cares for them since their parents died of AIDS); another one pays out weekly, which she uses to restock her market stall. In addition, she belongs to another informal credit and savings group in which she can take out small, short-term loans if needed periodically, and the entire amount is distributed among members of the group just before Christmas (last year she received $109 during the holiday season). She also belongs to an informal funeral insurance group to ensure that her remains are transported to her home village after she dies. Prudence keeps a few dollars around the house and has long-term savings locked up in a cow that is looked after by her brother in her home village. Finally, she also has a loan from Faulu, a Kenyan MFI, which she is using to upgrade her home to rent out some rooms to secure regular income in her old age.

Amina is a housewife in Pathrail, Bangladesh. She relies heavily on her neighbors for financial services. She alternately lends to and borrows from them in a complex web of reciprocal arrangements. But these arrangements can be unreliable, because sometimes the neighbors do not have money to lend or demand an extra-high price. Sometimes she has had difficulties recovering the money she lent out to others. Amina is also a member of a savings club, from which she borrows only when the neighbors cannot help out. This savings club liquidates just before the main Eid festival, providing her with a useful amount just at the right time. Amina hides a small amount of savings in a mud bank (hidden from her husband in the thatched roof of her house) only for emergencies. She also borrows from BURO, Tangail, an MFI from which she can borrow for her husband's rickshaw business and for emergencies that cannot be covered through more informal means. Amina is considering using one of BURO's contractual savings products to save for her daughter's wedding, which she believes will occur in about five years.

Marcelino was forced to flee from his village in rural Colombia a few years ago after guerilla violence threatened his family's safety. With around $300 in cash and not much else, he and his family joined thousands of others in Barrio Nelson Mandela, a shantytown just outside of one of Colombia's most beautiful cities, Cartagena. Marcelino was focused on getting money to improve the family's living conditions. They were living in a plastic tent, a situation that he found unacceptable. The MFI Fundación Mario Santo Domingo opened a lending operation in the area with the express purpose of helping migrants like Marcelino. With his first $95 loan, he opened a tiny variety store. Just one year later, Marcelino now owns the most successful butcher shop in the neighborhood. With profits from the store, he moved his family into a concrete-block home on the main road. The home, which contains a small storefront and counter, doubles as his business.

Sources: For the Prudence and Amina stories, Wright, *Understanding and Assessing the Demand for Microfinance,* 1, 2; and for Marcelino, www.accion.org.

FIGURE 2.1 How Poor Are Microfinance Clients?

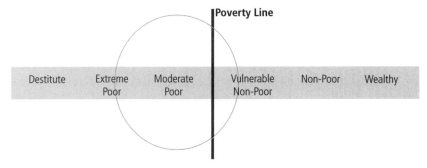

Source: Cohen, "The Impact of Microfinance."

This profile of traditional microfinance clients was reinforced by research that used a mix of qualitative and quantitative methods to compare clients of seven MFIs with nonclients in four countries (Bolivia, Bangladesh, Uganda, and the Philippines). See table 2.1 for a description of the qualitative research results).[3] The research confirmed the following:

- Most clients come from moderately poor and vulnerable non-poor households, with some clients from extreme-poor households also participating;
- Programs that explicitly target poorer segments of the population generally have a greater percentage of clients from extreme-poor households; and
- Destitute households are outside the reach of microfinance programs.

Self-reported data from 2,931 MFIs collected by the Microcredit Summit suggests that a higher proportion of very poor clients are served. These institutions report that two-thirds of their collective clients fall far below the poverty line or live on less than $1 per day.[4]

Experience with CGAP's Poverty Assessment Tool underscores the fact that those MFIs that attempt to reach very poor people tend to succeed. For instance, Nirdhan Uttan Bank Ltd. in Nepal actively targets very poor women. A poverty assessment conducted with that organization found that it reached clients that were poorer on average than the general population in the areas where it works.[5]

Delivering financial services to larger numbers of ever poorer and more remote clients than are currently reached presents a challenge to the microfinance community. Reaching the very poor is not always easy—and particularly difficult to do in a sustainable manner. The overall concentration of current clients around the poverty line suggests that innovations are necessary to better meet the needs of a broader range of potential clients, extending from the extreme poor to the vulnerable non-poor.

---

[3] Ibid, 3, 30.

[4] Daley-Harris, *State of the Microcredit Summit Campaign Report 2004,* 3.

[5] www.microfinancegateway.org/poverty/pat/closer.html.

TABLE 2.1 Whom Do Microfinance Institutions Reach?

	Philippines (CARD)	Uganda (UWFT)	Bolivia (4 programs)	Bangladesh (BRAC)
Destitute	Negligible	Negligible	Negligible	Negligible
Extreme poor	Some	Few	Almost none	~40%
Moderate poor	Many	Many	Many	~35%
Vulnerable non-poor	Some	Many	Many	~25%

Source: CGAP, "Microfinance and Risk Management: A Client Perspective."
Note: CARD = Centre for Agriculture and Rural Development; UWFT = Uganda Women's Finance Trust; BRAC = Bangladesh Rural Advancement Committee.

BOX 2.2 To target or not to target?

The question of client targeting has remained a hot topic throughout the history of microfinance. Targeting means using specific methods to identify the poor (for example, checking for assets like a tin roof or shoes, or participatory wealth ranking through which the community itself decides who is poor and who is not). Not surprisingly, institutions that target the poor tend to reach poorer clients. This is a good argument for targeting—at least for those institutions that aim to reach the very poor as their core mission. Critics of targeting argue that "Those that place emphasis on serving only the 'poorest of the poor' are effectively saying: 'According to our survey, you are not-so-poor: go away and have a serious crisis in your household and come back to us when you are really one of the poorest of the poor...then we will serve you.'"[a]

Conversely, providing financial services to a broader range of clients may result in reaching larger numbers of the very poor on a permanent basis. A more diverse clientele may lend itself more easily to financial viability, which in turn can translate into greater outreach. Institutions that cover their costs by mixing lower-cost, larger loans to less-poor people with higher-cost, very small loans to poorer people can attract larger amounts of capital and grow more quickly. This strategy of diversifying risk through a varied portfolio can reach many poor people, while also allowing those who are less poor (but still excluded and vulnerable) to obtain services.

In September 2003, CGAP hosted a debate about new U.S. legislation that would require some proportion of U.S. Agency for International Development funds to go to partners that target the poorest (defined as those who either live on less than $1 a day or who are among the bottom half below a country's poverty line). The partners would furthermore have to prove that they had done so by using a credible poverty measurement tool. Proponents felt that mandates were necessary to counteract everyday management and financial pressures, which may tend to crowd poverty outreach off the MFI's list of priorities. However, opponents responded that such directives increase service delivery costs by placing additional burdens on MFIs, making it more difficult to serve the poor—and everyone else who might be excluded.

[a] Wright and Dondo, "Are You Poor Enough?" Client Selection by Microfinance Institutions, 5.

How Poor People Use Financial Services

Poor people need a whole range of financial services, many of which they get from informal sources (see chapter 3 for a description of both informal and formal financial service providers). They need many different kinds of services to solve a wide range of financial problems at different points in time. Stuart Rutherford's groundbreaking book, *The Poor and Their Money*, points to three main categories of events that call for spending more money than might be available around the house or in the pocket: life-cycle events, emergency needs, and investment opportunities.[6]

Life-cycle events include those once-in-a-lifetime occurrences (birth, marriage, death) or recurrent incidents (school fees, holidays like Eid or Christmas, harvest time) that every household faces. In Bangladesh and India, the dowry system makes daughters' marriages an expensive business. In parts of Africa, burying deceased parents can be quite costly. Other life-cycle events include home-building, widowhood, old age, and the desire to bequeath a lump sum to heirs. These needs can usually be anticipated, even if their exact date is not always known. The awareness that such outlays are looming on the horizon is a source of great anxiety for many people.

Emergencies include personal crises like sickness or injury, the death of a bread winner or the loss of employment, and theft. Many emergencies are completely outside the control of the household, like war, floods, fires, cyclones, and (for slum dwellers) the bulldozing of their homes by the authorities. All these emergencies create a sudden need for cash.

Opportunities to invest in businesses, land, or household assets also pop up periodically. Business investments are only one of several kinds of investments that poor people make. They also want to invest in costly items that make life more comfortable—better roofing, better furniture, a fan, a television. Naturally these investments involve money.

Poor clients need more than credit. Today, microenterprise credit (credit to meet the running costs of small businesses) is the principle product offered by most specialized MFIs. To meet their various requirements, clients find themselves adapting microcredit to many uses. All too often the fit is far from perfect. Thus, to come up with the financial outlays required by life-cycle events, emergencies, and opportunities, more than microcredit is needed. Poor people need a range of options, from credit (beyond enterprise finance), to savings, to money transfer facilities, and insurance in many forms. Equity Bank in Kenya is an example of a bank that has enjoyed success among poor and low-income clients by offering diverse services. It has grown exponentially since introducing computerized systems in 2000 and offering a range of financial services, including agricultural

---

[6.] The following paragraphs draw heavily from Rutherford, *The Poor and Their Money*, 8.

loans, emergency loans, salary advance, business development loans, ordinary and contractual savings accounts (in which clients can save for a specific purpose), and money transfers. In just four years, Equity's client base swelled from 75,000 to nearly 450,000; this growth trend has continued into 2005, with around 50,000 new clients opening accounts in the first quarter alone.[7]

Figure 2.2 illustrates the link between typical financial needs and financial services for poor and low-income households.

Credit. The microfinance "revolution" has been marked by the introduction of credit methodologies that prove that poor people are bankable. They can take out loans and pay them back. In fact, microcredit clients often repay their loans more reliably than customers in the commercial banking sector. They are also willing and able to pay the typically high interest rates that are necessary for providers to cover the (relatively high) cost of offering very small loans.

Traditionally, the core of successful microcredit is the promise of permanent access to future credit that motivates clients to repay to ensure their access to this service. Another key success factor is use of collateral substitutes to reduce risk. Poor people do not have collateral, and this is the characteristic that primarily excludes them from formal credit sources. To address this, some microfinance pioneers introduced group-based joint liability schemes, in which individuals in a group guarantee each other's loans. Other programs rely on local knowledge through loan officers "on the street" and nontraditional forms of collateral, such as animals or refrigerators, rather than group schemes. Another critical element of successful microcredit is ensuring that client households have sufficient cash flow today (rather than projected cash flow assumed to emerge from the financed activity) to cover their interest and principal repayments. One method for making sure borrowers can service loans is to

FIGURE 2.2 Poor Clients Need a Variety of Services

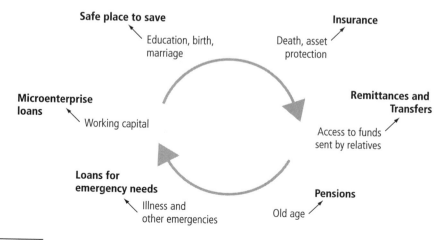

Safe place to save — Education, birth, marriage

Insurance — Death, asset protection

Microenterprise loans — Working capital

Remittances and Transfers — Access to funds sent by relatives

Loans for emergency needs — Illness and other emergencies

Pensions — Old age

[7]. Wright, *Understanding and Assessing the Demand for Microfinance*, 3, 4.

collect small and very frequent repayment installments that can be met comfortably from ordinary household cash flow.

However, frequent, regular loan repayments have drawbacks, especially when serving the very poor. While this feature helps people pay back loans a little bit at a time, it also requires a steady flow of income. Market vendors with rapid turnover can cope with frequent repayments, whereas farm families highly dependent on the vicissitudes of planting and harvesting cycles might find them more difficult to manage. Regular loan repayments also increase the costs of doing business for clients, as they spend time in regular meetings with their groups or loan officers. In recognition of this challenge, Grameen Bank, the pioneer of regular weekly loan repayments, has moved to making repayment terms and schedules more flexible. In the future, technology such as 24-hour automated teller machines or cell phone banking may further expand clients' options for accessible and convenient loan repayment.[8]

Lessons learned (both successes and shortcomings) from microenterprise credit can be applied to other kinds of pro-poor lending. Poor and low-income people want choice. Over the last few years, many MFIs have successfully introduced innovative credit products, including loans for housing improvements, emergencies, and consumption purposes. For instance, in 2000, Mibanco in Peru added Micasa, a housing improvement loan product. The loans are designed to help households finance incremental improvements to their homes, rather than to purchase or build a new home, as is the case with traditional mortgage lending. At the end of 2004, Mibanco has around 14,000 Micasa clients with a portfolio of $17.5 million and portfolio at risk (greater than 30 days) on its Micasa portfolio of just 2 percent.[9] This means that only 2 percent of the loan portfolio has any payments that are late more than 30 days.

Despite the significant progress made in delivering microcredit to millions, the majority of poor people still lack access to formal credit, whether or not they are entrepreneurs. The future will likely bring further innovations in lending for things like agriculture, consumption purposes, emergencies, housing, and education.

Savings. Poor people want to save, and many of them do save. But they are constrained by the multiple demands on their low incomes and a lack of available deposit services. Often referred to as the "forgotten half" of microfinance, savings is a critical financial service for poor and excluded households.

Poor people want secure, convenient deposit services that allow for small balances and transactions and offer easy access to their funds. In fact, globally there are many more savers than borrowers—CGAP's 2004 survey of "alternative" financial institutions around the world uncovered four times as many savings accounts as loans.[10] In the four years between 2000 and 2004, the number of savings accounts opened at Bank Rakayat Indonesia (BRI) increased by an average

---

8. See chapter 7 for more on technological innovations in financial services for the poor.
9. Brown, "Building the Homes of the Poor, One Brick at a Time: Housing Improvement Lending at Mibanco," 5; and interview with Cesar Fernández Fernández, marketing director, Mibanco.
10. Christen, Rosenberg, and Jayadeva, "Financial Institutions with a 'Double Bottom Line'."

of 1 million per year.[11] Clients (many of them poor) seem to be "voting with their feet" as they open up savings accounts in droves.

With so many savers, why do development professionals still mainly concentrate on microcredit? Mostly because very little is known about the service, design, and convenience of all those savings accounts, in terms of really meeting the needs of poor people. It is likely that the quality is not all that good. Perhaps more worrying, relatively few people within the mainstream development community consider savings a key to development and poverty reduction. Compared with credit, few resources have been dedicated to transferring knowledge and skills about how to deliver appropriate deposit services to poor people.

At the same time, many banks and others licensed to take deposits from the public have not entered into this market in a purposeful way. They see the costs of managing large numbers of small accounts and tiny transactions as prohibitive. Generally, they have not invested in development to match deposit products with the needs of poor clients and to balance services with what they can profitably offer. A notable exception is Grameen Bank, which recently introduced a number of very popular deposit services into their product mix, including a pension savings account. This savings product responds to poor Bangladeshi clients' need for longer-term savings, especially Grameen clients who are, as a whole, getting older and more attracted to the idea of saving for their old age. For a 10-year term, Grameen pays 12 percent per year interest, nearly doubling clients' deposits. Savers can take their money as a lump sum or as monthly income. Many clients like the option so well that they save more than the required minimum and, in less than three years, Grameen mobilized pension deposits totaling $37.2 million.[12]

The consequence of the scarce availability of appropriate savings services is that most poor people save in informal ways—by tucking cash under the mattress, buying animals or jewelry that can be sold off later, joining village savings circles, or giving money to neighbors for safekeeping (see box 2.3 for an analysis of savings patterns in Mexico). The problem with these methods of saving is that they are risky—cash can be stolen, animals can get sick, the neighbor can run off. They can also be fairly illiquid. It is impossible to cut off the leg of a cow and sell it if only a small amount of cash is needed.

In contrast, those with safer, more formal options to save benefit both themselves and the larger economy. In Uganda, one study revealed that those with access to formal savings in banks saved three times as much as those who had only informal savings mechanisms available. In Rwanda, more than half a million small savings accounts drew $40 million into circulation in 2001, money that would otherwise have stayed underneath mattresses. The national impact of offering secure and accessible savings can be critical to bolster domestic economies.[13]

[11.] Robinson, "Why the Bank Rakyat Indonesia Has the World's Largest Sustainable Microbanking System," 12.

[12.] Hirschland, *Savings Services for the Poor: An Operational Guide,* 143.

[13.] UNCDF, "Challenges and Prospects in the Mobilization of Domestic Resources through Microfinancial Intermediation."

BOX 2.3 How people save in Mexico

Mexicans save, regardless of their socioeconomic status, using formal and informal mechanisms. The majority save small amounts for short-term needs, such as dealing with emergencies as they arise or for consumption.

Of the 11 types of savings cited in a recent study, 2 were formal and 9 were informal. Most respondents used a mix of instruments, for example, saving in a bank for a future land purchase or other long-term goal and in a *tanda* (rotating savings and credit association) to pay off a short-term loan or purchase something for the home. Three categories of savings were analyzed in depth: formal financial savings, informal financial savings in *tandas,* and savings in physical assets.

Use of savings instruments varied according to demographic characteristics. The poorest respondents, those living in rural areas (including farmers), and residents of the south tended to save in physical assets. *Tandas* were preferred by the middle class, housewives, and salaried workers; those in mid-size towns; and those living in the Bajío region. The use of banks was concentrated among wealthy, professional people living in urban areas and in the north.

Source: Campos Bolaño, *El Ahorro Popular en México: Acumulando Activos para Superar la Pobreza.*

Money transfers.[14] Recent interest in the estimated $126 billion per year in international remittances going to developing countries has highlighted poor people's need to move money from one place to another.[15] Money transfers encompass more than just remittances, which are defined as the portion of migrant-worker earnings sent to family members or other individuals in their place of origin. Remittances include both domestic and international transfers.

Massive numbers of poor people have relatives living in other countries or cities and face serious constraints to sending and receiving this money. Currently, moving money from point A to point B, whether internationally or domestically, can be costly and, in some cases, dangerous for poor people. And sometimes the intended receivers never see the money. In many countries, there simply are no domestic transfer systems at all. In Ghana, for instance, market studies for the vast rural bank network revealed that clients encounter difficulty accessing transfers from urban areas. Crime made it especially difficult for traders, who carry large sums of cash for business purposes. In response, the Apex Bank, the central treasury for the Ghanaian rural banks, introduced a money transfer system with a turnaround time of between 15 minutes and 24 hours. The program is growing quickly, with some 24,000 transfers made within the first year of operations—a testament to the high level of demand for such a service.

The sheer amounts and numbers of transactions involved in money transfers offer a promising opportunity to bring more people into the financial system.

[14.] This section borrows heavily from Isern and Deshpande, "Crafting a Money Transfers Strategy: Guidance for Pro-poor Financial Service Provider."

[15.] Ratha and Maimbo, "Remittances: An Economic Force in Many Countries."

MFIs, with their roots in poor communities, increasingly seek alliances with money transfer companies, banks, and others to make safe, convenient, and lower-cost transfer services available to poor people (see chapter 7 for more on remittances and transfers as a "cross-cutting challenge").

Microinsurance.[16] Few poor households have access to formal insurance against such risks as the death of a family breadwinner, severe illness, or loss of an asset including livestock and housing. These shocks are particularly damaging for poor households, because they are more vulnerable to begin with. Microinsurance is the protection of low-income people against specific perils in exchange for regular monetary payments (premiums) proportionate to the likelihood and cost of the risk involved. As with all insurance, risk pooling allows many individuals or groups to share the costs of a risky event. To serve poor people well, microinsurance must be responsive to priority needs for risk protection (depending on the market, they may seek health, car, or life insurance), easy to understand, and affordable.

Microinsurance is a new product and still at the experimental stage. There is much interest among MFIs to provide microinsurance in partnership with insurance companies. Existing microinsurance schemes that attempt to deliver life or health insurance find it difficult to become sustainable. The big challenge is finding the right balance between offering adequate protection with affordability for poor households.

As shown in figure 2.3, several different types of insurance might be relevant for poor and low-income clients. The more complex the insurance, the more difficult it is to implement, and the less successful it is in serving poor households. Credit life insurance is the most common and ensures that the

FIGURE 2.3 Most Common Types of Microinsurance Products

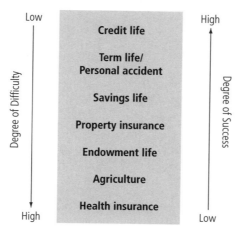

Source: Churchill, Microinsurance Products.

---

[16] This section borrows heavily from Latortue, "Microinsurance: A Risk Management Strategy."

"debt dies with the debtor." It is actually used to protect lenders, not the families, from the death of their clients and is often offered directly by MFIs. Term life or personal accident insurance is often offered alongside credit life insurance to cover the family if a borrower dies. An example of this kind of insurance is the work of the U.S.-based insurance company AIG in East Africa, which pays out $800 for the accidental death of the borrower, $400 for the spouse, and $200 for dependents.

Savings life insurance is often offered by credit unions and stimulates savings (see the example of COLUMNA in Guatemala in box 2.4). Property insurance is nearly always linked to a loan and may help a borrower continue repaying his or her loan only if something happens to the property (usually livestock). In some cases, replacement of the property is also covered. Endowment policies combine long-term savings and insurance with emergency loans against the savings balance. In this case, the premium payments accumulate value. Delta Bangladesh offers this kind of policy.

Agricultural insurance is particularly tricky, and no evidence exists of viable programs. The problem is that insured farmers are less likely to pursue sound practices and therefore are more likely to lose their crops. It is difficult to calculate the probability of loss because so many factors can influence crop yields. At the same time, premiums that farmers can afford are not usually sufficient to cover claims and administrative costs. Recent innovations that link insurance to rainfall and other weather conditions are promising, because they may be more measurable, objective, and viable.

BOX 2.4 Microinsurance: The case of COLUMNA, Guatemala

In 1994, the Guatemalan National Federation of Credit Unions (FENACOAC) and nine member cooperatives created their own insurance company, COLUMNA. Today, more than half a million Guatemalans, mostly members of 35 primarily rural credit unions, have bought insurance policies through COLUMNA. Cooperative members have a life insurance policy protecting their savings, contributions, and credit balances. Also, 54,000 members have a microinsurance policy for funeral services and accidents called *Plan de Vida Especial* (Special Life Plan).

The Special Life Plan is a group life insurance product that offers a benefit between around $1,200 and $6,200 in case of death and an additional sum to cover accidental death and disability. The low insurance premium (between $7.80 and $39.00) is paid annually. The product is marketed and distributed through the credit unions, benefiting from their wide geographic coverage. Some sell the policy when the member joins the credit union or applies for a loan, in which case the amount of the policy is added to the loan and repaid monthly. COLUMNA has retained its risk levels according to its solvency capacity and has had appropriate reinsurance coverage. The plan has been profitable; over the past four years, the estimated profit for the Special Life Plan has averaged 26 percent of the net written premium.

Source: Based on Herrera and Miranda, "COLUMNA, Guatemala: Good and Bad Practices Case Study."

Health insurance is probably the product for which there is the greatest demand among poor and low-income households; however, like agricultural insurance, it is difficult to provide this insurance viably. Several different delivery models exist, and many argue that this type of insurance should not be commercially sold, but rather be considered a natural right as part of a government's social protection program. Health insurance is likely the most difficult product to offer because (1) a third party is necessarily involved (for example, the health care provider); (2) a number of classical insurance problems apply (those more likely to get sick are also more likely to sign up, those who are insured are more careless and overuse health services), which makes insurance costly for all involved; and (3) the only policies that are affordable to poor people are those that are highly restrictive in terms of the kinds of benefits offered.[17]

The Impact of Financial Services on the Lives of Poor People

A deeper and more inclusive financial system benefits poor people both indirectly, through increased growth, and directly as they gain access to needed services. Increasingly, a growing body of research shows that deeper financial sectors better support growth and poverty reduction.[18] When financial institutions are effective, they mobilize savings for investment; facilitate and encourage inflows of foreign capital; and ensure that capital goes to its most productive use.[19] All these effects lead to higher levels of economic growth. Growth, in turn, tends to reduce overall poverty in many countries. (Although it does not guarantee poverty reduction when that growth is concentrated in the hands of the better-off.)

Measuring direct impact is about understanding how financial services affect the lives of poor people and their families. The research on this topic has focused on microcredit. For the most part, the benefits of savings and insurance, especially in reducing the vulnerability that is a permanent feature in the lives of the poor, have not been quantified. Because microcredit looks at only one piece of the puzzle, whatever impact has been proven for it likely understates the potential impact of an inclusive financial system.

Existing assessments largely reveal that microcredit has a positive impact on borrowers. Most assessments have looked at how microcredit has affected the individual person or household, while others have examined the impact of credit on the client's microenterprise or community. Impact studies suggest a positive impact on reducing poverty[20]:

[17.] Churchill, *Microinsurance Products.*

[18.] See, for instance, the survey by Levine, "Finance and Growth: Theory and Evidence," and recent research by World Bank economists Beck, Demirguc-Kunt, and Levine, "Finance, Inequality and Poverty," and Honohan, "Financial Development, Growth and Poverty: How Close Are the Links?"

[19.] DFID Financial Sector Team, *The Importance of Financial Sector Development for Growth and Poverty Reduction,* 7.

[20.] The examples in the following paragraphs are drawn from the literature review in Littlefield, Morduch, and Hashemi, *Is Microfinance an Effective Strategy to Reach the Millennium Development Goals?*

- In Indonesia, borrowers increased their incomes by 12.9 percent compared with increases of 3 percent in control-group incomes. Another study of BRI borrowers on the island of Lombok reports that the average incomes of clients had increased by 112 percent and that 90 percent of households had moved out of poverty (the data were collected by interviewing 121 women randomly selected from clients who had received credit at least one year before the interview).
- A study of Society for Helping Awakening Rural Poor through Education (SHARE) clients in India documented that three-fourths of clients who participated in the program for more than two years saw significant improvements in their economic well-being (based on sources of income, ownership of productive assets, housing conditions, and household dependency ratio) and that half of the clients graduated out of poverty.
- Freedom from Hunger clients in Ghana increased their monthly incomes by $36 compared with $18 for nonclients. In addition, clients significantly diversified their income sources. Eighty percent of clients had secondary sources of income versus 50 percent for nonclients.

Studies include not only the impact of credit on income levels, but also incorporate information on how microcredit might improve poor people's lives in other ways. For instance, some studies look at how microcredit has contributed to improving health care, children's education and nutrition, and women's empowerment (see box 2.5).

Regardless of the dimension studied, much of the research points to the importance of long-term access to services before the real impact can be seen. It takes time and repeated use of financial services, often combined with other services, to make a dent in poverty. This finding is among the most compelling arguments for ensuring permanent, financially sustainable provision of credit to the poor.

With such impressive results, it is tempting to overestimate the power of microfinance for solving all development ills. In fact, microfinance is *not* the sole solution for reducing poverty. Financial services, and especially credit, are not usually appropriate for the destitute (for instance, those who go hungry or without a cash income). It is sometimes forgotten that the other word for credit is debt. Loans to the destitute may in fact make the poor poorer if they lack opportunities to earn the cash flow necessary to repay the loans. Basic requirements like food, shelter, and employment are often more urgently needed than financial services and should be appropriately funded by government and donor subsidies.[21] Microfinance should not be seen as a substitute for investments in basic education, health, and infrastructure.

Some providers, like BRAC's Income Generation for Vulnerable Groups Development (IGVGD) program, have found innovative ways to combine credit, training, and government grant programs (in this case, food aid) to help extremely poor women get a foot on the bottom rung of the economic ladder. Over a 10-year period, two-thirds of the more than 1 million women enrolled in

---

[21.] Robinson, *The Microfinance Revolution*. Vol. 1, *Sustainable Finance for the Poor,* 20.

BOX 2.5 Impact of microfinance—beyond income poverty

Microfinance has an impact on more than just the income levels of poor clients. It also reduces their vulnerability to shocks and allows them to make investments in better health and education for their families. A survey of the impact of microfinance on the Millennium Development Goals highlighted some of the following results.

How does access to financial services improve education?

Greater access to financial services and increased incomes allow poor people to invest in their children's future. Studies on the impact of microfinance on children's schooling show the following:

- In Bangladesh, nearly all girls in Grameen Bank client households received schooling, compared with 60 percent of girls in nonclient households. Basic education competency (reading, writing, and arithmetic) among 11- to 14-year-old children in BRAC client households doubled in three years (from 12 percent in 1992 to 24 percent in 1995). Of course, these programs specifically focus on education as a core value and service for clients.

- In Uganda, Foccas clients spent one-third more than nonclients on their children's education.

How does access to financial services improve the health of children and women?

Access to financial services allows clients to seek health care services when needed, rather than wait until an illness has reached crisis proportions. Studies show that financial services have had a strong positive impact on the health of women and children, especially in those programs that combine credit with training on health issues:

- In Bolivia, Credito con Educación Rural (CRECER) clients had better breast-feeding practices, responded more readily with rehydration therapy for children with diarrhea, and had higher rates of diphtheria, pertussis, and tetanus (DPT3) immunization among their children.

- In Uganda, 95 percent of Foccas clients benefited from a microcredit program that combined financial services with education practices to improve the health and nutrition of their children, compared with 72 percent for nonclients. In addition, 32 percent had tried an AIDS prevention technique, twice the percentage for nonclients.

How does access to financial services empower women?

The ability to borrow, save, and earn income enhances poor women's confidence, enabling them to better confront systemic gender inequities. Studies show that this empowerment takes different forms:

- In Indonesia, female clients of Bank Rakayat Indonesia (BRI) were more likely than nonclients to make joint decisions with their husbands concerning allocation of household money, children's education, use of contraceptives, and family size.

- In Nepal, 68 percent of Women's Empowerment Program members said they made decisions on buying and selling property, sending daughters to school, marrying children, and family planning.

- In India, Self-Employed Women's Association (SEWA) clients organized in a union have lobbied for higher wages, the rights of women in the informal sector, and resolving neighborhood issues.

- In Bangladesh, Bolivia, Nepal, the Philippines, and Russia, clients of microfinance programs have run for local government office and won.

Source: Littlefield, Morduch, and Hashemi, *Is Microfinance an Effective Strategy to Reach the Millennium Development Goals?*

the program have climbed out of destitution and have graduated to become regular credit clients of mainstream microfinance programs.[22]

Debates within the microfinance community have focused on the quality of impact studies. Many other factors contribute to improvement (or deterioration) in a household's well-being. So it is difficult to isolate the impact of a few small loans. Also, success in using microcredit for business depends on local economic conditions outside the control of clients and the institutions that serve them. Highly rigorous and reliable impact assessments that employ scientific methods of inquiry cost a lot of money, and some experts question whether they are worth the investment. They contend that the observed fact that borrowers repay loans and then come back to borrow again testifies to the usefulness and presumably positive impact of the loan. Conversely, the donor community justifiably wants proof to ensure that the subsidies spent on this activity work in terms of reducing poverty.

Other observers are more concerned with how MFIs can use impact information more as a market research tool to improve their services to the poor.[23] If an institution cares about poverty reduction and understands the impact of its services on its clientele, then it can take steps to adjust its current services or introduce new ones to meet these objectives—and ultimately improve performance. Helping clients improve their economic condition can make good business sense.[24]

Conclusion

The definition of microfinance clients is expanding to incorporate everyone without access to financial services. Available information on current clients indicates that a relatively narrow range of clients are being served by specialized MFIs. Most clients concentrate around the poverty line, with representation from the very poor and some vulnerable non-poor. Current microcredit clients are largely entrepreneurs in the informal sector. Many potential clients remain excluded.

Poor clients need a variety of financial services, not just short-term working capital loans. Just like everyone else, poor people need a wide range of financial services that are convenient, flexible, and reasonably priced. Depending on their circumstances, poor people need not only credit but also savings, cash transfers, and insurance.

Microfinance can be a powerful instrument against poverty. Existing evidence on the impact of microfinance probably understates the value of financial services for poor people, because studies focus only on one piece of the puzzle: microcredit. Studies show that permanent access to sustainable microcredit enables the poor to increase incomes, build assets, and reduce their vulnerability to external shocks. Microfinance allows poor households to move

---

[22.] Hashemi, "Linking Microfinance and Safety Net Programs to Include the Poorest," 2.

[23.] See the ImpAct Web site for more on this topic: www.ids.ac.uk/impact.

[24.] Chapter 7 further discusses the issue of impact as a key aspect of measuring social performance of microfinance.

from everyday survival to planning for the future, investment in better nutrition, and improved living conditions, children's health, and education. If microcredit alone offers this kind of impact, then access to a broader range of services likely improves the lives of poor people even more dramatically. Future studies will hopefully offer more insight on the additional impact of savings, transfers, and insurance services.

However, microfinance, especially microcredit, is not always the answer. Microcredit is not appropriate for the destitute and hungry who have no reliable income or means of repayment. In many cases, small grants, infrastructure improvements, employment and training programs, and other nonfinancial services may be more appropriate for destitute people.

The challenge moving forward is to better understand the financial service requirements of those who are currently excluded from the financial system and ways to respond to these needs that have the potential to be self-sustaining. But better understanding is not enough. This understanding needs to be translated into permanent access to high-quality, affordable, and convenient financial services offered by a range of financial service providers. Only when supply begins to meet demand will poor people have the means to take control over their financial lives and chart their own paths out of poverty.

Chapter 3

Financial Service Providers: The Micro Level

In an inclusive financial system, a variety of financial service providers is required to meet poor clients' diverse demands. No one single type of financial service provider can do it alone; a range of providers is needed. Unfortunately, the lack of strong, competent retail-level institutions remains the main bottleneck to extending financial services to large numbers of poor people.

Potential service providers range from informal to formal. Their level of formality depends on the sophistication of their organizational structure and governance as well as the degree of oversight or supervision by governments. For instance, highly informal providers have simpler organizations (if any) and are not supervised by a government entity, and formal institutions are the mirror image. At the informal end of the spectrum, there are moneylenders, community savings clubs, deposit collectors, and agricultural input providers, traders, and processors. Private and public banks are the most formal. The middle ground is inhabited by member-owned institutions, nongovernmental organizations (NGOs), and nonbank financial institutions. Note that not all institutions line up perfectly along the continuum (see figure 3.1). Some large cooperatives in Africa and elsewhere operate as regulated financial institutions, giant NGOs in Bangladesh serve millions of clients each and are fairly formal, and some rural banks in countries like the Philippines and Ghana are tiny and somewhat informal, although they may be regulated in theory (if not practice).

Over the past 25 years, microfinance has involved a tremendous movement from informal toward formal providers. Specialized MFIs have proven that the poor are "bankable." Today, formal institutions are rapidly absorbing the lessons learned about how to do small-transaction banking. Many of the newer players in microfinance, such as commercial banks, have large existing branch networks, vast distribution outlets like automatic teller machines, and the ability to make significant investments in technology that could bring financial services closer to poor clients. Increasingly, links among different types of service providers are emerging to offer considerable scope for extending access.

FIGURE 3.1 The Spectrum of Financial Service Providers

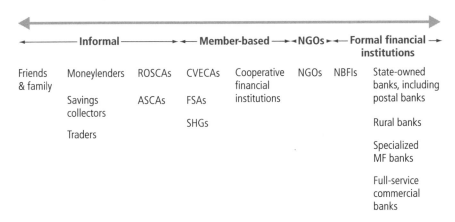

Note: ROSCAs = rotating savings and credit associations; ASCAs = accumulating savings and credit associations; CVECAs = Caisses Villageoises d'Épargne et de Crédit Autogérées; FSAs = financial service associations; SHGs = self-help groups; NGOs = nongovernmental organizations; NBFI = nonbank financial institution.

This chapter looks at the landscape of financial service providers. It addresses the following questions: Which kinds of financial service providers currently offer financial services to poor and low-income clients? What are their respective characteristics, strengths, and weaknesses? How can they work individually and as a group to reach large numbers of poor clients?

The Landscape of Financial Service Providers[1]

In its survey of the supply of formal financial services to poor people, CGAP identified the following types of financial institutions serving low-income clients: state-owned agricultural, development, and postal banks; member-owned savings and loan institutions; other savings banks; low-capital local and/or rural banks; and specialized MFIs of varying types. These institutions almost always have a double bottom line because they pursue both financial and social objectives.

Specialized MFIs—including NGOs, nonbank financial institutions (NBFIs), commercial banks that specialize in microfinance, and microfinance programs in full-service commercial banks—account for about 18 percent of the roughly 750 million total combined savings and loan accounts (see figure 3.2). Financial cooperatives make up another 5 percent. Government-owned financial institutions, including postal savings banks, dominate the scene, with about three-quarters of the accounts. When looking at credit only, MFIs account for 33 percent of the loans (57 percent if China and India are excluded).

[1.] This section draws from Christen, Rosenberg, and Jayadeva, "Financial Institutions with a 'Double Bottom Line': Implications for the Future of Microfinance."

FIGURE 3.2 Savings Accounts and Active Loans by Institutional Type

Savings accounts by institutional type

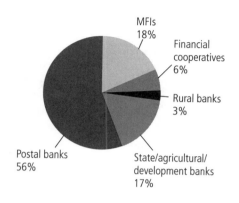

MFIs
18%

Financial
cooperatives
6%

Rural banks
3%

Postal banks
56%

State/agricultural/
development banks
17%

Active loans by institutional type

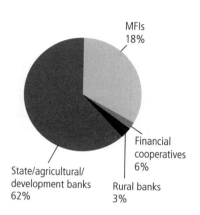

MFIs
18%

Financial
cooperatives
6%

Rural banks
3%

State/agricultural/
development banks
62%

Source: Christen, Rosenberg, and Jayadeva, "Financial Institutions with a 'Double Bottom Line.'"

Service providers also vary by region or country. For instance, banks and NBFIs have greater outreach in Latin America than other regions; credit and savings cooperatives dominate in West and Central Africa; and community banks (especially rural banks) are prevalent in certain countries like Ghana, Indonesia, and the Philippines.

Informal Providers

Most poor people obtain financial services through informal arrangements with friends and neighbors, not the formal institutions surveyed by CGAP. Interestingly, these informal arrangements take on similar forms—from Mexico to Senegal to Bangladesh. Informal financial service providers can be divided into two rough categories: individual providers and collective clubs or associations. (There are some exceptions, as supplier credit and pawnbrokering are typically supplied by companies; these will be discussed below.)

Individual informal providers: moneylenders, savings collectors, pawnbrokers, traders, processors, and input suppliers. The most common informal provider is a friend or a relative who lends money to help out in a pinch or to take advantage of an opportunity. In addition, a number of people make their living, either on a full- or part-time basis, by offering financial services to individuals in their community.

Moneylenders are perhaps the most well-known. Often reviled for exploiting poor people, moneylenders actually offer a valued financial service in many communities. Some argue that more formal lenders can learn much from moneylenders, including their knowledge of the credit market; development of personal relationships with clients; tested methods of evaluating the repayment capacity and character of prospective borrowers; quick and easy credit procedures carried out in locations convenient for borrowers; and repeat lending to those who repay on time. However, moneylenders can be very expensive. For instance, a standard moneylender loan in the Philippines uses the "5/6 loan"—that is, for every five pesos borrowed in the morning, six must be repaid by evening. This amounts to a daily interest rate of more than 20 percent.[2]

Deposit collectors—people who collect and store savings—are common in many societies, including South Asia and West Africa. A safe place to hide money can be hard to find. Deposit collectors often not only do not pay interest on the deposits they gather but they also charge for the service. In India, clients are willing to pay fees up to an equivalent of 30 percent annualized interest rate for someone to keep their money. This seemingly perverse behavior is due to the fact that there simply are no other good options for saving. Also, people often like to save for a specific purpose, like school fees, and rely on the discipline imposed by savings collectors to ensure they can meet these obligations.[3]

Pawnbrokering is another form of informal lending, although in many countries this practice has become more formal and regulated. Pawnbrokers lend on the basis of collateral. Unlike other lenders, though, they take physical possession of the collateral. Pawnbrokering usually entails a high volume of small advances made for relatively short periods. Given the processing, valuation, and storage of the pledged item, transaction costs might appear quite high as a percentage of the small amount lent. These costs, however, are partly offset because the pawnbroker does not take time to evaluate the borrower or monitor the loan.[4]

Especially in agriculturally dependent rural areas, traders, processors, and input suppliers are important (many would argue the most important) sources of credit for farmers. Credit is built into existing business relationships. Agribusiness lenders already do business with farmers by buying their produce for processing or marketing; input suppliers already sell seeds and fertilizers to them. Credit may be in cash or in kind, such as seeds and fertilizer. Clients often repay loans by selling their crops at a discount or having the loan amount deducted from the proceeds of their harvest. Credit may be combined with other services, like advice from a fertilizer vendor on how to apply the fertilizer for best results. Leading agribusiness companies across southern Africa were estimated to provide around $91 million in credit to more than 530,000 rural households between 2001 and 2003. Four out of every five rice mills surveyed by the Food and Agriculture Organization (FAO) in India offer advance payments to farmers to cover input costs.[5]

[2] Robinson, *The Microfinance Revolution*, Vol. 1, 172, 199.
[3] Rutherford, *The Poor and Their Money*, 15.
[4] Skully, *The Development of the Pawnshop Industry in East Asia*, 1.
[5] This paragraph draws heavily on Christen and Pearce, *Managing Risks and Designing Products for Agricultural Microfinance: Features of an Emerging Model*, 26. Chapter 7 explores rural and agricultural finance further as a "frontier challenge."

Clubs: ROSCAs and ASCAs. Collective forms of informal service providers include rotating savings and credit associations (ROSCAs) and their close cousins, the accumulating savings and credit associations (ASCAs). ROSCAs show up around the world—called merry-go-rounds in Kenya, *tandas* in Mexico, chit funds in India, *Kibati* in Tanzania, and *Esusu* in Nigeria. They are defined as associations of participants who make regular contributions to a central "pot." The pot is given, in whole or in part, to each contributor in rotation or chosen by lottery. The funds are managed by the members themselves. An ASCA is similar except that some members borrow and some do not and the pot grows over time, ROSCAs liquidate each cycle while ASCAs endure across cycles. Box 3.1 gives examples of ROSCAs and ASCAs in Asia.

The prevalence of ROSCAs and ASCAs throughout the world amply demonstrates that participants value their benefits. ROSCAs and ASCAs have many advantages: they are efficient and cost little to run, they are transparent and easy for members to understand, no outsiders are involved, no cash is stored since it passes from member to member, and the risks of misappropriation are low. They often run for a fixed period to avoid bookkeeping, disputes, fraud, and capture by powerful elites. One expert asserts that "ROSCAs could reasonably claim to be the most efficient intermediation device around, since at each round the savings of many are transformed instantaneously, with no middlemen, into a lump sum for one person."[6]

ASCAs share many of the benefits of ROSCAs, with added flexibility because they offer more opportunities for those who want to borrow, can be used for

---

BOX 3.1 Variations on the ROSCA and ASCA theme

Lottery ROSCAs: A typical ROSCA in Dhaka, Bangladesh, is run by a small shopkeeper. Many members pay when they can, often between meetings, sometimes in installments. The shopkeeper keeps records of who has paid and follows up on late payers. These managers accept tips from members as a reward for this work. A lottery avoids the problems of any perceived unfairness in the order the money is distributed. For each round, names are drawn randomly. The lottery itself generates a certain amount of excitement, attracting a crowd of onlookers, in turn helping to make the process public and transparent.

Initial-investment ASCAs: In the hills of the northern Philippines, there are ASCAs where members make only one initial investment, which is often quite small. These investments are pooled and lent out at high interest rates (up to 10 to 15 percent a month) to the member(s) most in need of cash. As borrowers repay their loans with interest, the fund grows quickly. Those who contribute their initial investment but do not borrow see their investment grow. Some ASCAs close and distribute profits after three years to reduce risks. Even after so short a time, at 15 percent a month, a saver who put in an initial $1 could multiply his or her capital 133 times.

Source: Rutherford, *The Poor and Their Money,* 35, 36.

[6.] Rutherford, *The Poor and Their Money,* 52.

purposes like insurance, and can last longer than ROSCAs. But because the money does not rotate evenly, ASCAs need more management skills to run well and may suffer more fraud.

With such a broad array of informal financial services available to them, how can it be said that poor people lack access to financial services? The problem is that these informal services, while appealing and useful for many reasons, have serious drawbacks. First, they can be expensive (especially in the case of the individual providers like moneylenders or pawnbrokers). Second, they are often rigid. For instance, ROSCAs and ASCAs require regular deposits of identical amounts, and an individual's money is tied up until it is their turn to access the funds. Third, ROSCAs can be highly risky—participants lose money when someone fails to continue contributions after taking an early hand. This system might also be inconvenient if a member's need for money occurs before (or after) their "turn." Also, costs can be less than transparent and difficult to understand, as is the case in some agricultural trader or processor credit systems. All informal financial services are vulnerable to collapse or fraud, where people can lose their money, whether because of corruption, lack of discipline, or collective shocks like a natural disaster or a bad harvest.[7] Finally, borrowing from family and friends can be associated with stigma or a loss of dignity, especially if borrowers become dependent on others.[8]

Member-Based Organizations

Building on what works in the informal system, many forms of member-based financial organizations exist throughout the world. Credit unions or savings and credit cooperatives are more formal, whereas other organizations border on informal, although usually with more formal organizations behind them as promoters. Member-based organizations typically rely on their members' own savings as the main source of funds. Many member-based organizations (especially the more formal cooperatives) are grouped into federations at the regional or national level. These federations can offer supervision, liquidity management, refinancing, and/or technical support to the federated cooperatives. Because of their low costs and closeness to their members, member-based organizations may hold the key for reaching remote communities.

Although they have been around for decades, self-help groups (SHGs) in India have attracted much attention over the past few years as a source of rural financial services, especially for poor women. The current model links informal SHGs of 10–20 people with sources of finance, such as NGOs and commercial banks. SHGs start by collecting members' savings and, if all goes well, may eventually gain access to bank loans. SHGs tend to reach the very poor. Surveys show that more than half of SHG members are from the poorest groups: landless and marginal farmers.

Recent years have seen exponential growth in linkages between Indian SHGs and public and private banks. In 2003, the number of SHGs linked to banks was

---

[7] Robinson, *The Microfinance Revolution*, Vol. 1, 24.
[8] Ruthven, *Money Mosaics: Financial Choice and Strategy in a West Delhi Squatter Settlement*, 19.

around 800,000, compared with just 33,000 in 1999.[9] Perhaps the most important bank involved is the National Bank for Agriculture and Rural Development (NABARD), an apex bank that launched its bank-SHG link program in 1992. NABARD's goal is to expand financial access to 20 million poor households by 2008. By March 2004, the NABARD program had cumulatively lent $867 million to 560 banks, which in turn extended loans to 1.1 million SHGs serving approximately 16 million poor households.[10] For its part, the State Bank of India was lending to nearly 175,000 SHGs in 2004, compared with around 12,000 groups four years earlier.[11]

For all their promise, SHGs are very fragile; even a slight deterioration in loan portfolio quality can seriously compromise their survival. A push to lend too much or grow too fast can result in groups that do not work over the long term.[12] In addition, most SHGs offer inflexible loan terms that do not necessarily correspond to members' cash flows or product demands, and repayment frequency can be rigid. SHGs do not capture large amounts of savings, and most of this savings is compulsory to gain access to loans (as opposed to voluntary deposits that respond to the market demand of poor clients for savings instruments).[13]

Financial service associations (FSAs) and Caisses Villageoises d'Épargne et de Crédit Autogérées (Self-Managed Village Savings and Credit Banks, or CVECAs) in Africa represent twists on the member-based theme, with an emphasis on remote rural areas. FSAs rely initially on building up a strong equity base through members' shares, with the goal of leveraging that equity by taking loans from banks at commercial interest rates. Start-up costs of these organizations have been subsidized by international development assistance agencies (often referred to as donors), and NGOs have done the promotional work to launch them. Comprehensive data are difficult to find on FSAs. As of 2000, roughly 160 FSAs operated in eight countries with more than 50,000 shareholders.[14] More recent data from Kenya show that 67 FSAs in 18 districts served 46,700 members at the end of 2004.[15] The question remains whether FSAs can become self-sufficient (independent from donor grants).

CVECAs, originally promoted by the French-based Centre International de Développement et de Recherche (CIDR), grew out of an interest in improving the traditional cooperative model in West Africa. CVECAs were first developed in the Dogon region of Mali in the late 1980s. Additional CVECAs were replicated in Mali and other countries in Africa, each of them adapting the original model to suit the local environment.[16] At the end of 2003, the CIDR networks reached 220,000 members with average loans of about $130. Nearly

---

9. Srivastava and Basu, *Scaling-up Access to Finance for India's Rural Poor,* 2.

10. www.nabard.org.

11. Harper and Arora, *Small Customers, Big Market: Commercial Banks in Microfinance,* 73.

12. Srivastava and Basu, *Scaling-up Access to Finance for India's Rural Poor,* 2, 12.

13. Prakash, Pillai, Hashemi, and Isern, *Self-help Groups in India: Value for Money?* 14, 16.

14. Jazayeri, *Financial Services Association (FSA): Concept and Some Lessons Learnt,* 19.

15. Duursma, *Community-Based Microfinance Models in East Africa,* 14.

16. Pearce and Reinsch, *Caisses Villageoises d'Epargne et de Crédit Autogérées* (CVECAs), 1–3.

all clients live in rural areas, and 70 percent of all loans went to agriculture or agriculture-related activities.[17]

Financial cooperatives (sometimes called credit unions or savings and credit cooperatives) take the principle of member ownership to increasingly formal levels. Cooperative financial institutions began in Europe nearly 150 years ago, and the movement has now spread around the globe, with nearly 29 million members throughout developing and transition countries (see table 3.1).[18] In many countries, some financial cooperatives have evolved into large, successful financial institutions. In West Africa more than 3.7 million clients were reached as of the end of 2004, mostly through credit cooperatives. Another good example is Kenya, where the Savings and Credit Societies (SACCOs) are recognized as a serious part of the financial system. The more than 3,000 SACCOs have nearly 5 million members and assets close to $1 billion.[19] In Central Asia, 72 percent of microfinance borrowers and 86 percent of depositors are members of credit unions.[20]

Financial cooperatives are owned and controlled by their members and are usually nonprofit. Members often share some common bond, such as where they work, live, or go to church. These institutions provide financial services: savings, checking accounts, loans, insurance, and fund transfer services (although the weaker and smaller ones are not capable of offering transfers). But instead of making money for shareholders (like banks do), credit unions and financial cooperatives return some earnings in excess of operational costs to their members. These benefits come in the form of dividends on member shares, increased

TABLE 3.1 Financial Cooperatives in Developing and Transition Countries

	Financial Cooperatives	Members	Savings (million $)	Loans (million $)	Average Savings/ Member ($)	Average Loan Balance/ Member ($)
Asia	14,085	6,010,725	10,948	825	1,821	137
Africa	7,856	7,162,689	1,872	1,658	261	231
Latin America and Caribbean	2,113	12,065,323	10,173	9,776	843	810
Eastern Europe and NIS	4,606	3,635,513	1,575	1,351	433	372
TOTAL	**28,660**	**28,874,250**	**24,569**	**13,611**	**851**	**471**

Source: World Council of Credit Union's Statistical Report, 2003, www.woccu.org.
Note: NIS = Newly Independent States.

[17] Email interview with Renée Chao-Béroff, research director, Centre International de Développement et de Recherche.
[18] World Council of Credit Unions, www.woccu.org.
[19] Ndii, *Role and Development of Microfinance and Savings and Credit Cooperatives in Africa*, 1.
[20] Pytkovska, *Overview of Microfinance Industry in the ECE Region in 2003*, 1, 2.

interest on savings, decreased rates for loans, or new and better services. Leadership is drawn from the members themselves, and sometimes, in smaller cooperatives, management is often voluntary as well. Voluntary management is, by definition, less professional and may present a risk to the financial health of the cooperative. In most financial cooperatives, each member has one vote: power is not distributed according to the proportion of shares held.[21]

As table 3.1 shows, financial cooperatives have relatively small average savings and loan balances per member. However, because they draw from a broad base of members, it is not clear how many of the clients of financial cooperatives are indeed poor. There is some evidence that, in some countries, the clientele of financial cooperatives is at least as poor (if not poorer) than those of other, more specialized MFIs (see box 3.2).

Financial cooperatives could potentially reach poorer people, especially in remote towns and villages. In the Philippines, for instance, credit cooperatives

---

BOX 3.2 Institutional determinants of poverty outreach in microfinance

Do financial cooperatives and/or rural banks reach people as poor as those reached by specialized NGO-MFIs? In partnership with others, CGAP used its Poverty Assessment Tool to test this question in Senegal and Ghana. The University of Maryland conducted similar research in Peru.

The research indicates that that conventional wisdom is wrong—institutional type does not necessarily influence the poverty level of clients. For banks, financial cooperatives, and NGOs alike, the most important factor appears to be where they place their branch offices.

In Senegal, the study found that FENAGIE-PECHE, a multipurpose cooperative, reached the largest proportion of very poor people among its clients: two-thirds of its clients were among the poorest third of the population. FENAGIE-PECHE sought membership from rural fishing communities, and therefore selected clients who were poorer than MFI clients. Other cooperatives—like Agence de Credit pour l'Entreprise Privée (ACEP), Cooperative and Mutual Solutions (CMS),

and Programme d'Appui aux Mutuelles d'Épargne et de Crédit au Sénégal (PAME-CAS)—serve a broad range of clients, but because they are so big, they reach large absolute numbers of poor clients.

In Ghana, the analysis indicated that rural banks had greater depth of outreach than NGOs. Twenty-six percent of rural bank clients were among the poorest 20 percent of the population of Ghana, compared with 16 percent of NGO-MFI clients. Many of the rural banks are located in the northern region, where poverty is most intense, and where NGOs are generally absent.

In Peru, the Center for Institutional Reform and the Informal Sector (IRIS) at the University of Maryland surveyed clients from six different financial institutions and control groups and found that the cooperative in the sample achieved the deepest poverty outreach, followed by a regulated microbank network and a rural savings and loan bank. Again, placement of branches mattered more than institutional form.

Sources: Email interview with Syed Hashemi, senior microfinance specialist, CGAP; and Central Bank for West Africa (BCEAO) and CGAP, *Determining the Outreach of Senegalese MFIs,* 2.

---

[21] World Council of Credit Unions, www.woccu.org.

play a big development role in rural areas (even though they are larger in urban areas).[22] They reach remote areas not served by banks, and a 2001 survey showed that 24 cooperatives had 41,248 clients with average outstanding loan balances of only $98 each.[23]

Two key conditions must be met for financial cooperatives to be successful: (1) the number of members must be small enough so that they can monitor each other easily (or systems similar to those found in formal financial institutions must be put in place to protect depositors), but large enough to ensure that (2) a single group of net borrowers does not dominate. A cooperative can become unstable if these conditions do not hold. As in other financial institutions, if management is not sufficiently monitored, then the risk of fraud and other mismanagement is dangerously high. Also, when a structural conflict arises between borrowers (who prefer low interest rates and low repayment pressure) and net depositors (who want high interest rates and conservative investment of their deposits), borrowers often "win" because they are often more influential and wealthy, leading to risky lending that puts members' savings in danger.[24] Another potential weakness comes from conflicts between elected board members who are volunteers and hired professional management with technical training and background.

A challenge to the future potential of member-owned institutions of all kinds is the need to improve their supervision. In some countries, such as those of the West African Monetary Union, banking authorities supervise cooperatives, but in others they do not. For example, a new law in Mexico delegates supervision of financial cooperatives to their federations. In most countries, the authorities charged with overseeing cooperatives of all kinds—not just financial cooperatives—also supervise financial cooperatives. These entities do not usually have the requisite skills, and the general lack of financial oversight leaves the safety and soundness of these organizations vulnerable, which is especially problematic when they hold poor people's savings.

On the other hand, some qualitative evidence from Uganda suggests that poor people are less likely to lose their savings in un- or undersupervised member-based institutions than in informal savings mechanisms. Recent focus group research revealed that nearly all clients saving in the informal sector report some savings losses. In contrast, losses were reported by only a small proportion of those saving in formal financial institutions and in semiformal institutions (including credit unions).[25]

Nongovernmental Organizations

NGOs emerged to fill the void left by the failure of banks to serve the poor effectively and have been the true pioneers of the microfinance world. Since the mid-1980s, NGOs have carried out their work with an increasing commitment

[22] Llanto, *Micro Finance and Rural Finance Options in the Philippines*, 31.

[23] Charitonenko, *Commercialization of Microfinance, The Philippines*, 16.

[24] Ledgerwood, *Microfinance Handbook*, 103.

[25] Wright and Mutesasira, *The Relative Risks to the Savings of Poor People*, 2.

to financial sustainability. Although the exact number of NGOs is not known, the Microcredit Summit Council has collected information on about 3,000 MFIs (most of which are NGOs) that provide financial services to more than 80 million clients.[26] Estimates of worldwide NGOs offering financial services reach up to 9,000.

Some NGOs dedicate themselves completely or mostly to microfinance, while others offer microfinance in addition to other services. NGOs can be completely indigenous or affiliated to international networks. Probably the best-known national NGOs include Bangladesh Rural Advancement Committee (BRAC), ASA, and PROSHIKA in Bangladesh, which have a combined clientele of a staggering 5.6 million people. But other smaller NGOs exist throughout the world. International networks have played an important role in spreading microfinance, starting up and supporting NGOs in all regions of the globe.[27]

Although NGOs have clearly led the way in the development of microfinance, they face a number of constraints and most have not grown as strongly as a result. For example, the average growth rate of the number of borrowers among institutions reporting to the Microcredit Summit equals about 15 percent per year from 1999 to 2003.[28] They are often donor dependent, particularly the smaller ones, because many were launched with donor funds. Their governance structures are unsuited for bearing fiduciary responsibility, since board members do not represent shareholders or member-owners with money at stake. The range of financial services they can offer is restricted. NGOs cannot usually mobilize savings legally; this function is limited to banks and other intermediaries supervised by banking authorities.

The past 10 years have shown two (somewhat opposing) trends among microfinance NGOs: commercialization and pushing the poverty frontier.

Some leading NGOs are increasingly behaving in a "commercial" way. The rationale for this approach, often referred to as seeking sustainability, is to become independent from unpredictable donor financing and tap commercial sources of funding to fuel growth and reach more poor people. In fact, data from the MIX Market suggest that sustainable institutions (those that cover their costs through revenues) reach much larger numbers than unsustainable ones. Of the 146 NGOs reporting data for 2003 to this database, only half (53 percent) are sustainable, but those sustainable institutions reach more than 90 percent of the total reported number of clients.[29]

Successful NGO commercialization has demonstrated to formal financial institutions that microfinance is a good and profitable business. But commercialization means different things to different NGOs. For a multipurpose NGO offering an array of (often socially motivated) services, it might mean professionalizing its microfinance activities and separating them operationally and

---

[26] Daley-Harris, *State of the Microcredit Summit Campaign Report 2004*, 3.
[27] International networks are discussed further in chapter 4.
[28] Adrian Gonzalez, research analyst, CGAP/The MIX, based on Microcredit Summit database.
[29] Data from the MIX Market www.mixmbb.org/en/index.html consulted in July 2005. Sustainability is defined as those institutions covering at least 110 percent of their costs with revenues. Note that MFIs reporting to the MIX Market are on average more profitable than other MFIs, and findings should not be generalized to the entire universe of financial institutions serving the poor.

BOX 3.3 Experiences with NGO transformation

Several NGOs have transferred into formal financial institutions, especially in some Latin American countries (Bolivia, Peru), Eastern Europe, Kenya, and now Uganda. The experience so far is that, although costly, the transformation process allows institutions to provide better services, improve their access to financing, and ultimately increase the number of clients they can reach on a permanent basis.

Fondo Financiero Privado para el Fomento a Iniciativas Económicas (FFP-FIE) is a nonbank financial institution that began as an NGO in 1984 in La Paz, Bolivia. FIE considered becoming a formal financial entity early in its history and was given a pathway when the Bolivian government created a legal structure for microfinance formalization, called Fondos Financieros Privados (FFPs, or Private Financial Funds). The application process was long and arduous. FIE's first application in 1995 was rejected, partially because of the dominant role the NGO wanted to play in ownership of the new financial entity. After three more years of preparation, FIE finally formed an FFP (FFP-FIE) in 1998. At the end of that year, FFP-FIE had 20,040 active borrowers, 121 savers, and total assets of more than $17 million.[a] Six years later, FIE had nearly 45,000 active borrowers, and nearly 31,000 savings accounts with more than $60 million in assets. As of 2004, FIE NGO held just under half of the shares; other major shareholders include the Andean Development Corporation (CAF), OIKO-CREDIT, Hivos-Triodos Fonds, Vincent Emanuel Burgi, and the Swiss Development Corporation.[b]

Opportunity Bank Montenegro (OBM) started as an NGO in 1999, with the intent to turn into a commercial bank from the outset.[c] By mid-2002, OBM was a licensed bank. It made major investments in computer systems, human resources, banking operations, and deposit mobilization. It also incurred costs in renovating the head office and branches, installing vaults and security equipment, hiring additional staff, and implementing new procedures. In 2003, OBM covered its costs and reported 5,700 clients with an outstanding portfolio of nearly $17 million. The Bank has a total of 13 common stock shareholders. Opportunity International, a U.S.-based nonprofit organization, owns 75 percent of the common shares and 100 percent of the preferred shares. Minority shareholders include Rabo Investment Advisory Services (part of the RaboBank Group) and Dutch, British, and U.S. individuals.[d]

[a] Based on www.ffpfie.com; performance data from the MIX Market: www.mixmarket.org.
[b] Email interview with Enrique Soruco, general manager, Fondo Financiero Privado para el Fomento a Iniciativas Economicas, Bolivia.
[c] This example draws from Coates and Wilson Shrader, *Turning an NGO into a Bank*. Data from www.opportunity.org.
[d] Interview with Mark Crawford, chief financial officer, Opportunity Bank, Montenegro.

financially from the other services offered. For a specialized NGO, commercialization might entail transformation into a licensed financial intermediary (see box 3.3). In microfinance, the term "transformation" refers to the process by which a nonprofit organization or an NGO becomes a regulated financial institution.[30]

The trend toward commercialization has led to concerns about "mission drift," or the tendency of increasingly commercial NGOs to abandon their tra-

---

[30.] www.accion.org/micro_glossary.asp.

ditional poor clientele. This concern is particularly acute for transformed MFIs. Profitability is a key objective for any licensed financial institution. Some assert that the only way to do microfinance on a profitable basis is to focus on easier-to-reach, wealthier clients who take out larger loans and make larger deposits. The evidence on mission drift seems mixed. In some cases, average loan sizes increase as MFIs mature and become more commercial, which could be a sign that more wealthy clients are being served, but this does not necessarily mean that poorer clients are being abandoned.

Larger loan sizes might also mean that existing clients are increasing their capacity for debt. Over time, a larger proportion of clients are repeat borrowers (as opposed to first-time borrowers who typically have smaller loans). This phenomenon will increase the average loan size even if there is absolutely no change in the MFI's strategy for reaching a certain poverty level among its clientele. In other cases, such as CARD Bank in the Philippines, average loan sizes are still very small, even while the institution remains profitable and transforms into a bank. Loans at CARD have remained below 20 percent of the gross national income (GNI) per capita of the Philippines over the past several years.[31]

The question of mission drift leads directly to another hot debate among microfinance NGOs: whether MFIs can really reach very poor people and be profitable. Intuitively, the trade-off between these two objectives seems obvious—wealthier clients take larger loans and make larger and fewer transactions, which would appear to be cheaper to manage. However, some institutions achieve both. For instance, 139 out of 231 institutions reporting data for 2003 to the *MicroBanking Bulletin* were profitable (even after adjusting for donor subsidies). Of those 139, the 41 that target the poorest clients averaged better profitability than all 139 profitable institutions combined. Those 41 institutions also reach more than three times more clients than the other financially sustainable institutions put together. In other words, what the MIX refers to as the low-end institutions out-performed the overall sample of institutions reporting to the bulletin.[32] Analysis of a more recent MIX Market dataset finds no significant relationship between loan size and profitability. This means that institutions with larger loan sizes are not necessarily more profitable.[33] These data demonstrate that it is possible to reach very poor people profitably—or at least that serving very poor people is not necessarily less profitable than serving the less poor.

While some microfinance NGOs have been commercializing, many others push to reach poorer or more remote clients, high-risk groups like families suffering from HIV/AIDS, or people displaced by conflict or natural disasters. This trend of pushing the poverty frontier does not necessarily conflict with commercialization and sustainability, but it may take longer to cover costs and become sustainable while working with these kinds of clients.

---

[31] Data from the MIX Market www.mixmarket.org.
[32] Interview with Adrian Gonzalez, research analyst, CGAP/The MIX. Regional distribution of the 41 low-end institutions: Asia = 19 (including 7 in South Asia); Latin America and the Caribbean = 11; Middle East and North Africa = 5; Sub-Saharan Africa = 4; Eastern Europe and Central Asia = 2.
[33] Adrian Gonzalez, research analyst, CGAP/The MIX based on MIX Market data.

Many (but not all) NGOs that target poorer clients work through informal or semi-formal member-based organizations, as well as group lending models. Examples include Foundation for International Community Assistance's (FINCA's) village banks, Pact's WORTH model, and CARE International's MMDs (*Mata Masu Dubara,* Women on the Move) program. The latter two programs function much like SHGs and border on more informal systems.

FINCA is the pioneer of the village banking method of microcredit, which pulls together 10–50 neighbors who form a group that decides who gets to take out loans and for how much. Loan sizes range from $50 to $500. In 2003, FINCA's network had 15 affiliates in 14 countries in the Americas, Africa, and Asia. FINCA serves more than 50,000 borrowers through more than 1,800 village banks.[34] Beyond the number served, the power of the FINCA village banking model is that many others have copied and adapted it. Pact, an international NGO specializing in capacity building for local organizations, has developed a village banking–type model in southern Nepal. As of 2003, their collective savings were estimated at nearly $4 million.[35] CARE's MMD project in 2003 offered 70,000 poor women in Niger access to a permanent system of savings and credit through their own community-based organizations.[36]

CGAP's Pro-Poor Innovation Challenge, a competition among smaller and younger MFIs, has uncovered a number of NGOs involved in reaching poorer and more remote clients. For instance, the International Justice Mission (IJM) helps former bonded laborers in India access financial services, through a pilot program linked to a local MFI, including help to open individual savings accounts at local banks to manage the reintegration funds they receive from the government upon their release. Alternativa Solidaria (AlSol) in Mexico formed a partnership with Zurich International to offer microinsurance for vulnerable clients in Chiapas to cover burial services of loved ones in this violence-ravaged region.[37]

Given the twin trends of commercialization and pushing the poverty frontier, the questions asked today are as follows: what exactly is the role of both international and domestic NGOs in building inclusive financial systems? Can they be used to scale up the numbers of clients reached, as in the case of Bangladesh, where 60 percent of the 24.6 million microfinance clients are served by financial NGOs?[38] Since they legally are not allowed to mobilize savings and usually are blocked from access to their country's payments systems, how can NGOs ever offer the variety of services demanded by poor clients? Are the constraints to scale (governance, donor dependency) too weighty to be easily overcome?

There is not much agreement within the microfinance community about the answers to these questions and the future role of NGOs as financial service providers. However, it seems clear that with more than 20 years of experience

---

[34.] www.gdrc.org/icm/finca and www.villagebanking.org.
[35.] Odell, *Moving Mountains: Appreciative Planning and Action and Women's Empowerment in Nepal,* 5.
[36.] www.careusa.org.
[37.] CGAP, *Pro-poor Innovation Challenge,* www.cgap.org.
[38.] Credit and Development Forum, "Microfinance Statistics," 19, 23, 248.

and a strong mission to serve the poor, NGOs have a straightforward advantage in at least two ways: to find innovative solutions for reaching increasingly poor and vulnerable groups and to link these innovations to commercial sources of funding to reach larger scale. This research and development function may not be feasible or attractive for other micro-level organizations.

Formal Financial Institutions

To a large extent, the very existence of microfinance is owed to the historic inability or unwillingness of banks and other formal financial institutions to serve the poor. But formal financial institutions, especially banks with some social mission, hold enormous potential for making financial systems truly inclusive. They often have wide branch networks; the ability to offer a range of services, including savings and transfers; and the funds to invest in systems and technical skills. Formal financial institutions can use these strengths to reach massive numbers of poor people, both on their own and in partnership with other financial service providers, including NGOs. CGAP research identified 225 formal financial institutions involved in microfinance in some way.[39] From funding or entering into strategic partnerships with existing MFIs to direct provision of financial services to the poor, formal financial institutions are rapidly entering the fray.

However, formal financial institutions are not all cut from the same cloth. They include both government-owned banks and private commercial banks, with a lot of variation within each category. Note that financial cooperatives are also formal, since they are registered, licensed, and regulated by government entities, but they were discussed under "member-owned institutions" above.

Government-owned development, agricultural, savings, and postal banks. Public banks often have large numbers of savers and extensive branch infrastructure. A CGAP survey found more than 400 million savings accounts in these banks. In many cases, especially in rural areas, they are the only formal option available to poor people (and everyone else). Government-owned banks were often founded with social or development objectives in mind and in many cases have some mandate to serve the poor and unbanked, often in rural communities.

Unfortunately, few government banks are first-rate institutions. They suffer several serious shortcomings: a legacy of subsidized loans often captured by elites, weak loan collection, dependence on large subsidies, political domination, and a lack of responsiveness to the demands of poor clients.[40] However, some notable exceptions offer hope that, when the right conditions hold, these immense "sleeping giants" could play a big role in scaling up financial services for the poor.[41] Here are a few examples:

[39.] CGAP. *Review of Commercial Bank and Other Formal Financial Institution (FFI) Participation in Microfinance.*

[40.] Christen, Rosenberg, and Jayadeva, "Financial Institutions with a 'Double Bottom Line'," 3, 11; see chapter 5 for further discussion of the role of government in direct and indirect provision of financial services.

[41.] See chapter 5 for a more extensive discussion of the success factors for state-owned banks.

- Bank Rakayat Indonesia's (BRI) microbanking division is the largest—and one of the best-performing—MFIs in the world. BRI is a government-owned bank. Today, it serves more than 30 million savers and 3 million borrowers from 4,200 outlets. One of the first banks to recognize the potential of poor clients, over the past 20 years it has consistently operated its microbanking services on a profitable basis.[42]

- The postal networks provide a valuable source of savings and transfer services for millions. In the Middle East and North Africa, for example, postal banks serve more than 25 million people and play an important role in extending access to services in rural areas, among public servants and pensioners.[43] In some countries like Benin and Kenya, the number of postal savings accounts equals or exceeds the number of savings accounts in all other banks combined.[44]

- The National Microfinance Bank (NMB) of Tanzania, with its 115 rural branches was created in 1997 in a spin-off of assets of the state-owned National Bank of Commerce.[45] As of December 2004, NMB had more than 1 million depositors and 145,650 loan customers.[46]

- The Agricultural Bank of Mongolia (Ag Bank) went from receivership in 1999 to a successfully privatized state bank today. It is the main rural financial services provider in the country, offering deposit and loan products throughout its network of 379 branches (the largest in the country). As of February 2004, Ag Bank had around 377,000 deposit accounts and 128,000 loans outstanding.[47]

Private commercial banks and NBFIs. Four kinds of private financial institutions are or can be involved in microfinance: small community or rural banks, NBFIs, specialized microfinance banks, and full-service banks with microfinance as a line of business.[48] The first three categories of financial institutions are more likely to see poor clients as a key market. Full-service commercial banks have been slower to realize the potential of poor clients.

Rural or community banks have emerged in specific countries like Ghana, Indonesia, the Philippines, Nigeria, Tanzania, and others. In Ghana, rural and community banks are owned by members of the community through purchase

---

[42.] Robinson, "Why the Bank Rakyat Indonesia Has the World's Largest Sustainable Microbanking System," 4, 5; and Harper and Arora, *Small Customers, Big Market,* 18.

[43.] Boon, *Worldwide Landscape of Postal Financial Services (Middle East and North African Region),* 2–3.

[44.] Kamewe, "Reinventing Postal Savings Institutions in Africa: A New Role as Large-scale Microfinance Providers."

[45.] Dressen, Dyer, and Northrip, "Turning Around State-Owned Banks in Underserved Markets," 58–67.

[46.] Interview with Robert Dressen, group vice president, Economics, Business, and Finance, Development Alternatives, Inc.

[47.] www.worldbank.org.

[48.] Although NBFIs are by definition (and by title) not banks, they are included in this section on commercial banks because they have very similar characteristics from the perspective of serving poor clients.

of shares. In 2001, there were 115 rural and community banks with more than 1.2 million depositors and 150,000 borrowers.[49] The Philippines has both rural banks, which are owned and organized by individuals living in a given community, and cooperative rural banks, which are owned and organized by cooperatives and other farmer associations. Today, there are more than 780 rural and cooperative rural banks covering more than 85 percent of the municipalities and cities of the Philippines.[50]

NBFIs include mortgage lenders, leasing companies, consumer credit companies, insurance companies, and certain types of dedicated MFIs. Some of these actors have shown an interest in the microfinance market, most recently insurance companies (see box 3.4). NBFIs can also specialize in microfinance. The Private Financial Funds in Bolivia, for example, include five institutions with more than 250,000 microloans.[51] Other examples include Compartamos in Mexico and Share in India. Both transformed from microfinance NGOs into NBFIs, and both are highly successful. Compartamos is the largest dedicated MFI in Latin America, with around 310,000 poor women borrowers and more than $134 million in assets as of the end of 2004. Share is one of the more prominent MFIs in India, with nearly 300,000 clients and more than $16 million in assets in mid-2004.[52] From a legal and regulatory perspective, it is often

---

BOX 3.4 Microinsurance providers

Insurance for poor people is still rare, but it is offered by formal insurers, MFIs, health institutions, agricultural and health cooperatives, traditional societies (for example, funeral societies), and many other types of institutions. MFIs have extensive networks and already offer financial services to poor clients, so they could play a more active role. Some MFIs recognize their lack of experience and technical proficiency and team up with professional insurance providers. FINCA International in Uganda, for example, formed a partnership with AIG, a large international insurance and financial services firm. MFIs can also enter into joint ventures with formal insurers and share both risk and management. A few, like the Self-Employed Women's Association (SEWA) Bank in India, directly provide health and property insurance. The community-based insurance model, where policyholders own and manage the insurance program directly is usually used in health insurance, like UMASIDA in Tanzania. In other cases, mainstream insurers get involved in providing services directly. For instance, La Equidad (Colombia) offers property insurance relevant for poor clients, and Delta Life in Bangladesh offers life insurance to both higher- and lower-end clientele.

Sources: www.microfinancegateway.org/microinsurance/faq.htm#Q3; and an interview with Michael McCord, microinsurance expert.

[49.] Steel and Andah, *Rural and Micro Finance Regulation in Ghana: Implications for Development and Performance of the Industry,* 6.

[50.] Charitonenko, *Commercialization of Microfinance, The Philippines,* 13; and www.rbapmabs.org.

[51.] Interview with Gonzalo Paz, consultant.

[52.] Email interview with Carlos Labarthe, co-executive director, Compartamos; www.sharemicrofin.com.

easier to get a license to operate as an NBFI. But NBFIs are generally restricted by law in the range of services they can offer. For example, neither Share nor Compartamos can mobilize savings.

Specialized microfinance banks include both transformed NGOs or NBFIs and banks that were dedicated to microfinance from the outset. Perhaps the most well-known microfinance bank is BancoSol in Bolivia. In 1992, the micro-credit NGO PRODEM joined with ACCION International, Calmeadow Foundation, Bolivian banks, and other investors to establish BancoSol, the first private commercial bank in the world dedicated exclusively to microfinance. In 1997, BancoSol became the first microfinance bank to issue dividends to shareholders. BancoSol now reaches more than 47,000 clients and remains a market leader in Bolivia. By 2005, ACCION Investments joined a consortium of investors that purchased 47 percent of BancoSol's shares.[53]

A new generation of microfinance banks has cropped up in Central and Eastern Europe and the Commonwealth of Independent States. In 2003, there were 15 microfinance banks serving 190,000 borrowers, with the KMB Bank in Russia and the ProCredit Bank in Georgia having the largest number of borrowers (29,000 and 28,000, respectively).[54] Perhaps the most interesting dimension of microfinance in this relatively new region is its rapid growth and the focus on commercial viability from the beginning.

Banco Solidario, a specialized microfinance bank in Ecuador, has tapped into a high-potential market: Ecuadorians living in Spain and Italy who want to send cash home to family members, save for their eventual return, and buy homes in their places of origin. In 2002, they introduced a new product: *mi familia, mi país, mi regreso* (my family, my country, my return), which has allowed more than 62,000 clients to access around 19,000 sales locations in Spain and Italy to bank with Banco Solidario.[55]

A recent comparison of licensed MFIs (including both NBFIs and banks) to commercial banks in developing countries revealed that the former are more profitable than the latter. The microfinance NBFIs and banks averaged a 3.3 percent return on assets, whereas the commercial banks averaged 2.1 percent.[56] This finding is illustrated in figure 3.3, which shows how specific specialized microfinance banks often outperform the regular commercial banks in their countries. Not surprisingly, this fact has begun to attract the attention of more mainstream banks.

Mainstream commercial banks are relative newcomers in financial services for the poor. Traditional banks find it difficult to do microfinance for a host of reasons: they are not necessarily committed to serving poor people; they may lack the right organizational structure, financial methodologies, and human resources to attract and retain poor clients; their processes are not cost-effective

[53] www.accion.org.
[54] Pytkovska, *Overview of the Microfinance Industry in the ECE Region in 2003*, 4.
[55] www.banco-solidario.com and email interview with Juan Carlos P Peñafiel S., chief of migrant products, Banco Solidario.
[56] Adrian Gonzalez, research analyst, CGAP/The MIX, based on *MicroBanking Bulletin* no. 9 and no. 10, and ratings from Rating Fund (for MFIs); and BANKSCOPE (for commercial banks).

for very small transactions; and regulations sometimes prohibit uncollateralized lending. Many banks simply enjoy large margins on their traditional business and do not feel the pressure of competition to search out new markets. But many banks are overcoming these obstacles, often through the application of technology, such as automated teller machines and cell phone banking.

As shown in figure 3.4, banks have become involved in microfinance in a variety of different ways, from a low-level commitment like renting out office space to a local NGO-MFI (ProCredit Bank in Georgia) to directly serving poor clients as a main business line (Equity Bank in Kenya). In some cases, an initial arm's length relationship with a specialized provider like an NGO can evolve into a deeper involvement.

The ICICI Bank, India's second largest bank with total assets of around $33 billion as of 2004, has a network of 530 branches and service counters and more than 1,880 automatic teller machines.[57] ICICI is moving into microfinance in a big way. Prompted in part by regulation that requires all banks to lend to priority sectors, ICICI entered the market in 2001 by extending credit on a wholesale basis to specialized MFIs. It also proposes to finance a network of village Internet kiosks as points of sale for financial services, form a partnership with MFIs that will act as loan service agents, and collaborate with social entrepreneurs to establish greenfield MFIs (microfinance start-ups). The ICICI Bank views NGOs and other specialized MFIs as partners to help it tap into the low-end market.

FIGURE 3.3 Relative Profitability of Specialized Microfinance Banks

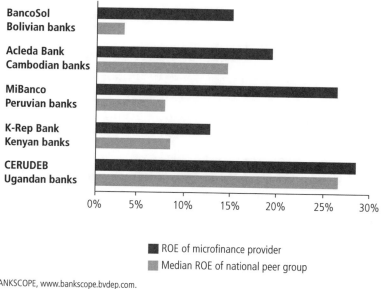

■ ROE of microfinance provider
■ Median ROE of national peer group

Source: BANKSCOPE, www.bankscope.bvdep.com.
Note: All data as of end of 2003. CERUDEB = Centenary Rural Development Bank Ltd.; ROE = return on equity.

[57.] www.icicibank.com.

FIGURE 3.4 Levels of Commercial Bank Involvement in Financial Services for the Poor

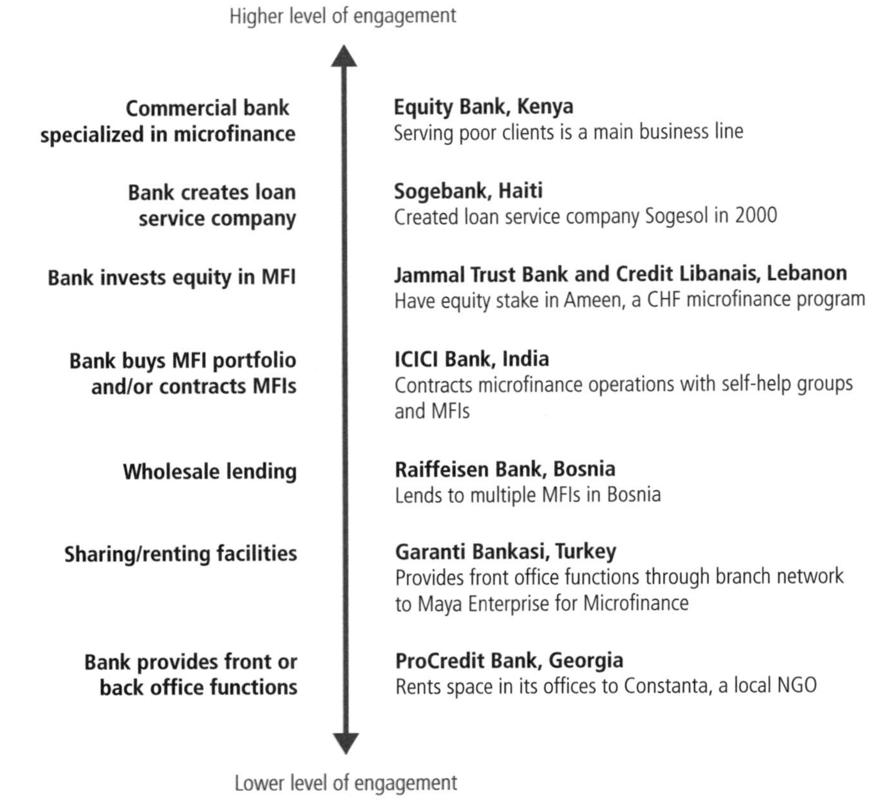

Higher level of engagement

↑

Commercial bank specialized in microfinance	**Equity Bank, Kenya** Serving poor clients is a main business line
Bank creates loan service company	**Sogebank, Haiti** Created loan service company Sogesol in 2000
Bank invests equity in MFI	**Jammal Trust Bank and Credit Libanais, Lebanon** Have equity stake in Ameen, a CHF microfinance program
Bank buys MFI portfolio and/or contracts MFIs	**ICICI Bank, India** Contracts microfinance operations with self-help groups and MFIs
Wholesale lending	**Raiffeisen Bank, Bosnia** Lends to multiple MFIs in Bosnia
Sharing/renting facilities	**Garanti Bankasi, Turkey** Provides front office functions through branch network to Maya Enterprise for Microfinance
Bank provides front or back office functions	**ProCredit Bank, Georgia** Rents space in its offices to Constanta, a local NGO

↓

Lower level of engagement

Source: CGAP.
Note: CHF = Cooperative Housing Foundation; MFI = microfinance institution; NGO = nongovernmental organization.

After two years of involvement, ICICI's microcredit portfolio grew from $16 million to $63 million, and the bank forecasts a potential $1 billion portfolio from this market.[58]

Commercial banks are well placed to invest in technological innovations that can bring financial services closer to where poor people actually live and work. It is likely that opening branches in every village will never pay off financially for a bank. But extending access to financial services through cell phones or working through agents like the town general store, telephone kiosk, or other points of sale could massively increase access at a relatively low cost (see box 3.5). For more on the role of advanced technology in microfinance, see Chapter 7, "Cross-Cutting Challenges."

---

[58] The ICICI Bank, *ICICI Bank's Microfinance Strategy: A Big Bank Thinks Small,* and Harper and Arora, 112.

BOX 3.5 Unconventional distribution channels

Recognizing the need to reduce costs to reach poorer clients, a number of innovators are exploring ways to piggyback financial service delivery onto nonfinancial infrastructure, such as cell phones, retailers' points of sale, Internet kiosks, post offices, and even lottery outlets. Here are some examples:

- In Brazil, Caixa Economica operates 8,961 federal lottery kiosks and has 1,690 branches, covering all 5,561 municipalities in the country. In 2003, it also had point-of-sale terminals at 2,250 retail establishments (including supermarkets and pharmacies), where clients can deposit and withdraw money from checking/savings accounts, make payments, and receive social benefits.

- In South Africa, Capitec has combined convenient branches along transportation routes (for example, train and bus stations, taxi stops) and the rapid rollout of debit cards and automatic teller machines among 200 of these branches to stimulate savings

among low-income earners in addition to short-term loans. This campaign paid off: between February and August 2004, the number of savers jumped from around 18,000 to more than 60,000.

- Cell phone companies in several African countries are developing low-cost, cell phone–based banking services using short message service technology, often connected to mobile banking. In South Africa alone, there are around 19 million mobile phone users, according to Cellular Online, many of which are held by poor customers. Transactions include balance inquiries, bill payments, money transfer, transaction alerts, account servicing, and so on.

New information technology holds promise to reduce risk and cut delivery costs as well. Smart cards, fingerprint readers, and personal digital assistants are being taken up by banks and MFIs in Bolivia, Mexico, India, and South Africa.

Sources: Littlefield and Rosenberg, "Microfinance and the Poor: Breaking Down the Walls between Microfinance and Formal Finance"; Reille and Ivatury, *IT Innovations for Microfinance;* Cellular Online (www.cellular.co.za); and DFID Financial Sector Team, *Banking the Underserved: New Opportunities for Commercial Banks.*

As promising as commercial banks are for building inclusive financial systems, many question whether these banks will ever reach very poor or remote clients. In fact, this is a legitimate question. It is likely that the hardest-to-reach clients will remain outside the realm of possibility for most commercial banks, at least in the near future. However, with their extensive branch infrastructure, capacity to invest in innovative technology solutions to lower the costs of reaching large numbers of people—many of whom are currently excluded from accessing financial services—banks will undoubtedly play an enormous role in building inclusive financial systems. In fact, in the future, reaching massive scale will likely rely on public- and private-sector banks.

Conclusion

Microfinance today is about building sound domestic financial intermediaries that can provide financial services to poor people on a permanent basis. The

TABLE 3.2 Pros and Cons of Different Financial Service Providers

Service Provider	Examples	Strengths	Weaknesses
Informal	Moneylenders ROSCAs ASCAs Input suppliers	• convenient and fast • close to clients • low-cost operations (ROSCAs and ASCAs) • accessible to poor and remote	• some are insecure and unstable • limited scope of operations • rigid (clubs) • expensive (moneylenders)
Member-owned	SHGs FSAs CVECAs Financial cooperatives	• indigenous • low-cost operations • accessible to poor and remote • profits used to benefit members	• governance challenges (risk of capture by net borrowers, manager-dominated) • in many countries, lack of effective financial supervision • scope of operations limited to members • limited products offered
NGOs	International network affiliates Domestic NGOs	• knowledge of poor clients • social mission-driven • more willing and able to take risks to work at frontier	• many donor dependent • limited range of services: limited or no voluntary savings • small scale (except South Asia) • high-cost operations in many cases (with major exceptions)
Formal Financial Institutions	Government-owned banks Rural or community banks NBFIs Mainstream commercial banks	• broad range of services • large branch infrastructure and points of sale • own capital • resources to invest in technology and innovation	• profit motive may dilute social mission • difficult to reach very poor and remote clients • products often do not always meet the needs of the poor

Note: ROSCAs = rotating savings and credit associations; ASCAs = accumulating savings and credit associations; CVECAs = Caisses Villageoises d'Épargne et de Crédit Autogérées; FSAs = financial service associations; SHGs = self-help groups; NGOs = nongovernmental organization; NBFIs = nonbank financial institutions.

lack of sufficient retail-level capacity remains the main constraint to extending financial services to poor people.

Financial sustainability is necessary to reach significant numbers of poor people on a permanent basis. But building financially sustainable institutions is not an end in itself. It is the only way to make an impact far beyond what donor agencies and most governments can fund. Sustainability allows the continued operation of the microfinance provider and the ongoing provision of financial services to the poor. What is more, it appears as though the trade-off between reaching very poor people and financial viability is less acute than originally thought. A number of financial providers have managed to offer high-quality financial services to very poor people—and cover their costs while doing so.

In fact, the type of financial institution (such as NGO, rural bank, or financial cooperative) is less important for reaching very poor and remote clients than other factors like the geographic placement of branches and institutional mission.

No single type of financial service provider can meet all the needs of all those who remain excluded from the traditional financial system. Table 3.2 shows that each type of service provider has strengths and weaknesses when it comes to building inclusive financial systems.

Retail-level service providers are the building blocks upon which the rest of the financial system can be constructed. Working individually and in partnership, they will likely continue to innovate while delivering to poor people financial services that are increasingly cost-effective, convenient, and secure.

Chapter 4

Financial Infrastructure: The Meso Level

Inclusive financial systems comprise more than just the clients and those that serve them directly. Financial institutions cannot operate in a vacuum. They rely on a well-functioning financial infrastructure or "architecture" and a web of other service providers. This is called the meso level.

What exactly is the meso level? The meso level is perhaps the least understood component of the financial system within the microfinance community. As shown in figure 4.1, it extends from financial infrastructure to systems that promote transparency about the performance of financial institutions, technical service providers that offer training and consulting services, and professional associations and networks. An effective meso level is critical for the functioning of the financial system as a whole and especially for expanding access to financial services for poor people.

- **Financial infrastructure** refers to the payments and clearing systems that allow funds to flow among financial institutions and facilitate rapid, accurate, and secure transactions processing. Institutions that serve poor clients need access to these systems to allow their customers to move money around the country and/or from outside the country.

- Information systems for **transparency** serve several purposes. Accurate information on performance allows managers to make sound decisions about how to improve their operations. This information also helps investors to weigh risks and returns in making funding decisions. Finally, information about clients reduces risk and lowers costs.

- **Technical support services,** when available through international or local consultants and training centers, offer advice, training, and systems support to complement and improve financial institutions' existing expertise on specific technical problems and build knowledge at the country, regional, or global level. These service providers also lend credibility to financial services aimed at poor people by increasing the professionalism of the field overall.

FIGURE 4.1 Meso Level: Financial Infrastructure and Services

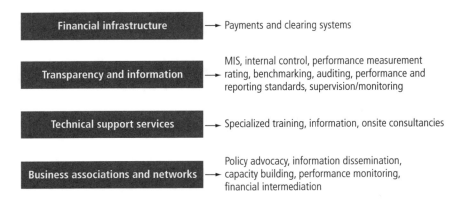

• ***Business associations and networks*** allow institutions to advocate collectively for policy changes and share costs of financial infrastructure and services.

At least three core issues at the meso level—all related to the delivery of services—are hotly debated. The first question is whether infrastructure and services should be microfinance-specific or whether microfinance skills should be absorbed by existing mainstream providers that work more broadly with private-sector clients. As microfinance markets mature and begin to integrate into the financial system, these mainstream service providers (such as rating agencies, auditors, management consultants, and bank training institutes, among others) are starting to adapt to meet the needs of financial institutions that serve poor clients. In the meantime, larger and often more efficient service providers, such as large audit firms, may not consider microfinance as a viable market. Or they may not know enough about microfinance operations to adapt their services. Often, the result is suboptimal quality of services offered (for instance, by assigning junior or less-experienced staff to microfinance). Consequently, specialized microfinance support services are required in many situations, particularly when microfinance is not as well integrated into the financial system.

The second question is which service providers are the most appropriate: domestic or international ones? The focus of this chapter (and most of this book) is on building inclusive *domestic* financial systems within developing countries. In some countries, especially those with competitive or high potential microfinance markets such as Bolivia and India, domestic providers are making a brisk business out of offering their services to MFIs and other financial institutions that serve poor and low-income clients.

International and regional service providers, however, have played a particularly important role and will likely continue to do so. This is especially true for organizations that facilitate information exchange (such as the Microfinance Information eXchange [MIX] and the Microfinance Gateway); rating agencies (such as Fitch and Standard & Poor's); technology vendors (such as MicroBanx Systems, LLC, Temenos eMerge, and Soft Corporación); consulting firms (such as Development Alternatives, Inc., Chemonics, and International Project Consult); and professional networks (such as ACCION International, Appui au Développement Autonome, Centre International de Développement et de Recherche, Groupe de recherche et d'echanges technologiques, FINCA International, Women's World Banking the Microfinance Center for Eastern Europe and the Newly Independent States, and the African Microfinance Network). There are economies of scale in servicing larger regional or global markets from the perspective of the service providers. Financial institutions also benefit from exchange of know-how and technology from other countries.

A third question is whether meso-level support services should be provided on a purely market basis, or whether they should be subsidized by donors or governments. To ensure their permanent availability, many of these services can and should be offered by the private sector on a commercial basis. This "market development approach" proposes a clear vision of numerous, competitive, and locally available suppliers selling a gamut of services to large numbers and types of enterprises (including financial institutions).[1] In many countries and regions, however, the supply of competent service providers is limited. The challenge becomes whether and how to support the emergence and strengthening of the supply of these services in the most effective way.

Because of the meso level's wide-ranging nature and relative newness to the microfinance field, less is currently known about how to build effective services. Nonetheless, going forward, financial infrastructure, technical service providers, and professional associations and networks will play an increasingly important role in supporting more diverse and complex financial systems that serve poorer and more remote clients on a large scale.

Payments Systems

Safe, efficient, and reliable payments systems are critical to the effective functioning of the financial system.[2] Payments systems allow the transfer of money among participating financial institutions, usually banks. Payments instruments include cash, checks, traveler's checks, money orders, debit and credit cards, wire transfers, and automated teller machines—in short, most of the types of instruments that those who live in industrial countries take for granted. Access to the payments system can allow financial institutions that serve the poor to offer higher-quality services and increase their outreach in rural and remote areas.

In many countries, the payments system is owned by the top banks, restricting access to smaller banks and others. In fact, the very financial institutions that are closest to the poor (such as community or rural banks, savings and credit cooperatives, and microfinance nongovernmental organizations [NGOs]) do not always have access to their countries' payments systems. But poor families are often quite mobile. A schoolteacher who receives his pay-

---

[1] Miehlbradt and McVay, *BDS Primer,* 12.

[2] Bank for International Settlements, *Core Principles for Systemically Important Payment Systems,* 1.

check in a rural area might want to withdraw savings when he travels to the capital city. A microentrepreneur may prefer to make a loan repayment in a different location from where she took out the original loan. Institutions that can only offer transactions in one fixed spot are at a disadvantage.

Modern transfers systems are characterized by several levels of sophisticated electronic subsystems. Electronic fund transfers (EFTs), also known as electronic banking, allow customers to access their accounts at any time through automated teller machines, buy items with debit cards using point-of-sale devices in their neighborhood store, and receive their paycheck through direct deposit into their checking or savings accounts. An EFT switch is a computer system that allows the transfer of electronic messages among different devices through interconnected terminals and computers that form a network. Financial institutions use switch and network services, often by sharing resources among themselves or using outsider providers, including nonfinancial companies. Finally, real-time gross settlement systems (RTGS) are mechanisms for instantaneous large-value fund transfers made between banks, both as interbank transfers and on behalf of customers. These systems use settlement accounts at the central bank to offer real-time transfers of funds and secure transactions.

Many developing countries are heavily cash based with shallow or nonexistent electronic payments systems. However, transfer of know-how and technology can allow these countries to leapfrog from a cash-based economy directly to technologically advanced electronic systems.[3] For example, if people can transfer funds and make payments through their cell phones, they can bypass formal payments systems and automatic teller machines altogether. Box 4.1 gives examples of two radically different types of money transfers systems in Afghanistan and Uganda.

Because financial institutions that serve the poor often lack direct access to the payments system, they must work through public- and private-sector banks. Increasingly, MFIs are finding new ways to forge new alliances to bring financial services closer to poor households. For instance, Fundación para el Apoyo a la Microempresa (FAMA) in Nicaragua lacks access to the payments system. It linked up with a network of rural credit unions to distribute international remittances. Credit unions can receive remittances from overseas, but they are not present in urban areas. FAMA offers the credit unions a way to access urban markets.[4] Developments such as this promise to accelerate the pace at which increasingly poor and remote clients gain access to financial services, such as remittances, and lower the costs of services.

Transparency and Information Infrastructure

Financial transparency is defined as the widespread availability of relevant, accurate, timely, and comparable information about the performance of finan-

---

[3.] Chatterji, *The Domestic Architecture of Financial Sectors in Developing Countries,* 10.
[4.] World Council of Credit Unions, *A Technical Guide to Remittances: The Credit Union Experience,* and www.woccu.org/development/remittances/index.php, 8.

cial institutions.[5] Transparency is fundamental for building inclusive financial systems that reach significant scale. It can enhance the performance of financial institutions. The right information helps managers identify areas for improvement and make better decisions to improve their institutions. Freely available information also allows managers to compare themselves with their peers, giving them strong incentives to boost performance.

Transparency also attracts funders. Accurate, standardized information allows private investors and public donors to make informed funding decisions. Increased participation of investors in turn provides the resources to fund more rapid growth of financial services for the poor.

Finally, transparency also better informs clients, which could lead to increased competition among financial service providers as clients gain knowledge and comparison shop among their options. This competition, driven by better-informed clients, could eventually drive prices down as service providers attempt to attract clients with more favorable interest rates. Financial institutions that fully disclose their financial performance and interest rates are more likely to gain the trust and confidence of their clients, especially depositors.

Transparency involves a range of activities, entities, and tools that spans the spectrum from production and verification to reporting and use of information. As shown in figure 4.2, financial transparency in microfinance relies on the proper functioning of several distinct processes.

---

[5] Transparency on social performance is also important. However, this section deals only with financial transparency—social transparency is treated as a cross-cutting issue in chapter 7.

FIGURE 4.2 The Transparency Spectrum

MIS	Internal Control	External Audit	Performance Measurement	Benchmarking	Performance Reporting Standards	Rating	Supervision/ Monitoring
Consultants (national/international) IT service providers (national/international) Auditors			CAMEL PEARLS Other assessment tools	MIX MicroBanking Bulletin	CGAP SEEP	Rating Agencies (specialized and "mainstream")	Banking authorities, MIX monitoring services

Source: Adapted from CGAP.

Note: MIS = management information systems; MIX = The Microfinance Information eXchange; ACCION International's CAMEL = Capital adequacy, Asset quality, Management, Earnings and Liquidity (diagnostic and management tool); PEARLS = Protection, Effective Financial Structure, Asset Quality, Rates of Return and Cost, Liquidity, Signs of Growth (set of financial ratios to monitor the financial stability for credit unions); SEEP = Small Enterprise Education and Promotion.

- **Information systems** (sometimes referred to as management information systems or MIS) help financial institutions gather and report timely, accurate, and useful data. The MIS is at the base of the transparency spectrum, and the quality of information at this stage affects all the other levels.

- **Internal controls** and **external audits** help verify the quality, integrity, and accuracy of the information provided by financial institutions.

- **Performance measurement** allows management and external actors, such as bank supervisors, investors, or clients, to monitor a financial institution's performance over time.

- **Benchmarking** compares performance results with those of similar institutions, for example, comparing performance among institutions in different regions or at different levels of development, so that managers and others can know where an institution stands in relation to its peers.

- **Performance standards** are absolute norms that financial institutions seek to attain. Standards can evolve from benchmarking, but are different from benchmarking because they refer to an absolute target.

- **Ratings** are independent assessments of credit or overall institutional risk of a financial institution based on a standardized methodology, including quantitative and qualitative analysis. They are often used by relatively uninformed investors in decisions about whether to fund a financial institution.

- **Supervisory** bodies and investors use all the information contained throughout the spectrum to determine the degree of risk a financial institution presents to depositors and the financial system as a whole.[6]

[6.] Miller, *The Role of Performance Information in Deepening Microfinance Markets.*

Transparency-related service providers. Transparency and its benefits depend critically on the availability of a suite of related services and tools, ranging from reliable information software to high-quality auditors and rating agencies, to credit bureaus that capture clients' credit histories. Unfortunately, these services are not uniformly available to many financial institutions in developing countries.

Information services. Standard banking software packages do not always accommodate the idiosyncrasies of microfinance, such as the many small and frequent transactions required. Yet specialized software providers and vendors that can adapt standard software or develop customized products are not always accessible in all microfinance markets, and the level of computerization among MFIs is highly uneven. Computerized systems can make a big difference in the accuracy and timeliness of performance information, as well as improvements in efficiency by streamlining processes (although a big exception is ASA in Bangladesh, which is one of the world's most efficient MFIs with manual systems). Figure 4.3 shows that computerization significantly improves the efficiency of standard business operations, such as detecting late payments on loans or writing financial reports. Institutions operating in regions with less computerization generally take longer (sometimes much longer) to complete these basic tasks.

External audits. External audits of financial institutions that serve the poor often fail to produce a reliable picture of their finances. Traditional audit firms are not aware of many of the risks involved in providing a multitude of microloans that are not secured by traditional collateral, nor are they familiar with the kind of documentation that is different from conventional lending. For this reason, conventional audits may not accurately reflect the true level of risk of MFIs. To assess the loan portfolio properly, auditors would have to get out into the villages and urban neighborhoods to review specific borrowers' experience much more than they would for conventional banking to test whether the portfolio

FIGURE 4.3 Level of Computerization and Impact of Information Infrastructure

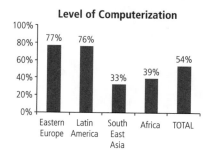

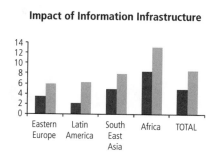

■ Days needed to detect unpaid loans
■ Days needed to write financial report

Source: CGAP, Survey on Information Infrastructure in Microfinance.

on the books actually exists as recorded. High-volume transactions in widely dispersed and remote locations can make this type of audit expensive.

Some auditors treat MFIs as welfare organizations instead of banking institutions. This approach will also miss the critical issues of the risks involved in financial operations. In these cases, auditors tend to look only at whether donor money was spent properly, not whether the financial institution as a whole has accurate financial reports.

Auditors need to invest in developing specialized skills if they are to respond to the needs of microfinance. Yet incentives to make these investments may be weak, especially in those countries where the market of financial institutions that serve the poor is not big enough to support a more specialized practice.

Ratings. In the area of assessing creditworthiness and rating, much progress has been made over the past few years. The number of MFI ratings has skyrocketed. It is estimated that the number of specialized MFI ratings and evaluations increased from 50 ratings a year in 2001 to 250 a year in 2004 (see figure 4.4 for a regional distribution of ratings funded by the Rating Fund).[7] In 2001, CGAP and the Inter-American Development Bank created the Rating Fund

FIGURE 4.4 Geographic Distribution of Ratings Funded by the Rating Fund

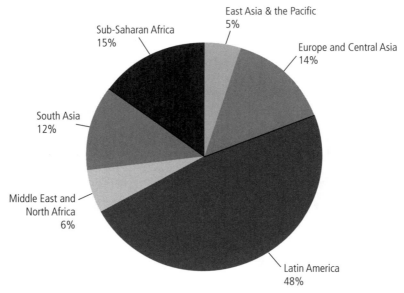

Source: The Rating Fund, www.ratingfund.org.

[7.] ADA (Appui au Développement Autonome), an internal unpublished survey conducted under the auspices of the multidonor Rating Fund that covered six microfinance specialized rating agencies: PlanetRating, M-CRIL, MicroRate, Microfinanza, CRISIL, and ACCION International.

(today, the European Commission and the government of Luxembourg are also funding partners). The main objective of the Rating Fund is to build a market for microfinance rating and assessment services and improve the transparency of performance, attracting social and commercial investors. Beyond those ratings funded through the Rating Fund, many of the other ratings are likely subsidized by other donors and social and private investors. The question of whether a true market—free from subsidies—exists for ratings is controversial among raters and other experts. It remains doubtful whether sufficient demand would exist to sustain specialized microfinance raters without donor subsidies.

One of the most interesting developments is that "mainstream" or formal rating agencies have entered into the business of conducting microfinance ratings. Today, for instance, 9 of the 14 raters certified under the Rating Fund program are formal rating agencies, including the local, largely independent affiliates of well-known firms like Fitch and Standards & Poor's.[8] This trend is promising for integrating financial services for the poor into the larger financial system.

Credit bureaus. Credit bureaus are another critical building block of transparency. Credit bureaus (sometimes called registries) provide information sharing among financial institutions and other sources about payment habits and current debt of individual clients. Credit bureaus organize this information into a database and sometimes sell access to the information for a fee. The incorporation of microfinance into mainstream credit bureaus is an example of how financial services for the poor are increasingly becoming an integral part of the financial system in many countries. In fact, specialized microfinance credit bureaus may not make sense at all, because clients may bank with several types of institutions at the same time.

The kind of information shared through credit bureaus varies. The simplest form is data exchange on past client delinquency, sometimes referred to as "blacklists." In Haiti, for example, financial institutions improved the quality of their loan portfolios by informally circulating monthly paper blacklists.[9] Other bureaus collect more comprehensive data about client histories—both bad and good. For example, Long Range Company (LRC) *Kreditni Biro* in Bosnia and Herzegovina is a private business that began issuing credit reports in June 2001. LRC maintains client-based information about credit and other financial liabilities and issued more than 3,000 credit reports as of January 2005.[10]

The main impact of credit bureaus is to lower credit risk to institutions. Credit bureaus also lower the transaction costs of lending, by reducing the amount of time financial institutions spend evaluating loan applications. They

---

[8.] Diaz Ortega, CGAP Rating Fund Project Evaluation, 11.

[9.] Haider, "Credit Bureaus: Leveraging Information for the Benefit of Microenterprises," 5.

[10.] As of March 2005, 25 banks, 18 microcredit organizations, 2 leasing companies, 10 insurance companies, and 21 public utility companies (among others) provided information to and used information offered by Long-Range Company (LRC). Interview with Senada Havic, general manager, LRC, Bosnia and Herzegovina, March 25, 2005.

can contribute to greater competition among financial service providers as they compete for the clients with the best credit histories and raise incentives for borrowers to repay their loans (borrowers know they can be locked out of credit markets if they have a bad credit history).[11] A recent study of 123 countries worldwide suggests that countries with credit bureaus have nearly 9 percentage points greater financial development compared with countries without them (measured as the ratio of credit to the private sector to GDP).[12]

Although the benefits are great, in many markets, financial institutions remain reluctant to share information about clients with competitors. Also, participation in credit bureaus places heavy demands on financial institutions' information systems. Many MFIs are far from being able to meet those demands.

The structure and ownership of credit bureaus can also have a big impact on their effectiveness. Credit bureaus take two basic forms: voluntary schemes run by the private sector, often owned by the financial institutions and lenders that report to them; and registries managed by bank supervisors or other government entities. Private bureaus have some advantages, because they can include a wider range of financial institutions and other lenders. However, private credit bureaus, which are exclusive and owned by a limited group of financial institutions, risk reducing the scope of the database. Government-run registries tend to include only regulated financial institutions, and bank secrecy laws often limit access to the information to these regulated banks. Government-run registries can oblige banks to report data, something that private ones cannot. Box 4.2 gives the story of how a public system in Peru transformed into a more inclusive private system.

Training

Technical training and capacity building remain the most sorely needed meso-level services in most microfinance markets. Financial institutions rely on a host of technical service providers that offer specialized training, information, and onsite consultancies to staff in areas like strategic planning and implementing employee incentive systems. Financial institutions that need this support can be divided into two categories, each with their own technical requirements: specialized MFIs, often NGOs, that may need to boost their financial management and other operational skills; and existing banks (commercial, postal banks, and so on) that typically have to adjust their systems, procedures, and staff skills to introduce products for lower-end retail clients (microfinance).

Technical support services encompass a wide range of topics, including the following:

- Financial Management
- Field Staff Training

- Strategic Business Planning and Projection

---

[11] Haider, "Credit Bureaus: Leveraging Information for the Benefit of Microenterprises," 5.

[12] These data and that presented in the next paragraph from Inter-American Development Bank (IADB), *Unlocking Credit—the Quest for Deep and Stable Bank Lending,* 176.

BOX 4.2 Transforming and modernizing credit bureaus in Peru

The public credit bureau system in Peru was slow, outdated, and limited to regulated banks before a new law allowed for private credit bureaus (Centrales Privadas de Información de Riesgos, CEPIRS) in 1996. CEPIRS offer the same information provided by the public bureau managed by the Superintendency of Banks and Insurance plus additional information from the Chamber of Commerce, department stores, utilities companies, tax authorities, and so on. CEPIRS also verify addresses, employment, housing conditions, business premises, identity cards, and civil status.

Today, one firm, Infocorp, controls 80 percent of the market with a database of more than 7.5 million registries available to 1,700 lending clients. Currently, the average number of consultations per month is 900,000. Around 88 percent of all consultations to the database turn up some information on the potential client, with negative information coming up in approximately 25 to 28 percent of the cases. By March 2005, Infocorp had incorporated more than 104 MFIs (including Cajas Municipales, Cajas Rurales, Edpymes, Cooperativas de Ahorra y Credito y ONGs), some through Consorcio de Organizaciones Privadas de Promoción al Desarrollo de la Micro y Pequeña Empresa or COPEME (a U.S. government-funded microfinance project), and became the subsidiary of the U.S. credit bureau, EQUIFAX.

The result is that Peru's largest and most profitable banks are quickly entering the microfinance market with small loans (as small as $100). Well-functioning credit bureaus are not the only factor driving the entry of banks into the system, but they do play an important role.

Sources: University of California and Food and Agriculture Organization Office for Latin America, *Credit Bureaus and the Rural Microfinance Sector: Peru, Guatemala, and Bolivia,* v; interview with Alfonso Higueras, commercial manager, Infocorp; and Young, "Credit Bureaus in Latin America: Expanding Financial and Other Services to the Base of the Pyramid."

- Specialized Microfinance Credit Technology
- NGO Transformation to Regulated Institutions
- Information Technology Solutions
- Human Resources Training/Management
- Employee Incentive Systems
- Market Research
- New Product Development
- Risk Management
- Business Process Mapping
- Branding/Marketing
- Costing and Pricing

These kinds of technical services are not always available to financial institutions in developing countries. The rapid growth and evolution of microfinance into an increasingly complex activity with a diversity of institutions, delivery mechanisms, and financial services partially explains the shortage of technical service providers—it is simply difficult to keep up. These services are often provided by international specialists funded by donor subsidies. When they are available locally, they can be supplied by national or regional state entities, private-sector providers (for example, training institutes, consulting firms, individual consultants), NGOs, and professional associations. Larger MFIs often develop internal training programs without relying as much on outside providers.

A number of internationally recognized training programs have sprung up over the past few years. Table 4.1 has a few examples.

TABLE 4.1 Examples of International Training Programs

Program	Location	Focus	Accomplishments
Microfinance Training Institute	Boulder, Colorado, United States; Turin, Italy	Three-week course covering microfinance basics, case studies, financial analysis, business planning, asset liability management, and the commercialization of microfinance.	Over the past 10 years, has trained more than 1,700 people from 124 countries.
Microenteprise Development Institute	University of Southern New Hampshire, United States	Three-week program on Microenterprise Development (including a specialized microfinance track), focusing on building and balancing financial and social impact and performance.	Over the past six years, has trained more than 525 practitioners from 80 countries and 300 organizations.
Bankakademie International	Frankfurt, Germany	Two-week Summer Academy in microbanking for mid-level and senior managers of financial institutions.	Each year since 1999, the Summer Academy welcomes around 25 participants; in 2004, the 26 participants came from 18 different countries.
CGAP Skills for Microfinance Managers	Global—through domestic partners	Three- to five-day courses on seven topics related to financial and operational management, aimed at managers of specialized MFIs.	As of the end of 2004 and after six years, 44 training partners, institutions, and individuals have offered the courses in 11 languages to 9,700 participants from 48 countries.
PlaNet University	Virtual—Internet	Offers 10 free online training modules on basic microfinance, financial analysis, new technology and information communication, and MFI viability.	Since 1999, there have been 2,900 participants; 8 training modules in English, 10 training modules in French.
Microfinance Management Institute (MFMI)	Global—through partnerships with six leading MBA programs[a]	Introduces a microfinance component into existing MBA programs.	Since March 2004, more than 350 students have participated in the microfinance electives. Fellowship program is set up with six universities.

Sources: Interview with Robert Peck Christen, president, the Boulder Institute of Microfinance Training for Sustainable Development; www.snhu.edu/MDI/; www.international.bankakademie.de; interview with Tiphaine Crenn, microfinance analyst, CGAP; interview with Mostaq Ahmmed, director training and technical support, PlaNet Finance; interview with Leslie Barcus, president of The Microfinance Management Institute (MFMI).

[a] The partners of this program created by CGAP and the Open Society Institute are the Asian Institute of Management in the Philippines, the Central American Economic Institute (INCAE) in Costa Rica, the Indian Institute of Management Ahmedabad, the Indian Institute of Management Bangalore, the Institute for Rural Management at Anand in India, and the University of Pretoria in South Africa. Each institution offers at least one elective in microfinance management on an annual basis. Some programs are setting up internships in which students can obtain practical experience working in local MFIs. Interview with Leslie Barcus, president, MFMI.

Networks and Associations

A number of specialized international, regional, and national networks and associations have cropped up in the microfinance world over the last few decades. They make important contributions at the meso level, by providing services directly or facilitating their members' access to services. They also provide a collective voice to financial service providers that serve the poor.

Generally speaking, "networks" or "network service organizations" refer to global or regional voluntary organizations of affiliated financial institutions. The term "association" means a member-based organization, mostly at the country level, but there are also some regional and global associations. These networks and associations offer many benefits to their affiliates and/or members: from providing a joint platform advocating a common cause to giving opportunities to learn from each other to promoting standards. As shown in table 4.2, the sheer numbers and massive growth of country-level and regional associations imply that they are valued by their members.

The Small Enterprise Education and Promotion (SEEP) Network is a "network of networks," based in North America, that supports enterprise development. It has identified five main categories of network services that may be provided by international or regional networks or national-level associations:

- **Policy advocacy,** like political lobbying and policy dialogue with governments and international bodies—this function can catalyze a national-level network;
- **Information dissemination,** including research, networking, and publications/documentation;
- **Capacity building,** offering technical services, including training courses and technical assistance;
- **Performance monitoring,** such as collecting industry data, self-regulation, and developing national performance benchmarks and standards (see box 4.3 for an example from Ghana); and
- **Financial intermediation,** including serving as second-tier (wholesale) financial institutions and distributing grant funds.[13]

TABLE 4.2 Regional and Country-Level Microfinance Associations

	2003	2004
Number of associations	34	47
Total active client base	4,500,000	15,538,001
Number of countries in which associations are active	45	80
Number of regional associations	5	6
Number of country-level networks	29	40

Source: Small Enterprise Education and Promotion Network, *Global Directory of Regional and Country-level Microfinance Networks.*

13. Small Enterprise Education and Promotion Network, *Global Directory of Regional and Country-level Microfinance Networks,* viii.

Despite great differences among specialized microfinance networks, the following common characteristics and trends can be observed:

• International and regional networks are assuming a larger ownership and governance role in their members;
• Members are increasingly becoming formal, regulated financial institutions;
• More networks promote performance standards and financial transparency among members; and
• Networks are attempting to cover more of their costs through fees charged to members for technical services.[14]

As a further step toward integrating microfinance more fully into the financial system, mainstream bankers associations are becoming more interested in social responsibility issues. Often the issue of how to serve poorer and more remote clients falls into that category. For example, the Mexican Bankers Association has taken on the challenge issued by the president of Mexico and has agreed to work toward increasing access to financial services for low-income people. In March 2005, the Banking Association South Africa consulted the Micro Finance Regulatory Council (the regulatory body for microfinance) for assistance on how to best implement the recently developed Consumer Credit bill to protect consumers in the credit industry. In Colombia, the banking association joined WWB affiliates and others to form a microfinance committee focused on performance standards, capacity, innovation, and policy change in that country.[15] A similar collaboration can be found in Mali, where the microfinance association (APIM/Mali) works closely with the banking association. They intend to create a joint professional education center for finance and microfinance issues.[16] Only time will tell if this type of commitment by bankers

---

[14.] Ibid, 14.

[15.] Mexican Banking Association, Annual Report April 2003–March 2004; Sizwekazi, "Banks, DTI nuke it out"; Barry, Welcome Remarks for the Federación Latinoamericana de Bancos-Women's World Banking (FELABAN-WWB) Seminar on Microfinance as a New Banking Opportunity.

[16.] German Agency for Technical Cooperation (GTZ), "Microfinance Associations (MFAs)—Their Role in Developing the Microfinance Sector," 44.

associations translates into something more than a political gesture, but the trend is certainly encouraging.

Conclusion

Different markets need different kinds of meso-level players. For instance, in countries with weak financial systems, fragile financial infrastructure, and limited experience in microfinance, it may be premature to create credit bureaus or invest in elaborate technological solutions. Conversely, more advanced or larger markets may require a wide array of competitive services to support the development of the financial system. Examples include e-payment infrastructure, consulting services, information and point-of-sale technology vendors, and specialized technical support.

The payments systems in many countries are inadequate to enable poor (and other) clients to move money around the country in a secure, cost-effective, and efficient manner. Yet the possibilities for some countries to leapfrog technologies and implement advanced electronic payment systems may help solve this problem in the future, potentially offering payment services for hundreds of millions of people.

Accurate, standardized, and comparable information on financial performance is imperative for integrating microfinance into the financial system. Bank supervisors and regulators, donors, investors, and, more important, the poor who are clients of microfinance need this information to adequately assess risk and returns. There is increasing convergence among specialized MFIs and banks around international financial reporting standards. Still, the lack of widespread adoption of standard terminology, ratios, and indicators remains a constraint, especially when it comes to the comparability of information between banks and other pro-poor financial service providers. At the same time, generating and sharing all that information is not costless to financial service providers, and not all of them will be able and willing to accomplish this, at least in the short term. They need better skills and incentives to become more transparent.

The lack of human and institutional capacity at the micro level remains the key constraint to extending access of financial services on the ground. Therefore, it is imperative to ensure that an adequate supply of technical service providers and education institutions exists to build the skills of existing and future managers and staff within financial institutions that serve the poor.

Networks and associations can optimize the collective ability of financial institutions to improve transparency on their performance, build up technical and managerial skills, negotiate with service providers and funders, and advocate for policy changes that make small-scale financial transactions possible.

The meso level of the financial system—the service providers that support the work of those directly offering financial services to poor people—includes a complex and varied set of actors. To reach massive scale with inclusive financial systems, better financial infrastructure and more service providers will be required than are currently available in most places. Increasingly, mainstream financial infrastructure and service providers should take on this task, rather than specialized (and potentially marginalized) microfinance providers. The challenge is to help build a more inclusive financial infrastructure and a permanent and competitive supply of these much needed meso-level services.

Chapter 5

Governments: The Macro Level

The role of government in building inclusive financial systems is a controversial topic. Several different perspectives coexist, and many of these perspectives are evolving rapidly. Should governments be involved in microfinance at all? Should governments themselves direct credit to those in need? Or should governments stay as far away as possible from the delivery of microfinance, leaving the private sector to do the job—as has been the case in leading microfinance markets like Bolivia and Bangladesh?

An emerging consensus holds that governments in fact *do* have an important role to play in ensuring favorable policy environments within which microfinance can flourish. A good policy environment allows a range of financial service providers to coexist and compete to offer higher-quality and lower-cost services to large numbers of poor clients.

Over the past few years, governments have become keenly interested in microfinance for the poor. For example, the G8 industrial countries discussed microfinance as a poverty-reduction strategy at their Sea Island, Georgia, USA, meeting in 2004 and endorsed a set of key microfinance principles set forth by CGAP. They called upon CGAP to launch a global microfinance initiative.[1] In developing countries, too, governments have become more involved, for better or for worse. And many, such as Tanzania and the Philippines, have introduced national microfinance strategies.

This heightened interest by governments in microfinance brings opportunities and risks. On the one hand, well-informed governments can implement policies that encourage the emergence of permanent, sustainable financial institutions that serve the poor. At the very least, they could eliminate policies that block microfinance. On the other hand, increased attention risks politicization. Many governments equate microcredit with handing out money to poor people. A danger of too much government involvement in microfinance is that political criteria, rather than sound credit administration, could drive decision making on topics such as who gets credit and where branch opera-

---

[1] CGAP, *Key Principles of Microfinance.*

tions are located. And the focus of political attention remains largely on loans, instead of the gamut of financial services required by poor people.

Governments typically get involved in the financial system in at least three ways:

- They *deliver financial services directly and indirectly,* often by disbursing credit to preferred groups or channeling resources to financial institutions through wholesale arrangements (either way, most of this funding comes from international donors). Governments are not good at offering credit directly to poor people, although government-owned banks (for example, postal banks) can succeed at savings mobilization or money transfer.

- They *set policies* that affect the financial system. These policies include ensuring macroeconomic stability, liberalizing interest rates, and establishing banking regulation and supervision that make viable microfinance possible.

- They can *proactively promote inclusion* by offering fiscal incentives or requiring financial institutions to serve poor or low-income people. There is much less conclusive experience on this third dimension, especially in developing countries.

This chapter examines the role of government in all three areas.

Government Involvement in Credit Delivery: Direct and Indirect

Historically, governments (both at national and local levels) have used credit to target specific economic sectors and populations. They have done this directly through state-owned banks and other credit schemes operated by government entities, and indirectly through wholesale funds. In many cases, international donor funding has fueled these credit schemes, as well as government budgets.

Direct credit delivery by governments. By and large, government credit programs have failed to deliver high-quality, permanent financial services to poor people, prompting massive closures of many state-owned development banks in the 1980s and early 1990s. Nevertheless, more than 40 percent of the world's population still lives in countries where the majority of banking assets are in state-owned (or controlled) banks. These banks continue to perform poorly, retard financial sector development and economic growth, concentrate credit in the hands of few, and increase the likelihood and costs of banking crises.[2]

Government credit schemes for the poor are usually heavily subsidized. There are at least three problems with these subsidized lending schemes (see box 5.1 for an example in India of one such scheme).[3]

- They are vulnerable to political patronage, often diverting credit to better-off (and more politically connected) borrowers.

---

[2] Caprio and Honohan, "Finance for Growth," 124.
[3] This discussion and the following few paragraphs are taken from Helms and Reille, "Interest Rate Ceilings and Microfinance: The Story So Far."

- Borrowers often view soft government money as grants or gifts and are less likely to repay loans from subsidized programs. This is especially true in countries with a history of forgiveness programs for agricultural or other lending. Default rates of 50 percent and higher in subsidized rural credit programs are typical worldwide.

- Low interest rates in government programs mean that lending institutions cannot cover their costs and thus require continuous government or donor subsidies to survive.

Another feature of many government credit programs is that they are often limited to specific, preferred sectors, regions, or populations. This targeting means that credit does not necessarily reach the most dynamic sectors of the economy. Even worse, directed credit does not always reach the intended beneficiaries. Research in Thailand noted that instead of benefiting poor farmers, government-secured lending programs reach better-off and more informed farmers with personal connections to the Agricultural Extension Service. The same study pointed out that subsidized loans were designed by agricultural officials with expertise in farming, but not finance, and do not reflect the true demands and requirements of poor farmers.[4]

In some exceptional cases, governments have played a positive role in delivering financial services to poor people. This is particularly true in terms of savings and transfers, in which state banks, including postal savings banks, are important sources of services for poor clients. As discussed in chapter 3, state-owned financial institutions reach hundreds of millions of account holders, many of whom are probably poor. The quality of those accounts and transfer

---

BOX 5.1 The case of the Indian Integrated Rural Development Programme

In the 1980s, the government of India introduced a variety of subsidized targeted lending programs, including the Integrated Rural Development Programme (IRDP). The program suffered from all three classic problems of subsidized lending schemes: diversion of funding to the better off, low repayment rates, and dependence on significant subsidies. The loan recovery rate on IRDP loans varied between 10 and 55 percent. A 1993 study on rural finance reported widespread credit diversion and low levels of awareness of repayment conditions. By contrast, leading MFIs in India (SHARE and BASIX) enjoy nearly 100 percent repayment rates. Other studies have shown that IRDP tended to favor better-off segments of the rural population, rather than poorer groups.

What is more, the program absorbed more than $430 million in subsidies between 1982 and 1997—an expensive endeavor for the Indian government, especially given the poor results.

Sources: Mahajan and Ramola, "Financial Services for the Rural Poor and Women in India"; World Bank, "Microfinance in India"; the Microfinance Information eXchange, www.themix.org; and Sharma, "Assessment of Rural Poverty in India," www.unescap.org/rural/doc/Beijing_march97/India.pdf.

[4.] Haberberger, "Creating and Enabling Environment for Microfinance—the Role of Governments Experiences from Thailand," 11.

services in meeting the needs of poor and low-income clients, however, is not as well understood.

A well-known example of a successful state bank is Bank Rakayat Indonesia (BRI), hailed as a worldwide best practice microfinance leader, with 31.3 million savers and 3.2 million borrowers in 2004.[5] Benefiting from interest rate liberalization in the early 1980s, BRI, then an inefficient and failing state bank with subsidized credit, experimented with commercial microfinance by creating a separate unit called the Unit Desas. As a result, it became a profitable enterprise that has allowed the entire bank to survive financially. The bank weathered the storm of the Asian financial crisis of 1997–99, with the number of savers increasing dramatically and the number of borrowers increasing as well—albeit more slowly.

By 2001, BRI received a better risk rating from an international rating agency than the country as a whole (BBB versus C), mostly because of a shift in strategy toward micro, retail, and medium-size business and away from corporate lending. BRI's Unit Desas remained nearly free from political influence and were not forced to manage government credit schemes—a huge success factor.[6] Upon partial privatization, in November 2003, BRI began trading on the stock exchange, and its microfinance track record attracted the most attention. Shares were oversubscribed at the initial public offering, and *Asia Money* named BRI "the best newly listed company in 2003."[7]

In Brazil, Banco do Nordeste (BN) launched CreditAmigo in late 1997– early 1998. The bank's president envisioned BN as a world-class microfinance provider and was determined to find a more effective way to reach the poor than directed credit lines. Early vertiginous growth led to deterioration of portfolio quality and heavy loan losses as hastily trained loan officers were pushed to lend without sufficient focus on repayment capacity and follow up. Subsequently, BN management committed to more prudent and careful growth, backed up by significant support from the World Bank and advisory services from CGAP and ACCION. By 2002, BN had nearly 119,000 outstanding borrowers in the CreditAmigo program. Although not immune to political pressure (management recently accepted a government-imposed interest rate cap for political reasons), it is still considered to be one of the better microfinance providers in Brazil.[8]

Although rarely successful on the credit side, the main features of microfinance that work well within state-owned banks are as follows:[9]

---

[5] Robinson, "Why the Bank Rakayat Indonesia has the World's Largest Sustainable Microbanking System," 4, 5.

[6] German Agency for Technical Cooperation (GTZ), "The Challenge of Sustainable Outreach— How Can Public Banks Contribute to Outreach in Rural Areas? Five Case Studies from Asia," 12.

[7] Interview with Marguerite Robinson, independent consultant; and Robinson, "Why the Bank Rakayat Indonesia has the World's Largest Sustainable Microbanking System."

[8] Schonberger and Christen, "A Multilateral Donor Triumph over Disbursement Pressure," 9; The Microfinance Information eXchange (MIX), www.themix.org; and interview with Robert Christen, president, Boulder Institute of Microfinance Training for Sustainable Development.

[9] Some of these features are borrowed from GTZ, "The Challenge of Sustainable Outreach—How Can Public Banks Contribute to Outreach in Rural Areas? Five Case Studies from Asia."

- full operational separation and autonomy from the rest of the bank operations;
- commitment of board members and government owners to professional and financially sustainable microfinance;
- bank management committed to providing viable financial services to poor clients;
- patience in allowing growth (especially in credit) to proceed at its own pace;
- no political influence on lending policies;
- freedom to set loan interest rates; and
- appropriate internal control mechanisms and regulations to avoid fraud within large decentralized structures, especially with branches in remote and inaccessible areas.

Recently, many governments have begun discussing the possibility of re-introducing state-owned agricultural or development banks. Examples include Afghanistan, Nicaragua, the Republic of Yemen, Jordan, and the West African region. These and other governments are particularly interested in filling the gap in agricultural lending left by the closure or insolvency of the previous generation of such banks. The question is whether this new generation of banks will repeat the mistakes of the past and distort markets or adhere to good practice principles that support creation of new, pro-poor markets. Unfortunately, given the track record and the built-in incentives to politicize credit allocation, it is highly unlikely that the world will see many good practice state-owned banks cropping up in the near future.

Indirect support through second-tier funds. Governments often channel funding to preferred sectors and populations indirectly through wholesale-level funds that pass those resources along to retail financial institutions.[10] These funds, sometimes called "second-tier" or "apex" funds, are often temporary and linked to the implementation of specific projects. One reason they are controversial is the likelihood that they may face political pressure to spend funds quickly, rather than allocating funding only to solid financial institutions that have demonstrated they can make effective use of them.

Also, second-tier funding is often subsidized, meaning that government funds are offered at a lower price than financial institutions can negotiate from other sources. Financial institutions (understandably) choose to take the subsidized funds rather than incurring more costly commercial debt or mobilizing deposits (see box 5.2 for the case of Bolivia). Tapping the easily available and cheap government funds can provide a potentially serious disincentive to integrating microfinance into the financial system by building relationships with domestic banks and investors and tapping domestic markets. Over time, this disincentive could damage the viability of the system and reduce the range of products available to poor people.

Those apex funds that are more successful tend to be the ones in which governments play a less important role in governance and management, and in

---

[10] For more on the characteristics, success factors, and extent of apex funds, see chapter 6.

which funds are offered at market or near-market rates. The Pali Karma Sahayak Foundation (PKSF) of Bangladesh is a relatively successful apex institution. It operates in a country with a critical mass of strong MFIs, it has access to a large pool of inexpensive and well-educated human resources, and it operates in an environment, despite government ownership, in which it can avoid most of the political pressure. Also, the organization's leadership has been committed to sustainability of the apex itself (meaning that it not likely to invest in poor-quality retail institutions).[11] However, the availability of cheap PKSF funds has probably retarded the accessibility of deposit services for poor people in Bangladesh, although this phenomenon has not been studied as much as the Bolivia case.

Policy Environment

Governments have an important role to play in setting policies that allow sustainable financial services for the poor to flourish. There are at least three types of policies that governments need to get right:

- macroeconomic stability,
- liberalized interest rates, and
- appropriate banking regulations and supervisory practices.

Other policies have an impact on microfinance, but their exact relationship is not as well known. These policies include establishing a favorable legal environment related to issues like contract enforcement, business registry, collater-

---

BOX 5.2 How the availability of cheap money discouraged savings in Bolivia

Most microcredit in Bolivia is offered by regulated institutions that are allowed to mobilize deposits from the public. But until recently, they were very slow to do so. The abundance of "easy money," primarily through government-run second-tier institutions, created a disincentive to mobilize savings. Bolivian-regulated MFIs considered savings to be more expensive and risky than subsidized funds. As of November 2004, the top regulated MFIs (BancoSol, Caja Los Andes, Fondo Financiero Privado PRODEM, and FFP-FIE) financed from 44 to 79 percent of their loan portfolio with savings. This proportion is lower (especially for FIE and Los Andes) than other mature MFIs that take deposits in other countries, such as Banco Caja Social (Colombia), Bank Rakayat Indonesia (BRI) (Indonesia), and One Network Bank (Philippines). These institutions report savings-to-loan ratios between 70 and 90 percent. At the same time, in Bolivia, only those MFIs strong enough to obtain a license to become a formal intermediary are allowed to access cheap second-tier funding. Paradoxically, this link between getting a license and access to the apex organization removes much of the incentive to mobilize deposits precisely among those institutions that would be the best placed to offer savings products to the poor on a massive scale.

Sources: Miller, "The Paradox of Savings Mobilization in Microfinance: Why Microfinance Institutions in Bolivia Have Virtually Ignored Savings"; and Gonzalez-Vega, "Microfinance Apex Mechanisms: Review of the Evidence and Policy Recommendations."

[11.] Levy, "Apex Institutions in Microfinance," 17, 20.

al confiscation, property rights, and taxation. Other increasingly hot topics related to providing financial services to poor clients are rules against money laundering and countering the financing of terrorism (see box 5.3).

Additional government policies and actions are important in an indirect way for building inclusive financial systems. These include policies regarding physical infrastructure (such as roads and bridges), telecommunications and technology development, health, education, and social policies, including social protection and welfare. Generally speaking, the better these other services, the lower the risks and transactions costs of doing business, and the higher the probability of innovation and expanded outreach of financial services.

Macroeconomic stability. Probably the most important single thing that governments can do to facilitate microfinance is to make sure inflation remains low. Inflation erodes the capital base of financial institutions; makes it difficult to mobilize resources, especially savings; and increases the volatility of interest

---

BOX 5.3 The potential impact of anti–money laundering and counterterrorism regulation on microfinance

Both money laundering (disguising the illegal origin of funds obtained through criminal acts) and use of the financial system to fund terrorist operations are serious problems. However, the implementation of measures to combat money laundering and financing of terrorism that were introduced following September 11, 2001, could have the unintended impact of restricting access to financial services for poor people. Developing and transition countries seek to comply with these regulations on international anti–money laundering and combating the financing of terrorism (AML/CFT) to gain access to global payments systems and bolster their reputation in international financial markets.

These measures can impede the delivery of financial services to poor customers, although such customers' transactions pose little threat to security. Customer due diligence or "know your customer" rules are perhaps the biggest challenge for financial service providers working with the poor. These rules require financial institutions to identify clients according to international standards set by the Bank of International Settlements in Basel, Switzerland. These rules often entail requiring clients to present identification like identity cards, passports, proof of residence, and so on. Financial institutions that serve the poor may find it difficult to verify identity and residence of their clients, because coming up with these types of identification can be tricky for poor clients working in the informal sector. This issue is particularly challenging when opening small balance savings accounts. The cost of compliance with these and other AML/CFT regulations could be especially high for financial institutions that serve the poor with many small transactions.

Furthermore, those that serve the poor tend to manage small transactions and deal with individuals, not companies or trusts. This means that large amounts would stand out and would be easy to identify. In this sense, poor people are relatively low risk, and some experts argue for making exceptions for small balance accounts to avoid harming poor peoples' access.

Source: Isern, Porteous, Hernandez-Coss, and Egwuagu, "AML/CFT Regulation: What Are the Implications for Financial Service Providers That Serve Poor People?"

---

rates, exchange rates, and other prices in the economy, including salaries. Financial institutions that depend heavily on foreign currency loans are even more vulnerable to macroeconomic shocks.[12]

Those countries where microfinance has flourished (like Bangladesh) tend to be the ones with relative macroeconomic stability. In Latin America, relatively stable inflation partially explains why a country like Bolivia has taken off. On the other hand, Brazil's "inability to shake off inflation" largely explains why it has little microfinance, despite its enormous potential.[13] At the same time, as box 5.4 shows, once microfinance is well established in a country, it seems to be particularly resilient to macroeconomic crises.

Liberalized interest rates.[14] Governments sometimes impose limits on the level of interest rates that financial service providers can charge on loans. The purpose

---

BOX 5.4 Coping with macroeconomic crises in Indonesia and Latin America

In contrast to the rest of Indonesia's banking sector (especially that part that served wealthier and corporate clients), Bank Rakayat Indonesia (BRI) managed not only to survive but to thrive through the Asian financial crisis of the late 1990s. Deposits did not decrease, in fact they increased because

- many poor clients were not directly affected by the currency crisis, because they operate in the domestic (often informal) economy;

- government safety net programs (food, employment, education, and so on) ensured that the economically active poor remained economically active and able to use financial services;

- savers valued the services offered, especially the fact that BRI savings were seen as extra secure because of the bank's relationship with the government; and

- high interest rates helped savers partially counter the ill effects of inflation and underemployment.

Financial crises can have an indirect effect on MFIs, due to the government's instinct to change policy course in the aftermath. For instance, Bolivia, Colombia, and Mexico have all experienced financial crises. These crises have created the impetus for new regulatory frameworks, for better or worse. In Bolivia, the mid-1980s crisis spurred wholesale liberalization of the financial sector that paved the way for microfinance to flourish. Mexico's crisis in the mid-1990s led the government to impose much stricter controls in the financial sector and to institute a new microfinance law. The effects of these measures on access of poor people to financial services have yet to be clearly identified.

Sources: Robinson, *The Microfinance Revolution.* Vol. 2, *Lessons from Indonesia;* and Trigo Loubiere, Devaney, and Rhyne, "Supervising and Regulating Microfinance in the Context of Financial Sector Liberalization."

[12.] Fernando, *Do Governments in Asia Have a Role in Development of Sustainable Microfinance Services?* 4.

[13.] Rhyne, *Mainstreaming Microfinance: How Lending to the Poor Began, Grew, and Came of Age in Bolivia,* 205.

[14.] This section borrows heavily from Helms and Reille, "Interest Rate Ceilings and Microfinance: The Story So Far."

of these limits, or ceilings, is to protect consumers from unscrupulous lenders and excessively high interest rates. Currently, about 40 developing and transitional countries have some kind of interest rate ceilings (see table 5.1).

Unfortunately, interest rate ceilings unintentionally hurt poor people in the end by making small transaction financial services unattractive to NGOs and financial institutions. It costs much more to make many small loans than a few large loans, and governments normally set ceilings with mainstream commercial banks in mind, not the more costly microcredit (see box 5.5 for an explanation of why microcredit interest rates are high.) These ceilings can make it difficult for microlenders to cover their costs, driving them out of the market (or keeping them from entering in the first place). Poor clients are either left with no access to financial services or must revert to informal credit markets, such as local moneylenders, which are even more costly. Ceilings can also lead to less clarity about the costs of loans, as lenders cope with interest rate caps by adding confusing fees to their services.

In the United Kingdom, recent research conducted by the Department of Trade and Industry sought to assess the impact of imposing interest rate ceilings. They studied countries with ceilings, such as France, Germany, and the United States. The research found that interest rate ceilings had a negative effect on low-income people, despite the fact that these ceilings are meant to protect them. In countries with ceilings, the choice of loan products offered by

TABLE 5.1 Interest Rate Ceilings in Developing and Transition Countries, 2004

Interest Rate Controls	Usury Limits	De facto Ceilings
Algeria	Armenia	Brazil
Bahamas, The	Bolivia[d]	China
China	Brazil[a]	Ethiopia
Libya	Chile	India
Morocco[a]	Colombia[b]	Lao PDR
Myanmar	Ecuador[b]	Pakistan
Paraguay	Guatemala	Vietnam
Syrian Arab Rep.	Honduras[a]	
Tunisia[a]	Indian states	
UEAC[b]	Nicaragua[c]	
UMOA[a]	South Africa[b]	
	Uruguay	
	Venezuela, R. B. de[c]	

Source: Helms and Reille, "Interest Rate Ceilings and Microfinance: The Story So Far," 9.

Note: UEAC = l'Union des États d'Afrique central; UMOA = l'Union monétaire ouest-africaine.

[a] A separate regulation on interest rate ceilings exists for the microfinance sector.

[b] Microfinance lenders are excluded from interest rate ceilings, or are authorized to charge additional fees.

[c] Interest rate ceilings apply only to institutions and individuals not regulated by banking authorities (including NGOs).

[d] Introduced in January 2004.

Interest Rate Controls: Banking laws that give the central bank the authority to fix the maximum lending rate for regulated financial institutions. These types of controls have mostly been abandoned with financial sector liberalization.

Usury Limits: Usually part of the civil code authorizing the government to set a limit on what private lenders may charge. Sometimes usury laws do not apply to regulated banks, but NGO-MFIs are often affected.

De facto Ceilings: Political pressure and/or the need to compete with large subsidized government lending programs keep interest rates below a specified level. Some countries have banking rate controls (or usury limits) and large subsidized government programs.

BOX 5.5 Why are microcredit interest rates higher than commercial bank loans?

Compare the costs of two hypothetical lenders, Big Lender and MicroLender, each of which lends $1 million. Big Lender makes a single loan, while MicroLender makes 10,000 loans of $100 each.

The costs of capital and loan loss risk vary proportionally with loan size. Both lenders need to raise $1 million to fund their loans and will have to pay the same market rate—say, 10 percent—for the money. If both lenders have a history of losing 1 percent of their loans to default each year, they will need a loan loss provision of that amount. Both lenders can cover the cost of their capital and their risk by charging 11 percent (10% + 1% = 11%) on the loans they make to their customers.

Administrative costs are not proportional to loan size. Making a single loan of $1,000,000 might cost Big Lender $30,000 (3 percent of the loan amount) in staff time and other expenses involved in appraising, disbursing, monitoring, and collecting the loan. Big Lender can cover all its costs by charging the borrower an interest rate of 14 percent (10% + 1% + 3% = 14%).

However, MicroLender's administrative costs for each $100 loan will be much higher than 3 percent of the loan amount. Instead of $3 per borrower, MicroLender is more likely to have to spend $20 or more per borrower. Big Lender has to deal with only a single borrower, but MicroLender has to manage 10,000 borrowers who typically do not have collateral, financial statements, or records in the database of a credit reporting bureau. Many of these clients may be illiterate. Lending to, and collecting from, such clients requires time-consuming personal interaction.

Assuming Big Lender's loan is repaid quarterly, it has to process four payment transactions per year. MicroLender's borrowers probably make repayments monthly or even more frequently, generating at least 120,000 transactions per year. While Big Lender's administrative cost is $30,000 per year, that of Micro-Lender is at least $200,000. Covering this cost requires a 20 percent charge on loaned amounts, resulting in an interest rate of at least 31 percent (10% + 1% + 20% = 31%). Note that administrative costs may be much higher in young MFIs that are too small to take advantage of economies of scale.

Source: Helms and Reille, "Interest Rate Ceilings and Microfinance: The Story So Far," 2.

financial institutions was more narrow (and less appropriate to the needs of poorer clients), which limits competition and forces them to either borrow more than they need or turn to more informal sources. For instance, the number of people admitting to borrowing from unlicensed or illegal lenders was twice as high in France and Germany as in the United Kingdom.[15]

In Nicaragua, evidence of a market contraction was seen after the national parliament introduced an interest rate ceiling for specific types of lenders, including NGO–MFIs, in 2001. Annual portfolio growth fell from 30 percent to less than 2 percent. The imposition of interest rate ceilings also caused several MFIs to leave rural areas, where risks and operational costs are higher. Perhaps most important, the Nicaraguan law has had a terrible impact on the

---

[15.] Department of Trade and Industry (DTI), *The Effect of Interest Rate Controls in Other Countries.*

transparency of lending costs to clients. MFIs stay afloat by adding commissions and fees to their loans, and many of these extra charges are difficult to comprehend. It becomes difficult for clients to understand the true cost of a loan and compare costs among providers. This lack of consumer understanding in turn thwarts competition—if customers cannot comparison shop, they cannot force prices down by "voting with their feet" and opting for the lowest-cost service.

However, concerns about the high costs of microfinance and predatory lending practices remain valid. Competition, is the single most effective way to reduce both microcredit costs and interest rates. Policies to promote competition among credit providers, combined with relevant consumer protection measures, such as fully disclosing the total costs of credit, can go a long way toward expanding the reach of sustainable microcredit while safeguarding consumer interests.[16]

In Bolivia, for instance, competition has reduced interest rates dramatically. Market pioneer BancoSol charged a combination of interest and fees equivalent to a 65 percent annual percentage rate when it began operating as a bank in 1992. Today, BancoSol operates in a highly competitive environment and has brought its interest rate down to 22 percent.[17] In Cambodia's relatively new but highly competitive microfinance market, interest rates have dropped from around 5 percent to 3.5 percent per month over the past few years. In some provinces where MFIs are particularly active, moneylenders have dropped their rates to match market rates.

Banking sector regulatory and supervisory practices.[18] Perhaps the highest-profile policy issue in microfinance over the past 10 years has been how to best treat microfinance regulation and supervision. As microfinance matures, it will likely migrate toward institutions that are licensed and supervised by the central bank and other financial authorities. In most countries, this shift requires some adjustment of existing banking regulations.

Most people have "prudential regulation" in mind when (and if) they think about regulating financial institutions. Prudential regulation aims to ensure the financial soundness of regulated institutions to prevent systemwide financial instability and protect depositors from losing their money. When a deposit-taking institution collapses, it cannot repay its depositors, which could undermine public confidence and stimulate a run on deposits (where everyone "runs" to their banks to pull their money out, causing even previously solvent institutions to fail). Examples of prudential regulation include capital adequacy norms (does the financial institution have enough equity in case of a crisis?) and reserve and liquidity requirements (does it have enough cash to pay off depositors if there were such a run?). However, prudential regulation means little without effective prudential supervision.

[16.] See chapter 7 for a discussion of consumer protection.

[17.] Interview with Julio C. Herbas Gutierrez, manager, Banco Solidario, S.A.

[18.] This section borrows heavily from Christen, Lyman, and Rosenberg, *Guiding Principles on Regulation and Supervision of Microfinance.*

Supervision involves monitoring to verify compliance with prudential regulations and taking steps to shore up the solvency of a regulated institution when compliance becomes doubtful. Prudential regulation and supervision are generally complex, difficult, expensive, and invasive. They require a specialized financial authority for their implementation.

For those financial institutions that capture deposits from the public (and thus would generally be subject to prudential regulation), some standard banking regulations need to be adjusted to accommodate microfinance (see table 5.2 for examples).

Governments should apply the more burdensome prudential regulation only when the financial system and depositor's money is potentially at risk. Otherwise nonprudential norms and regulatory approaches should be sufficient. Nonprudential regulations include measures like registration with some authority for transparency purposes, keeping adequate accounts, prevention of fraud and financial crimes, and various types of consumer protection measures. Specialized microcredit institutions that do not take retail deposits should not be subjected to prudential regulation. Some countries (especially in former communist regimes) prohibit unlicensed nonbank institutions (including NGOs) from lending. This is an unnecessary restriction that can stifle experimentation with microcredit. In these cases, reforms subjecting those that offer microcredit to nonprudential regulation may be a relatively simple and effective means of freeing up the development of large-scale microlending, as seen in Bosnia and Morocco.

The costliness and difficulty of effective prudential supervision, especially for smaller institutions, is a particularly thorny policy issue. Supervisory authorities typically have limited resources at their disposal. Authorities use the minimal capital requirement—the lowest amount of capital required to obtain a license—to ration the number of financial institutions that require supervision.

TABLE 5.2 Possible Adjustments to Prudential Regulations for Microfinance

Standard Banking Regulations	When Applied to Microfinance
Minimum capital requirements	Need to balance promotion of microfinance with the realistic capacity to supervise
Capital-adequacy ratios	May need more equity because of repayment volatility
Limits on unsecured lending	Impractical for character-based lending
Registration of collateral	Too expensive for tiny loans
Requirements for branches: security standards, working hours, daily clearing of accounts, limitations on location	May interfere with innovations that reduce costs and bring more convenient services to clients
Standard loan documentation requirements	May be too expensive and time-consuming for tiny loans

Source: Adapted from Christen, Lyman, and Rosenberg, Guiding Principles on Regulation and Supervision of Microfinance.

Many microfinance proponents feel that minimum capital requirements should be much lower for financial institutions serving the poor. Others argue that the minimum capital requirements should limit licensed institutions to a set number that supervisors can realistically monitor. Ineffective supervision may be worse than none at all, because poor (and other) clients could be lulled into a false sense of security.

Against this backdrop, it is easy to see that some small and remote financial institutions—savings and loan cooperatives, for instance—may not meet the applicable minimum capital requirements and, even if they did, they likely could not be effectively supervised. This commonly happens with member-owned financial cooperatives. In some cases, the authorities have decided to let these institutions continue to operate and take deposits without licensing and supervision by the banking supervisor. The rationale is that, even if they are unsupervised, these tiny institutions may be less risky than other informal forms of savings that a client would turn to if these institutions were shut down. This practical solution could help provide access to financial services to poor and remote clients who would not otherwise have access. However, customers should be made aware that no government agency is monitoring the health of these organizations or the safety of their deposits, and take heed.

There is some debate about supervising large financial cooperatives. With the exception of cooperatives in West Africa (see box 5.6), many financial cooperatives are not supervised by banking authorities. Instead, they are often supervised by the government entity charged with overseeing all kinds of cooperatives, for example, the ministry of agriculture or cooperative development. Unfortunately, these entities rarely have the financial skills to enforce prudential norms and thus they fail to ensure the safety and soundness of the financial cooperative system.

Some argue that banking supervisors should take on this job, because they are the only ones likely to do it properly. Others express concern that taking on yet another class of financial intermediaries would overstretch the already-thin resources of the banking authorities. A compromise option is delegated supervision, in which the banking supervisor retains authority over the cooperatives but empowers a third party (for example, a federation of financial cooperatives or independent auditors) to inspect and supervise them. This is used in the Kyrgyz Republic, where the central bank delegates supervision to a private company, and in Indonesia, where BRI is contracted by the central bank to supervise small village credit institutions called Bank Kredit Desas (BKDs).[19]

The jury is still out as to how well the delegated supervision model will work. Growing evidence suggests that success is more likely in countries where the party or parties to whom supervisory responsibilities are delegated are themselves closely monitored. Self-supervision is more problematic. When an entity solely under the control of the organizations it is supposed to be supervising is assigned this task, the results have not been favorable in virtually all developing and transition country situations.

---

[19] Asian Development Bank, *The Role of Central Banks in Microfinance in Asia and the Pacific*. Vol. 1. Overview, 57, 59.

Some countries have adopted microfinance-specific laws that introduce whole new regulatory categories of financial institutions. These laws might be a second-best option when it is difficult or impossible (often for political reasons) to reform existing banking sector laws. Box 5.6 gives examples of different specialized microfinance laws in Bolivia, West Africa, and Uganda.

BOX 5.6 Three approaches to specialized microfinance regulation and supervision

In **Bolivia,** a special law governing private financial funds (FFPs) permits NGOs to transform into specialized regulated financial institutions allowed to mobilize deposits and intermediate government funds. The minimum capital required is only around $1 million compared with about $3 million for banks (as of April 2005). FFPs are subject to the same (if not stricter) prudential supervision as banks and are monitored by the same Banking Superintendency.[a] The Superintendency requires all deposit-taking institutions (including FFPs) to submit their financial statements on a daily basis, an administrative burden that may discourage FFPs from entering into more remote rural areas with weak telecommunications infrastructure.[b]

In 1993, the Central Bank for **West Africa** (BCEAO) introduced the PARMEC Law (named after the project that produced it), regulating MFIs in eight member countries. The PARMEC Law includes special prudential standards for microfinance and subjects licensed institutions to an interest rate ceiling of 27 percent. However, most institutions charge fees on top of their stated interest rates, thus raising the effective cost to the borrower above this limit: they might find it difficult to survive if the ceiling were strictly enforced.[c]

One of the most recent countries to introduce specialized microfinance regulation and supervision is **Uganda.** Ugandan law adopts a tiered approach defining four categories of financial institutions that can offer microfinance services:

Tier 1: Commercial banks

Tier 2: Credit(-only) institutions

Tier 3: Microfinance-deposit-taking institutions (MDIs) allowed to take deposits from the public and supervised by the Bank of Uganda (central bank)

Tier 4: Non-deposit-taking institutions and small member-based institutions, mobilizing funds only from their members, which would not be regulated or supervised by the banking authorities.

The MDI law covers Tier 3 institutions. Passed in November 2002, it allows MDIs to accept deposits from the public and then on-lend those deposits to credit clients. MDIs can offer certain types of services, such as foreign exchange transactions or current accounts, only with the approval of the central bank. Along with the tiered structure, the most interesting aspect of the MDI law is the participatory process of consultation that produced it. Concerns were voiced on such issues as whether the minimum capital requirements (equal to $300,000 in late 2004) would exclude small institutions and what to do about high microcredit interest rates.[d]

[a] Association of Financial Entities Specialized in Microfinance (ASOFIN), *Regulatory Framework That Governs the Operation of the Microfinance in Bolivia,* 1.

[b] Miller, "The Paradox of Savings Mobilization in Microfinance: Why Microfinance Institutions in Bolivia Have Virtually Ignored Savings," 16.

[c] Ouattara, "Implementation of the PARMEC Law for Regulation of Microfinance," 4.

[d] Hannig and Braun, *Transforming NGOs: Becoming a Deposit-Taking Financial Intermediary,* 9, 20.

Some commentators caution against the "rush to regulate" microfinance through the introduction of laws creating new regulatory categories of depository financial institutions. They point to the more successful microfinance markets in Latin America, Bangladesh, and Indonesia, where microfinance was born and matured without special microfinance regulation. Potential dangers include (1) the political process of regulatory change can attract attention to microfinance and possibly result in suboptimal policies like interest rate ceilings; (2) overspecific regulation could limit innovation and competition; and (3) pressure to license deposit-taking institutions might result in the proliferation of low-quality institutions.[20] It is best to wait until there is a critical mass of strong candidates before promoting a specialized microfinance law (as was the case in Bolivia and Peru).

Another risk is that specialized microfinance laws, especially when they specify a particular institutional type, may end up marginalizing microfinance rather than integrating it within the financial system. Financial services for the poor stand a better chance of growing when larger financial institutions, including commercial banks, get involved. This is in fact happening in some Latin American countries like Ecuador. By keeping it completely separate, with its own special rules, those in the formal banking sector may not take microfinance seriously. Even worse, banks may find it difficult to enter the field under the regular banking laws if microfinance is relegated to a certain type of institution.[21]

Proactive Government Promotion

Governments, especially in developed countries, have used carrots and sticks to proactively entice or force financial institutions to serve those excluded from accessing financial services. More study and analysis about applying this proactive promotional approach in developing countries would be beneficial. There appear to be at least four models of government promotion to consider: priority sector lending or mandated minimum banking services, regulatory incentives, payment of government benefits through bank accounts, and matching deposits.

Priority sector lending. Some governments require banks to dedicate a certain proportion of their loan portfolios to specific, often social, purposes. For more than 35 years, the Indian government has mandated that banks orient 40 percent of their credit to strategic sectors of the economy. These priority sector rules are intended to benefit disadvantaged groups, including the poor. On the one hand, many of the existing microfinance programs might not have been established had it not been for this requirement, including some exciting new programs by the ICICI Bank. On the other hand, the system has been criticized because it forces banks away from lending that is efficient in terms of risk and return. Banks are being forced to lend to the less-creditworthy priority sectors,

---

[20.] Christen and Rosenberg, "The Rush to Regulate: Legal Frameworks for Microfinance," 15.

[21.] Espinosa, "Supervision and Regulation of the Microfinance Industry in Ecuador," 4.

which is not the best allocation of resources for the banks and for the economy as a whole.[22]

In 2002, the Colombian government directed banks to invest in microfinance, both directly and through lending to NGOs and commercial finance companies. While criticizing the overall concept of directed credit because of its potentially distorting effects, some experts think that this policy could catalyze the development of a viable microfinance market.[23]

Regulatory incentives. Some governments offer carrots (or incentives) to financial institutions to lend or open up accounts in specific communities. At least eight countries are known to have some kind of community reinvestment law: Australia, Brazil, Canada, India, Nigeria, South Africa, the United Kingdom, and the United States.[24] The best known strategy of this type is the Community Reinvestment Act (CRA), passed in the United States in 1977 to encourage deposit-taking financial institutions to lend in the communities where they operate, including low-income neighborhoods. CRA-motivated lending has introduced many banks to low-income consumers and has leveraged more than $1 trillion for economically disadvantaged communities, much of which otherwise would not have been provided.[25]

The future of the CRA is under debate because neighborhood branches no longer provide most neighborhood banking.[26] This has led many community development advocates to argue for expansion of the CRA to other types of financial institutions. At the same time, the CRA is costly, especially for smaller institutions.[27]

In a South African program under what is called the Financial Sector Charter, banks receive incentives to offer a basic entry-level bank account to low-income clients that is convenient, affordable, and user-friendly. This Mzansi account, launched in October 2004, has attracted about 1 million clients in less than one year. The aim is to put full-service banking within 15 kilometers of all South Africans, and automatic teller machines within 10 kilometers.[28]

Government payments. Increasingly, governments transfer benefits of various kinds through bank accounts. These accounts could, in theory, then be used to offer a broader range of financial services to beneficiaries. Over the past few years, the United Kingdom has instituted various methods to achieve what is re-

[22] Miller, "Political Economy of Directed Credit," 4.

[23] Trigo Loubiere, Devaney, and Rhyne, "Supervising and Regulating Microfinance in the Context of Financial Sector Liberalization," 9.

[24] Feltner, "A Global Survey of Community Reinvestment Laws: The Obligation of the Private Sector to Serve the Underserved in Several Countries," 1.

[25] Interview with Cheryl Neas, manager for policy, National Community Capital Association, April 2005.

[26] Apgar and Duda, *The Twenty-Fifth Anniversary of the Community Reinvestment Act: Past Accomplishments and Future Regulatory Challenges,* 169.

[27] Benston, "The Community Reinvestment Act—Looking for Discrimination That Is Not There," 10.

[28] Peachey and Roe, "Access to Finance," 52; and www.southafrica.info/public_services/citizens/consumer_services/mzansi.htm.

ferred to as "universal banking services," especially current accounts (or checking accounts) for the unbanked. As part of this effort, the government required social security benefits to be paid via automated transfers to a beneficiary's bank account. The government is working with the post office and banks to set up accounts that are free of charge and special Post Office Card Accounts that use swipe cards instead of checks.

In another program, the U.S. government urged banks to offer electronic transfer accounts to make federal benefit payments electronically.[29] In return, the government pays a fixed amount for each account opened. These accounts must comply with certain cost characteristics (for instance, they cannot cost owners more than $3 per month and could not have a minimum balance requirement). The Mexican government also pays out several welfare programs through public- and private-sector banks and other financial entities. One example is the "opportunities" program, which provides benefits for education, health, and nutrition that are directly transferred as cash to more than 4 million households.[30]

Matching deposits. In the United States, experimental Individual Development Accounts (IDAs) match deposits of working poor families at a ratio of 1:1, 2:1, or more. These savings accounts are meant for those saving for specific purposes, such as a home purchase, postsecondary education, or small business start-up. Account holders usually make monthly contributions to an account over one to four years. Many have never had a savings account before opening an IDA. Target clients include former welfare recipients, disadvantaged youth, refugees, and others. The savings and financial literacy components of the program attract financial institutions. In 2003 there were more than 500 IDA initiatives with more than 20,000 savers. There is some evidence that poorer Americans seize this savings opportunity less often than their better-off peers.[31]

Many other innovative government programs exist. Yet, there is still much to learn about promotional policies and incentives that could increase access to bank accounts and other types of financial services. Specialists working in developing countries should keep an eye on experiments in the developed world to learn lessons and apply the most relevant ideas to extend access to poor and low-income people.

Conclusion

The role of government in building inclusive financial systems is crucial but nuanced. There is a tension among the different roles that governments play.

[29] Peachey and Roe, "Access to Finance," 52.
[30] World Bank, "Mexico's Oportunidades Programme," 1.
[31] Comptroller of the Currency Administrator of National Banks, "Community Developments—Individual Development Accounts: An Asset Building Product for Lower-Income Consumers," 1; Duflo, Gale, Liebman, Orszag, and Saez, "Savings Incentives for Low- and Middle-Income Families: Evidence from a Field Experiment with H&R Block," 1.

Microfinance experts and many developing country officials increasingly concur that the government's best role is to offer a policy environment that allows competitive and diverse financial service providers to flourish. Some countries, like the Philippines, Jordan, Tanzania, and Uganda, have developed microfinance strategies that describe precisely what the appropriate role of government should be relative to the private sector. While not all countries need to articulate formal national strategies for microfinance, governments should incorporate finance for the poor into their overall development policies, such as financial sector reforms and poverty reduction strategies. This kind of policy coherence is vital, especially in countries with a history of heavy state involvement in the financial system and the economy as a whole.

The key actions for governments are to maintain macroeconomic stability, to avoid interest rate caps, and to refrain from distorting the market with unsustainable, subsidized, high-delinquency loan programs. Governments can also adjust banking sector regulation and supervision to facilitate microfinance while also protecting poor people's deposits. Governments can further support financial services for the poor by improving the legal framework for contract enforcement and collateral rights, ensuring practically and legally feasible systems of land titling, and ensuring that tax systems do not discriminate against different types of institutions engaged in microfinance—although the impact of these measures on poor people is less well understood. It also appears that governments might play a useful promotion role, by employing carrots and sticks.

Ten years ago, microfinance experts wanted governments to stay as far away as possible from directly providing microfinance, as justified by the poor track record of government-run retail credit programs. Many have also expressed skepticism about the need for regulating microfinance. Today, it is well understood that the government has a positive role to play in building inclusive financial systems. The challenge ahead is to convince governments—through demonstrated success and impact, not just philosophical arguments—to take on this constructive and powerful responsibility and to avoid repeating approaches that have failed in the past.

Chapter 6
Funders

Building inclusive financial systems will not happen automatically. Money and technical support are key ingredients, although the recipe actually calls for a lot *less* money and a lot *more* technical support than is commonly believed.

Recent years have seen an explosion in the number and types of international funding sources for microfinance. Beyond the traditional donor community, an array of socially motivated investors has entered into the fray. More attention is also being focused on domestic sources of financing.

In an ideal world with inclusive financial systems, domestic financial markets in developing countries would supply the bulk of the funding for microfinance. Financial service providers would rely on savings from the public, loans from the commercial banking sector, bond issues, and domestic stock markets. Limited amounts of international finance would complement the domestic funding market.

In the real world, most specialized MFIs are still far from integrating into domestic markets. Some financial service providers like government savings and postal banks already tap domestic financial markets (especially savings), as do a few leading specialized microfinance providers. But until now, international subsidies have played a huge role in jump-starting and strengthening microfinance. International donor agencies have injected grants and subsidized loans to fuel the development and growth of microfinance—making significant contributions at all three levels of the financial system discussed so far: micro, meso, and macro.

As microfinance has evolved from being mostly about the delivery of microenterprise credit to focusing on making financial systems more inclusive, public donors need to reinvent themselves as they define their most constructive role. The fundamental question is how to best use subsidies to stimulate (mostly) private entities to serve poor people with quality financial services faster than they would on their own.

The landscape of funding options in microfinance is highly dynamic and complicated (see figure 6.1). Existing funders range from those with primarily a social mission to alleviate poverty (international donor agencies and founda-

FIGURE 6.1 The Landscape of Funding Options for Microfinance

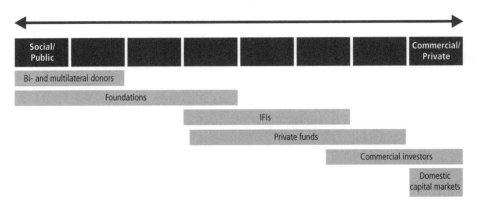

Note: IFI = international financial institutions (investment arms of public bilateral or multilateral institutions).

tions) to those with more commercial motivations (commercial investors and domestic capital markets), and many options in between. Important differences exist within each category. For instance, some socially responsible investors are more "social" and others more "commercial."

The biggest challenge for funders going forward is to identify their relative strengths in order to focus on the segments they are best positioned to serve—based on their objectives, the kinds of financing instruments they offer, their cost structures, their internal technical strengths, and their risk appetites. This chapter explores the roles, trends, and potential of international donor agencies, other international investors, and domestic funding sources.

International Donor Agencies and Foundations

In this chapter, the term "donor" encompasses a range of international development agencies (sometimes called international development partners), including the following:

- **Bilateral donors**—the aid agencies of governments in industrial countries

- **Multilateral development banks and organizations**—agencies owned by the governments of the industrial and developing world, such as the World Bank, the regional development banks, and UN agencies like the United Nations Development Program (UNDP) or the International Fund for Agricultural Development (IFAD)

- **Foundations**—privately owned nonprofit institutions through which private wealth is contributed and distributed for public and/or charitable purposes, such as the Ford Foundation, Argidius, or the Open Society Institute (OSI)

These donors spend an estimated $800 million to $1 billion *each year* on microfinance and credit projects. According to a recent survey of CGAP member donors, the World Bank, the Asian Development Bank, the Inter-American

Development Bank, and the European Commission are among the largest public funders of microfinance. According to information reported by them, these four donors alone had a microfinance portfolio (cumulative amount still committed) of $1.8 billion at the end of 2003.[1]

Donor agencies support microfinance using a range of instruments. The instruments at donors' disposal include policy support, technical assistance (support for experts to offer technical advice), grants, loans (which can be offered at subsidized or commercial interest rates, quasi-equity (usually low-interest loans that can be converted into equity), equity investments in those institutions that can sell shares, and guarantees. Different combinations of these instruments are used for a host of different types of projects, including the following:

- funding financial institutions' loan portfolios;

- providing technical support to financial institutions and governments (often called capacity building);

- improving financial institutions' ability to tap domestic capital markets through helping to forge relationships and guarantees;

- building the skill sets of technical service providers, such as local consulting firms or training facilities; and

- supporting the operations of networks and associations.

The most effective donors in microfinance are those that can directly fund private organizations in developing countries. Unfortunately, many donors, particularly the multilateral development banks, are able to work only with governments, usually with soft loans. This instrument might be valid for traditional aid activities like building roads, hospitals, and schools, but is less suitable for supporting the financial system in the private-sector domain. As discussed in chapter 5, most governments do not have a stellar track record when it comes to offering financial services.

Retail (micro-level) MFIs can be funded either directly by the donor or through wholesale funding institutions (apexes). These indirect channels are often set up with the intention of more efficiently channeling funds and sometimes technical support to multiple financial institutions. Another commonly used channel for funds is credit components of multisector projects. Box 6.1 discusses why both apex funds and credit components have not been especially effective.

Making aid more effective.[2] The good news is that donors interested in building inclusive financial systems have worked hard to form a common position about

---

[1] CGAP Charter Reporting 2004. The difference between the $800 million to $1 billion per year and this figure of outstanding projects is that the former is the flow of money that is spent year after year, some of which is in the form of loans that are repaid. The latter is the net amount still active as of mid-2005.

[2] This section draws on CGAP, *Building Inclusive Financial Systems: Donor Guidelines on Good Practice in Microfinance;* Helms and Latortue, *Elements of Donor Effectiveness in Microfinance: Policy Implications;* and Duflos, Helms, Latortue, and Siedek, *Global Results: Analysis and Lessons.*

how to do the right thing. Over the past 30 years, "what works" to optimize the impact of donors' subsidies has become clearer. In 1995, donor agencies codified good practice guidelines for supporting MFIs. These agencies recently produced updated guidelines titled *Building Inclusive Financial Systems: Donor Guide-*

BOX 6.1 Donors' least effective contribution

Two kinds of projects often perform poorly and usually do not result in permanent access to financial services for poor people: apexes (often called wholesale funding or second-tier funds) and credit components (also known as credit lines, revolving funds, and community development funds). Apexes and credit components share the dubious distinction of allowing donors to move relatively large amounts of funds into microfinance. Unfortunately, the large subsidies they absorb are not usually justified by their results.

Apex institutions channel funds, with or without supporting services, to multiple retail financial institutions in a single country or integrated market. (See Chapter 5 for the role of government in channeling apex funding.) Most apexes fail to deliver, because they are often designed as government-controlled entities and set up in countries without a critical mass of good financial institutions with the capacity to absorb the funding. Donors often use this mechanism, because it appears to be an easy way to move large amounts of money quickly. In some cases, apexes have turned to retail lending themselves when they were set up in countries without sufficient demand for wholesale funds (for example, K-Rep in Kenya and FondoMicro in the Dominican Republic). In extreme cases, apex funding is highly concentrated in a few or even one good financial institution. Banco Multisectorial de Inversiones (BMI) in El Salvador, for instance, held 90 percent of its portfolio in one MFI, Financiera Calpia (now called Banco ProCredit El Salvador).

Apexes present a paradox: to be successful in their intermediation role, they need enough financial institutions that are capable of absorbing the funds. But when a country has sufficient sustainable and credible financial institutions, they may already have access to commercial funds. Apexes may, in some cases, be redundant or crowd out domestic private-sector suppliers (at worst). Some cases, like India, prove that apexes can make a difference when a large number of smaller financial institutions that require risk-tolerant funding coincide with well-run apex organizations. On the whole, though, apexes have a spotty track record; it is simply difficult to keep politics out of the picture.

Credit components are funding for credit in larger donor projects in other sectors such as agriculture, education, health, or community development. They are often targeted at a particular group of people. Because they are part of larger programs, credit components are often designed by people lacking financial expertise. These people often confuse the objective of transferring resources to a particular group with that of offering financial services that will continue to benefit clients long beyond the life of the donor project. These credit components may lose money quickly as borrowers do not usually repay well (because they see the funding as a "gift" from government), cease functioning when a project is completed, create unsupportable levels of borrower debt, encourage donor dependence among beneficiaries, and crowd out domestic financial institutions.

Sources: Clark, "Credit Components"; CGAP, "Apex Institutions in Microfinance"; and Levy, "Apex Institutions in Microfinance," 6, 12.

---

lines on Good Practice in Microfinance.[3] This document, facilitated and codrafted by CGAP, contains lessons learned and operational guidance for donors and others working in microfinance. At the very least, the guidelines seek to enforce a sort of Hippocratic oath for donors to "do no harm."

The bad news is that donors do not consistently apply these good practice principles. A large proportion of the money they spend is not effective, either because it gets hung up in unsuccessful and often complicated funding mechanisms (for example, a government apex facility), or it goes to partners that are not held accountable for performance. In some cases, poorly conceived programs have retarded the development of inclusive financial systems by distorting markets and displacing domestic commercial initiatives with cheap or free money.

Donors often find it difficult to adhere to good practices because of the way they work (see box 6.2 for details). Development agencies could have a far greater impact (even with current levels of spending) by aligning their operations with good practice and sticking to what they are good at, individually and as a group. This approach worked well in India, where individual donors defined their best role relative to each other and the private sector. Donor flexibility provided a diverse and reliable funding base on which the MFI BASIX was able to secure its long-term growth. A mix of bilateral donors and the Ford Foundation offered funding to this innovative financial institution that allowed it to build a diverse funding base in preparation for commercial investors.[4] BASIX used the early funders to establish a track record as a reliable borrower. Subsidized loans dropped from more than 90 percent of total funding in early years to less than 50 percent in 2002, while Indian funding (as opposed to international funding) increased to nearly 40 percent.

Positioning donor funding. The role of donors in the future will change as progress toward inclusive financial systems gains momentum. Dependence on donor funding will diminish in relative terms as markets mature. Donors will need to find ways to complement—not replace—private domestic and international capital.

Donor subsidies still will likely be needed at all the levels of the financial system. The private sector alone will not address all the challenges posed by expanding and deepening the financial system, or at least will not do so fast enough to achieve the development benefits urgently needed. In the near term, purely commercial investors may find the cost of providing financial services too great, the rate of return too low, or the risk too high. Donors are needed to promote innovation with research and development on new products or technologies; improve financial infrastructure; encourage increased transparency on performance and competition among retail financial service providers; and finance skill-building at all levels. Donors can also influence do-

---

[3.] The earlier guidelines were called *Micro and Small Enterprise Finance: Guiding Principles for Selecting and Supporting Intermediaries* (known as the "Pink Book").
[4.] Dileo, "Building a Reliable MFI Funding Base: Donor Flexibility Shows Results."

BOX 6.2 Why do donors find it difficult to adhere to good practice and support effective microfinance?

Starting in 2002, a group of 17 bilateral and multilateral agencies launched a process to answer this question. The ministers and agency heads of these organizations, together with CGAP, embarked on a series of practical peer reviews. These reviews forced donor agencies to look in the mirror and to analyze their individual strengths and weaknesses. They realized that their own internal processes, systems, and incentives thwarted them from doing the right thing in microfinance. The leadership of the agencies then committed to determine their comparative advantage and act on it in collaboration with others. All agencies agreed to disclose the results of their reviews publicly on the Internet.[a]

Drawing on interviews with nearly 900 donor staff, the reviews offered concrete recommendations for change to each participating agency. The reviews also yielded five core elements of donor effectiveness (referred to as the "aid effectiveness star").

Box figure 6.2.1. The Aid Effectiveness Star

- Strategic clarity and coherence—does the agency know where it's going? Does its vision reflect good practice? And are its actions and programs consistent with that vision?

- Strong staff capacity—does the agency have sufficient staff with the right technical skills to design and manage good programs?

- Accountability for results—what is the level of transparency about programs and performance?

- Relevant knowledge management—does the agency learn from its own and others' experience (both good and bad)?

- Appropriate instruments—can the agency work directly with the private sector with the right type and range of instruments?

Source: Helms and Latortue, "Elements of Donor Effectiveness in Microfinance: Policy Implications."
[a] See www.cgap.org for more on the Microfinance Donor Peer Reviews and the overall CGAP Aid Effectiveness Initiative.

mestic and international financial policies that allow more inclusive financial systems to emerge and thrive.

Finally, donors should be prepared to take more risks than private actors, because they can more easily absorb the losses that might result. A higher appetite for risk means that donors should focus on funding institutions that commercial or socially responsible investors would avoid.[5]

International Investors

International investment in microfinance is on the rise. Socially oriented international investors include public investors (investment arms of bilateral and multilateral development agencies, often called international financial institutions or IFIs) that take a more commercial approach than the donors, and private funds of many different types (see table 6.1 for a list of IFIs and private funds active in microfinance). These funds could potentially increase the supply of financing where donor funding is no longer needed but commercial funding is not yet available. Collectively, private funds and IFIs have placed $1.2 billion in debt, equity, and guarantees in about 500 specialized MFIs and cooperatives. International investors will likely have an additional $650 million to place in the very near term.[6]

The creation of more than 50 funds over the past few years has captured the attention of the microfinance community and reflects the surging enthusiasm for microfinance. Private investors come in various shapes and sizes:[7]

* Independent equity funds specialized in microfinance: Profund, AfriCap

* Funds associated with and created by microfinance networks: ACCION Investments (ACCION Global Bridge Fund, ACCION Latin America Bridge Fund, ACCION Gateway Fund), Opportunity International, Développement International Desjardins (Investment Fund for International Development [FONIDI], the Partnership Fund, and the Guarantee Fund), and Internationale Micro Investitionen Aktiengesellschaft (IMI-AG)

* Funds created by private socially responsible investors: Gray Ghost, Unitus, Andromeda, Triodos, Oikocredit, responsAbility, and Société d'Investissement et de Développement International (SIDI)

The substantial growth of international investments in microfinance has been both beneficial and troubling. First, these funds provide a wide array of financial instruments to meet the financing needs of MFIs. Although equity has been relatively difficult for MFIs to obtain in the past, some funds are beginning to provide equity. This is important, because international investors can have a positive impact on the governance and management of MFIs when they become part owners. Besides debt and equity, other instruments offered by these

---

[5.] Jansson, *Financing Microfinance—Exploring the Funding Side of Microfinance Institutions,* 20.
[6.] Ivatury and Abrams, "The Market for Microfinance Foreign Investment: Opportunities and Challenges," 4.
[7.] Adapted from Rhyne, "Perspectives from the Council of Microfinance Equity Funds," 9.

TABLE 6.1 IFIs and Private Funds Investing in Microfinance

IFIs	Private Funds	

Multilateral
- AfDB (African Development Bank)
- AsDB (Asian Development Bank)
- CAF (Corporación Andina de Fomento)
- CABEI (Central American Bank for Economic Integration)
- EBRD (European Bank for Reconstruction and Development)
- EIB (European Investment Bank)
- IADB Multilateral Investment Fund (Inter-American Development Bank)
- IFC (International Finance Corporation)
- IIC (Interamerican Investment Corporation)
- OPEC Fund (Organization of Petroleum Exporting Countries)

Predominantly Debt Funds
- Alterfin
- ASN/Novib Fund (ANF)
- AWF Development Debt
- Calvert Foundation
- CORDAID (Catholic Organization for Relief and Development Aid)
- Creditosud
- Développement International Desjardins (Partnership Fund, FONIDI Fund)
- Dexia Microcredit Fund
- Deutsche Bank Microcredit Development Fund (DBMDF)
- Etimos
- Hivos-Triodos Fund
- LA-CIF (Latin American Challenge Investment Fund)
- Kolibri Kapital ASA
- Luxmint–ADA
- Partners for the Common Good
- PlaNet Finance Revolving Fund

Predominantly Equity Funds
- ACCION Gateway Fund
- ACCION AIM
- Global Microfinance Facility
- AfriCap Microfinance Fund
- IMI-AG (Internationale Micro Investitionen Aktiengesellschaft)
- La Fayette Participations, Horus Banque et Finance
- La Fayette Investissement (LFI)
- Opportunity International– Opportunity Transformation Investments
- ProFund
- SIDI (Société d'Investissement et de Développement International)

Bilateral
- AECI (Spanish Agency for International Cooperation)
- BIO (Belgiische Investerings Maatschappij voor Ontwikkelingslanden)
- DEG (Deutsche Investitions und Entwicklungsgesellschaft)
- FMO (Nederlandse Financierings Maatschappij voor Ontwikkelingslanden NV)
- Finnfund
- KfW (Kreditanstalt für Wiederaufbau)
- OPIC (Overseas Private Investment Corporation)
- ProParco (subsidiary of AFD)
- SECO/COSUDE
- USAID Development Credit Authority (United States Agency for International Development)

Guarantee Funds
- FIG (Fonds International de Garantie)
- ACCION Latin American Bridge Fund
- Deutsche Bank Microcredit Development Fund
- Developpement International Desjardins (Guarantee Fund)
- The DOEN Foundation
- ICCO (Inter Church Organization for Development Co-operation)
- Incofin
- ASN-NOVIB
- Oikocredit
- Rabobank Foundation
- Unitus Debt Fund

Mixed Debt and Equity Funds
- The DOEN Foundation
- Geisse Foundation
- ICCO (Inter Church Organization for Development Co-operation)
- Incofin
- Microvest
- NOVIB
- Oikocredit
- Open Society Institute
- Rabobank Foundation
- ResponsAbility Global Microfinance Fund
- Sarona Global Investment Fund
- ShoreCap International
- Unitus
- Triodos Fair Share Fund
- Triodos-Doen Foundation
- Unitus Debt Fund

Source: Ivatury and Reille, "Foreign Investment in Microfinance: Debt and Equity from Quasi-Commercial Investors," 3.
Note: Many debt and/or equity funds also offer guarantees.

FIGURE 6.2 Distribution of International Investments

Investment by region (volume)

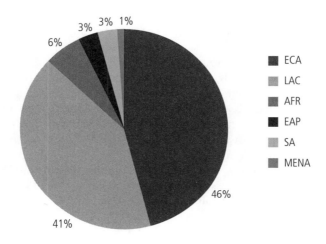

- ECA
- LAC
- AFR
- EAP
- SA
- MENA

Instruments used by funds

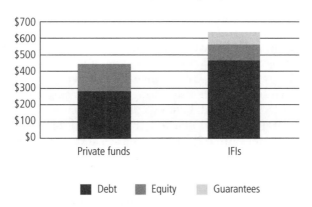

Debt   Equity   Guarantees

Source: Ivatury and Abrams, "The Market for Microfinance Foreign Investment: Opportunities and Challenges."
Note: AFR = Africa; EAP = East Asia and the Pacific; ECA = Eastern and Central Asia; LAC = Latin America and the Caribbean; MENA = Middle East and North Africa; SA = South Asia.

investors include quasi-equity (medium- to long-term soft loans designed to be repaid from profits, which are subordinated to other more secure loans and, in the context of microfinance, can eventually be transferred to equity in return for good institutional performance); purchases of bonds, certificates of deposit, and other instruments; and guarantees so that the financial institutions can obtain domestic bank loans, issue bonds, or float shares on the stock exchange.

The majority (around 90 percent) of international investment comes directly or indirectly from public funds. Many of the private funds obtain their financing from IFIs. But the approach of both IFIs and private funds is very risk-averse. This is reflected in the high level of concentration of investments, both geographically and in the types of instruments offered (see figure 6.2). Around 87 percent of the funds go to two regions, Europe and Central Asia (IFIs) and Latin America (private funds). Concentration may be even more acute, as private funds and IFIs compete for a small group of strong, regulated financial institutions. For instance, about one-third of all private funds have financed Banco Solidario in Ecuador and Confianza in Peru, and one-third of IFIs have invested debt or equity in a number of ProCredit institutions in Eastern Europe, the Balkans, and Central Asia.

The high concentration of funding raises doubts about whether sufficient market opportunities exist to support so many relatively small funds. Some observers predict increased consolidation as the fund market matures and subsidies for establishing funds dry up.[8]

Another level of concentration is the instrument used. Figure 6.2 shows that most money is offered as loans in foreign currency, which could pose problems for institutions that might not fully understand nor know how to manage foreign exchange risks (see box 6.3). Two examples of international lenders that have developed their own mechanisms to mitigate foreign exchange risk are provided by Triodos Bank and Oikocredit. Triodos combines local currency loans with currency swaps when those are available (for example, Indonesia, India, South Africa, Brazil, and Mexico) and, when not available, incorporates foreign exchange risk into the loan price. Oikocredit set up a Local Currency Risk Fund (LCRF), which is like insurance that protects its loans against exchange rate fluctuations. LCRF uses donor grants to ensure lenders' return on hard currency loans does not fall below a certain threshold.

Finally, some observers question whether there is an inherent conflict of interest in funds that offer both technical assistance and investment. Specifically, they ask whether the technical assistance may influence or interfere with the investment decision process. Will investors tolerate lower returns only as long as they can tap subsidies to offer technical support?[9]

All international investors in microfinance have one thing in common: they are willing to accept a more modest return on their investments in exchange for the social returns generated by microfinance. As attractive as financial services for the poor are to many socially minded investors, many MFIs may never attract purely commercial investors interested only in profits. The higher the emphasis on social returns, the more financial risk investors should be willing to take. Just as donors should allow their grantees and soft loan recipients to "graduate" to quasi-commercial investors like private investors and IFIs, so the

[8.] Goodman, *International Investment Funds—Mobilizing Investors toward Microfinance*, 15; and Ivatury and Abrams, "The Market for Microfinance Foreign Investment: Opportunities and Challenges," 9.
[9.] Goodman, *International Investment Funds—Mobilizing Investors toward Microfinance*, 15.

BOX 6.3 Managing foreign exchange risk

Financial institutions that finance some portion of their portfolio with hard currency loans face a risk of losses because of foreign exchange fluctuations, but this risk is not always well understood. Foreign exchange risk is the possibility of a loss (or gain) when exchange rates change. At least half of the 216 MFIs responding to a CGAP/Microfinance Information eXchange (MIX) survey had hard currency loans (dollars or euros). Half of these institutions were not hedging (or managing) the foreign exchange risk.

Suppose an MFI borrows $500,000 over three years at a 10 percent annual interest rate, with interest payments made every six months. The local exchange rate equals 10 DCs (domestic currency units) to $1 at the outset of the loan, but it devalues to 13.4 DCs by the end of the loan term. The amount of principal that would need to be repaid at the end of the three years equals $6.7 million (as opposed to the original $5 million), with an effective interest rate of 21 percent annually, nearly double the original 10 percent! Financial institutions should compare domestic alternatives with the 21 percent effective foreign rate, not the 10 percent rate offered on the loan contract. Of course, it is not always possible to know the direction of exchange rate fluctuations ahead of time. This is why financial institutions are well advised to manage foreign exchange risk—this kind of devaluation can really damage a financial institution's financial position. It could also harm poor clients by increasing the cost of foreign debt, resulting in higher interest rates charged to cover those costs.

A few options for managing foreign exchange risk include the following:

- **A local currency loan payable in hard currency with a reserve mechanism.** Borrowers reserve some proportion of the loan amount to make sure they can cover the costs of devaluation, thus protecting the lender against depreciation of the local currency over the life of the loan.

- **Back-to-back hard currency/local currency loans.** A dollar (or euro) loan is deposited in a bank in foreign currency, and the bank turns around and issues a local currency loan to the MFI using the foreign currency deposit as collateral.

- **Forward contracts and swaps.** These derivative products offered in financial markets are purely commercial instruments. For forward contracts, financial institutions borrow in hard currency and then enter into separate contracts to lock in the future rate at which it will buy the hard currency to repay the loan. Swaps involve exchanging financial obligations with another party, for instance, swapping a foreign currency loan for a local currency obligation of a third party.

Sources: Cavazos, Abrams, and Miles, *Foreign Exchange Risk Management in Microfinance;* Featherston, Littlefield, and Mwangi, "Foreign Exchange Risk in Microfinance: What Is It and How Can It Be Managed?" 3; and Fernando, "Managing Foreign Exchange Risk: The Search for an Innovation to Lower Costs to Poor People."

IFIs, with their low-cost public money, should move away from the same regulated MFIs they have funded over the past several years and encourage them to develop their own links to domestic capital markets. This means focusing more on the next generation of strong institutions, offering seed capital and support for the development or transformation of this new crop of stars.[10]

[10.] Goodman, *International Investment Funds—Mobilizing Investors toward Microfinance,* 18; and Ivatury and Abrams, "The Market for Microfinance Foreign Investment: Opportunities and Challenges," 12.

Domestic Funding Markets

Integrating microfinance seamlessly into domestic markets is the ultimate objective of building inclusive financial systems. Domestic funding has at least three advantages. First, the availability of deposit services (one source of domestic funding) is highly valued by poor and low-income people. Second, domestic funding helps financial institutions avoid foreign exchange risk. Third, it is more likely to come from commercially motivated sources, so it is not money that would have gone to some other social or development purpose if the financial institution had not captured it.[11]

Most domestic financial systems have excess liquidity—banks have been fairly successful in mobilizing resources, mostly from corporate, institutional, and wealthy clients. In fact, many financial institutions that serve poor and low-income people, such as large savings banks, postal banks, and other community banks and cooperatives, already rely on domestic markets, especially deposits. The large numbers of savings accounts among these institutions hint at the potential for mobilizing deposits on a massive scale from poor and low-income people. Beyond savings, other potential sources of domestic financing for microfinance include debt from commercial banks, certificates of deposit, and bonds as well as equity from private domestic individuals or funds, and floating shares on the stock exchange (although these domestic equity sources have not materialized much yet).

Most specialized MFIs have not taken advantage of the enormous opportunity presented by domestic funding markets as well as they could. Many prefer foreign investors. In a recent CGAP/MIX survey, MFIs and cooperatives cited better terms and conditions, especially apparently cheaper nominal interest rates, as the main reasons for seeking foreign investment over domestic sources (see table 6.2). To the extent that many international investors incorporate subsidies of some kind into their funding, this preference is not surprising. Financial institutions often overestimate the relative cheapness of foreign debt, however, because they fail to fully take into account the foreign exchange risk described in the previous section. Another problem with international debt, especially when subsidized, is that it can lower incentives to mobilize deposits.

A number of MFIs are beginning to access domestic funding sources. Regulated MFIs have begun to focus on domestic sources of funds and act as true financial intermediaries. Many have turned to deposit mobilization, which has many benefits. First, it allows financial institutions to better meet the needs of poor (and other) clients by offering a more diverse range of services. It also can lower the overall costs of financing and diversify the sources of funds. Savings, even small-balance savings, are usually relatively stable over time and can be more reliable than donors or other funders, who may change their strategies or decide not to fund.[12]

In Peru, as commercial banks have entered the market, regulated MFIs have looked for ways to reduce their costs to compete. To do this, they turned in-

---

[11.] Ivatury and Abrams, "The Market for Foreign Investment in Microfinance: Opportunities and Challenges," 14.

[12.] Robinson and Wright, "Mobilizing Savings."

TABLE 6.2 Why Microfinance Institutions and Cooperatives Seek
Foreign Investment

Motivating Factor for Seeking Foreign Investment	Percent of Respondents "Extremely Important"	Rating This Factor as or "Very Important"
	36 Regulated MFIs	112 Unregulated MFIs and Cooperatives
Lower interest rate	86%	78%
Easier or lower amount of collateral	69%	72%
Investor's willingness to negotiate	69%	66%
Tenor (length of loan)	61%	66%
Speed of disbursement	56%	65%
Ability to attract other lenders and investors	56%	60%
Better choice of products	44%	56%
Technical assistance provided with foreign capital	32%	54%
Prestige	31%	40%

Source: CGAP/MIX Survey of Funding Needs in Ivatury and Abrams, "The Market for Microfinance Foreign Investment: Opportunities and Challenges."

creasingly to deposits rather than borrowing to fund growth. Between 1997 and 2003, deposits as a percentage of total assets increased from 40 percent to 62 percent among 11 Peruvian MFIs.[13] Another example is Association of Cambodian Local Economic Development Agencies (ACLEDA) (see figure 6.3). The Cambodian MFI increased its number of savers from 3,800 ($1.95 million) in 2001 to 38,000 ($16.1 million) in 2004.[14]

However, many financial institutions have found that mobilizing savings is not always so easy, particularly among poor clients. The perceived high costs (especially of small accounts), specialized skills required, liquidity risk, and exposure in times of crisis, when depositors could rush to withdraw their funds, have sometimes dampened enthusiasm for deposit mobilization. Banks have found it difficult to balance poor clients' demand for safe, convenient, and accessible places to store money with their own requirements for financial viability. As seen in box 6.4, given the formal options available in most developing countries, a poor client may well prefer stashing cash under the mattress to opening a bank account. The challenge for regulated financial institutions that serve poor clients is to build the "business case" for deposits. Financial institutions need to see the many benefits of making investments in market

[13] Ivatury and Abrams, "The Market for Microfinance Foreign Investment: Opportunities and Challenges," 13.
[14] Fernando, *Micro Success Story? Transforming of Nongovernment Institutions into Regulated Financial Institutions*, 21.

FIGURE 6.3 ACLEDA Savings Growth

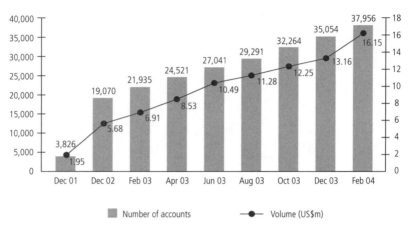

Source: Fernando, *Micro Success Story? Transforming of Nongovernment Institutions into Regulated Financial Institutions.*

BOX 6.4 Can banks beat the mattress?

Finmark Trust reviewed the product features of a typical bank account versus stuffing cash under a mattress. Based on an analysis of price, access, product features, service quality, and value placed on clients, the mattress emerges as more attractive than a bank account! Product features is the only category in which a bank account wins—specifically, banks are much more secure than the mattress, where relatives and neighbors could easily gain unwanted access to funds. As long as clients prefer the mattress and other informal savings mechanisms to opening bank accounts, it remains difficult for financial institutions to tap the deposits of poor and low-income people as a primary funding source.

	Price	Access	Product Features	Service Quality	Value Placed on Client	NET
Mattress	+ (free)	+ (anytime banking)	- - (insecure, risky)	0 (self-serve)	0	0
Bank account	- - (fees and commissions)	- - (limited hours)	+ (secure)	- - (intimidating)	?	- -

Key: +   =   strong
       - -   =   weak
       0   =   neutral
       ?   =   unknown

Source: Porteous, "Cooperative Banking in Context."

knowledge, product mix, systems, and marketing necessary to offer high-quality deposit services to poor and low-income clients.

Unregulated MFIs are more numerous than regulated ones. They have few options beyond foreign debt because they are not legally allowed to mobilize savings. They also often have unclear ownership structures that raise questions about who is accountable for bank loans in case of default. Domestic banks are generally unwilling to lend to them beyond a one-to-one debt/equity ratio, and they often require formal collateral like a mortgage on property.[15] The loan portfolio is the only significant asset for many conventional MFIs. Some banks have accepted these portfolios as collateral, which could be a breakthrough in domestic lending for some MFIs (see chapter 3 for an extensive discussion of partnerships between banks and MFIs that have allowed the latter to tap commercial funding). After all, portfolio quality in good microfinance is often quite high and may be a sufficiently secure guarantee.[16] International partners could help by strengthening the numerous smaller MFIs' skills at negotiating loans, introducing them to domestic banks, enhancing the credibility of their domestic partners, improving governance, and possibly offering guarantees (see box 6.5 for a discussion of guarantees).

A few leading MFIs (mostly, but not all, regulated ones) have made use of debt instruments on local capital markets. For instance, Compartamos in Mexico, Mibanco in Peru, and Women's World Banking (WWB) Cali in Colombia have placed bonds on their local markets, based partially on ratings from mainstream rating agencies like Standard & Poor's, Fitch, and Moody's.[17] BancoSol, the microfinance pioneer in transforming into a bank, listed itself on the Bolivian stock exchange and issued the equivalent of $3 million in bonds as long ago as 1997. In Eastern Europe, the ProCredit microfinance banks are also tapping into domestic capital markets. For instance, in June 2004, ProCredit Bank (Ukraine) issued $6.8 million in three-year bonds.[18] It is important to recognize that these investments are not purely driven by private market investments. These deals have also benefited from at least initial partial guarantees from donors and IFIs (like the International Finance Corporation and the U.S. Agency for International Development).[19]

In early 2005 an MFI called Faulu Kenya became the first African MFI to issue bonds to raise capital. Faulu issued $6.7 million worth of Kenyan five-year shilling bonds on the Nairobi Stock Exchange. Some pension funds, two microfinance wholesale institutions, and two commercial banks are the primary investors. Faulu's bond was partially guaranteed by a donor, Agence Française de Développement. The guarantee covers capital and interest of the issue for the benefit of Faulu's investors. Public scrutiny because of the bond issue over

---

[15.] Ivatury and Abrams, "The Market for Microfinance Foreign Investment: Opportunities and Challenges," 17.

[16.] Gibbons and Meehan, "Financing Microfinance for Poverty Reduction," 12.

[17.] Marulanda and Otero, *The Profile of Microfinance in Latin America in 10 Years: Vision and Characteristics*, 40; and Conger, "To Market, To Market," 22.

[18.] Ivatury and Abrams, "The Market for Microfinance Foreign Investment: Opportunities and Challenges," 13.

[19.] Jaquand, "Finding a Role for Public Donors in the Privatized World of Microfinance."

BOX 6.5 Can guarantees link MFIs to domestic funding markets?

Since the 1980s, international donors and/or governments have guaranteed loans from commercial banks to specialized MFIs, with mixed results. The purpose of these guarantees is twofold: (1) to help MFIs gain access to commercial funding from banks that would not otherwise be forthcoming; and perhaps more important (2) to forge long-term relationships among different players in the financial system that last beyond the life of a given guarantee. In theory, these instruments could serve as a catalyst to develop domestic funding markets. In practice, a few have worked, others have not, and yet others have not been picked up by MFIs and commercial banks they aim to help.

There is an estimated $300 million to $500 million in loan guarantees for microfinance. The most successful microfinance guarantee program is ACCION's Latin America Bridge Fund, which has more than $6 million in guarantees. USAID's Development Credit Authority has succeeded in creating initial links between strong MFIs and banks in Morocco, Colombia,

Uganda, and South Africa. Other guarantee funds are run by the international network Foundation for International Community Assistance (FINCA), the Latin American Challenge Investment Fund (LACIF), and Deutche Bank. A few MFIs have also used guarantees to float bonds on their domestic capital markets (for example, Compartamos in Mexico, MiBanco in Peru, and Faulu in Kenya).

The key to success of these programs appears to be the existence of banks truly willing to enter into new markets and the design of the guarantee itself. If too much of the loan between a bank and MFI is guaranteed, then the bank might not take the loan seriously, treat it more recklessly, and discontinue the relationship in the absence of the guarantee. Banks need to take on some part of the risk. At the same time, guarantees can be cumbersome and costly to set up. The ultimate impact of these guarantees in terms of forging permanent commercial links to domestic funding and capital markets has yet to be determined.

Sources: Freedman, "Designing Loan Guarantees to Spur Growth in Developing Countries," 18; Norell, Emory-Smith, and Bruett, "How Do International Networks Manage Grants, Investments, and Loans to Their Partners and Affiliates?" 3; and de Sousa-Shields and Frankiewicz, "Financing Microfinance Institutions: The Context for Transitions to Private Capital," 6.

the next five years will undoubtedly improve Faulu Kenya's performance as it commits to meeting interest and capital commitments. Spillover effects could benefit microfinance in Kenya and other countries, as markets take note of this emerging investment opportunity.[20]

On the equity side, few MFIs are listed on their local stock markets. And the results have been mixed. Some evidence from BancoSol in Bolivia indicates that these shares might sell at a discount compared with those of mainstream Bolivian banks, meaning that the domestic market might not value microfinance as seriously. At the same time, many of the original microfinance investors express concerns about the possible dilution of the social mission should broader (and more commercial) ownership be allowed.[21]

[20.] Xinhua News Agency, "France guarantees first microfinance bond issue in Africa"; and Macharia, "Faulu Kenya Issues KES 500 Million (US$7 Million) Bond to Assist Poor People: A Journey to the Capital Markets."
[21.] de Sousa-Shields and Frankiewicz, *Financing Microfinance Institutions: The Context for Transitions to Private Capital*, 48, 50.

Why have so few specialized MFIs issued bonds and raised equity on their domestic stock markets to date? And why have even fewer done it on a purely commercial basis, without the benefit of a guarantee from an IFI? Will many more follow suit and tap this potential source of funding? Some constraints remain, even in Latin America, one of the more advanced regions in terms of microfinance bond issues. First, regulatory obstacles in some countries, such as Peru, impede access by some types of financial institutions. Second, capital markets are not always familiar with microfinance, and investors may perceive it to be too risky. Third, the costs of issuing a bond are relatively high, and the small financing requirements of many specialized microfinance entities may not justify these costs.[22]

In most developing countries, capital markets are simply too underdeveloped to support large financing beyond deposit mobilization. Lack of competition and inefficiency in the banking sector mean that funds are expensive when they are available. Most of this funding is short term, and few markets can issue such longer-term financing. A lot of work remains to be done to build and fully tap into domestic funding markets and create truly inclusive financial systems.

Conclusion

An increasingly complex maze of international and domestic funders offers a range of financial instruments that could be used to build more inclusive financial systems. As shown in table 6.3, each of these instruments presents opportunities and limitations. At the same time, different funders have different strengths and should focus on those market segments that make the most sense, whether they are small, unregulated MFIs or large, high-potential regulated financial institutions. Other funders might be better adapted to helping build the financial infrastructure or to beefing up the government's ability to make good policy decisions. As the number of commercial funders grows, they bring welcome competition to what was once the sole domain of the donors. The key to being more effective as a group of funders is to identify and act on their relative strengths—as opposed to undermining one another and getting in each other's way.

Donor subsidies should stimulate or complement private capital, not compete with it. Furthermore, where possible, subsidies should be temporary, setting the stage for the private sector to take over. Donors can support more risk, have close relationships with governments, and fund initiatives with minimal private returns but large social benefits or public goods. Therefore, donors should focus on those activities that the private sector would not touch. Examples of appropriate donor activities include the long, difficult process of building up human capacity and skills; developing financial infrastructure components like rating agencies, credit bureaus, and auditors; working with governments to improve the legal and regulatory framework; and supporting experimentation—especially among those financial service providers that push the frontiers to reach extremely poor or remote populations.

[22.] Portocarrero Maisch and Soria, *Cómo deberían financiarse las IMF,* 54.

TABLE 6.3 Analysis of Alternative Funding Instruments

Instrument	Actor	Strengths	When/How to Use
International			
Policy Support	Donors	• helps governments make sound decisions and take a more constructive role	• needs specialized expertise by donor staff and advisors to be done properly
Technical Assistance	Donors	• builds much-needed human capacity at all levels, one of the most critical bottlenecks	• needs to be market-based and client-responsive to be effective • best for donors that can work directly with the private sector
Grants	Donors	• helps build equity that can later be leveraged on domestic and international markets	• important for supporting micro, meso, and macro level • best for start-up/young/risky financial institutions • when commercial sources not available, avoid distorting markets with money perceived as "too easy"
Loans			
Concessional	Donors	• source of cheap funds for microfinance	• avoid foreign exchange risk when in hard currency • if commercial alternatives exist, avoid distorting domestic markets and reducing incentives to mobilize deposits
Commercial	Donors, IFIs, Private Funds	• source of funds for cash-strapped financial institutions • focus on efficient microfinance operations	• for mature institutions • avoid foreign exchange risk when in hard currency • if commercial alternatives exist, avoid distorting domestic markets and reducing incentives to mobilize deposits
Quasi-equity	Donors, IFIs	• source of funds for financial institutions	• for mature institutions • same as concessional debt
Equity Investment	IFIs, Private Funds	• contributes equity that can be leveraged on domestic markets • governance role can improve overall management	• for mature, formal institutions that sell shares • avoid crowding out local investors
Guarantees	Donors, IFIs, Private Funds	• allows financial institutions to tap into domestic sources of finance	• structure guarantees such that they result in permanent relationships after the guarantee

TABLE 6.3 Analysis of Alternative Funding Instruments—*continued*

Instrument	Actor	Strengths	When/How to Use
Domestic			
Savings	Individual Savers	• independence from external funding, low cost over time	• only for regulated institutions • some institutions may need support to develop products and systems to lower costs and manage growth of deposits
Loans			
Concessional	Apexes, Government Credit Schemes	• apexes, if well-designed and administered, can help develop retail MFIs	• if commercial alternatives exist, avoid distorting domestic markets and reducing incentives to mobilize savings
Commercial	Commercial Banks	• integrates MFIs into mainstream (although it may not include longer-term financing required for some activities, for example, agriculture)	• for mature institutions • initial incentives or partnerships might be needed to jump-start funding between commercial banks and specialized MFIs
Bonds	Local Investors	• allows financial institutions to tap into domestic capital markets	• requires sufficiently developed secondary market; dependent on local shocks • may require initial incentives to get started in some markets
Equity			
Direct Investments	Local Investors	• builds an equity base that can be leveraged on domestic market • broadens governance structure	• only licensed financial institutions are eligible • avoid mission drift because of stockholder demands by balancing socially and profit-oriented owners
Stock Market	Local Investors	• allows financial institutions to tap into domestic capital markets	• only licensed financial institutions are eligible to sell shares on the market • avoid mission drift because of diluted ownership and stockholder demands

International investors may well continue to grow in importance, but the current market seems too fragmented to be sustainable. The proliferation of new funds, combined with a relatively small target market may mean some consolidation is necessary. The emergence of large numbers of private funds may be a fad or it may mean that international investors are beginning to see the value of microfinance (although balancing risk and returns is still not completely understood). Other potential problems include poorly managed foreign exchange risks for MFIs and the dampening of incentives to mobilize domestic resources because of relatively easy-to-access international funding.

At the same time, strong domestic funding markets, especially savings, are beginning to emerge in some places. Although they might not ever address the financial needs of all people in all countries, the use of domestic capital markets will hopefully accelerate as microfinance matures and financial systems become more inclusive. Regulated financial institutions are finding innovative and lower-cost ways to mobilize deposits from large numbers of poor and low-income people. Recent experiments in tapping into domestic capital markets through bond issues reinforce this tendency and promise to help financial institutions working with poor clients to strengthen their financial position. If these trends continue, the end result will be large-scale access to financial services among those currently excluded.

Finding the right mix between domestic and international sources of funding is an immediate concern for the future of microfinance. The goal is to build strong local financial intermediaries and to integrate microfinance fully into domestic financial markets in developing countries. But this goal is quite a long way from reality, especially when financial systems are weak and highly risk-averse. Donors and other international investors will likely play an important role for some time to come.

Chapter 7

Cross-Cutting Challenges

The preceding chapters offer a snapshot of today's microfinance and the challenges for building tomorrow's inclusive financial systems. They provide insight into how to push out the frontier of microfinance by addressing three core challenges: (1) scaling up quality financial services to serve large numbers of people (scale); (2) reaching increasingly poorer and more remote people (depth); and (3) lowering costs to both clients and financial service providers (cost).

Several other issues cut across the different levels of the financial system and contribute to meeting the core challenges of scale, depth, and cost. Although these cross-cutting issues are numerous, this chapter highlights five for more in-depth discussion because they pose particularly stubborn dilemmas that have proven difficult to resolve and/or they represent an enormous opportunity. The issues selected for this chapter are as follows:

- **Optimizing Technology.** Which advanced technology solutions hold the most promise for lowering costs and expanding the reach of financial services?

- **Leveraging Cross-border Remittances and Other Transfers.** How can financial service providers build on these large flows of funds to improve financial services for poor people?

- **Reaching Farmers and Other Remote Rural Clients.** How can financial service providers extend high-quality financial services on a viable basis to those currently beyond reach?

- **Measuring Social Performance.** What is the social return on offering financial services to poor and low-income people?

- **Protecting Poor Consumers.** What are the best ways to ensure poor and vulnerable consumers do not fall prey to predatory lenders and other unscrupulous practices?

Optimizing Technology to Reduce Transaction Costs (and Improve Quality)

Technology promises to reduce costs and improve transparency in delivering financial services, both of which can translate into increased access for large numbers of lower-income clients. Streamlined and automated processes allow financial institutions to extend services to harder-to-reach and more costly clientele by replacing people and branches with point-of-sale (POS) devices and the like. At the same time, reducing the "hassle factor" makes banking relationships attractive for more people. Finally, technology undergirds the information and reporting systems that are essential for efficient financial service delivery.

Despite the appeal of advanced delivery technologies, relatively few financial institutions have successfully deployed them to reach poor and low-income clients. The truth is that there is still insufficient experience to know whether they will work on a large scale. Several challenges remain, including the high cost and limited availability of existing technological solutions, consumer acceptance of technology, the lack of basic communications infrastructure in some countries, and inadequate government policies.

The range of technologies applicable to microfinance. As shown in figure 7.1, an array of technologies can be used to support financial services for poor people. These technologies range from software that supports the internal systems of financial institutions to debit or credit cards and linkages with clients' mobile phones.

FIGURE 7.1 Technology Map

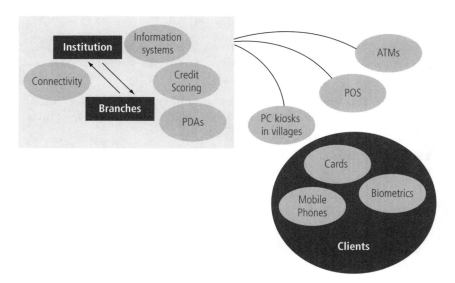

Note: ATM = automatic teller machine; PC = personal computer; PDA = personal digital assistant; POS = point of sale.

The following are brief definitions of technologies commonly used in micro-finance:[1]

- **Information Systems:** Custom-built or commercially available software that allows financial institutions to track transactions and create reliable financial reports. Getting this right is a critical building block for all other technology applications.

- **Connectivity:** Network connections (for example, dial-up, broadband, or satellite) that link staff and branches for real-time information exchange, transaction processing, and distance learning.

- **Personal Digital Assistants (PDAs):** Small handheld computers that help field staff more efficiently collect data, manage client records, and process loans.

- **Credit Scoring:** Automating or enhancing the loan approval process by computerized analysis of client characteristics and behavior to predict willingness and ability to repay.

- **Automatic Teller Machines (ATMs):** Machines that dispense cash or provide a wider range of services to cardholders. ATMs are relatively expensive to own and operate. Most require network connectivity and reliable power.

- **POS Devices:** Devices or systems, usually in retail outlets, that perform electronic transfers from one account to another, often using cards.[2]

- **Internet Banking:** The ability to conduct banking transactions from any location, such as Internet kiosks. This service is probably more relevant for higher-income clients.

- **Magstripe and Smart Cards:** Debit (or sometimes credit) cards that store customer information and account balances. These cards allow customers to access their accounts online via ATMs and POS devices. Smart cards have an embedded chip that stores complex information, allowing customers to complete transactions using remote devices that do not have an online real-time connection with the central server.

- **Biometrics:** A technology that measures an individual's unique physical characteristics, such as fingerprints, to recognize and confirm identity for security purposes.

- **Mobile Phones:** Millions of poor and low-income people have access to cell phones, and increasingly use text messaging (Philippine mobile users send 200 million text messages per day, for instance).[3] This technology offers an opportunity to operate virtual bank accounts with minimal infrastructure

---

[1] This section draws from Cracknell, *Electronic Banking for the Poor: Panacea, Potential and Pitfalls;* Ivatury, *Using Electronic Payments to Build Inclusive Financial Systems;* and the CGAP IT Innovations Series.

[2] CGAP, "Point of Sale for Microfinance: A CGAP Presentation."

[3] Miranda, "Philippines: Telecommunications and Broadcasting Market Brief."

investments. Mobile phones can also be used as a POS device by merchants, market vendors, and others.

Financial institutions can employ some combination of these technologies to reach clients directly, or in partnership with others. The large volumes of transactions required to ensure a return on technology investments (especially ATMs) drive financial institutions to leverage each other's networks. Also, by working with agents like local merchants and smaller MFIs, financial institutions can reach poorer or more remote rural clients without building expensive branch networks.

Benefits to clients and financial institutions. Technology-enabled delivery systems can benefit poor clients as long as six key criteria are met.[4] First, clients must perceive a benefit from the technology—for instance, convenience, the reduced risk of carrying cash, or the ability to transfer funds from one person to another. Second, clients must be comfortable with, and educated about, the technology. Third, user-friendliness is critical—if the technology is too difficult to understand or learn, clients will not use it. Fourth, to be successful, the technology needs to address cultural sensitivities around gender, class, and privacy. Fifth, customers must trust that the technology will not somehow "rip them off"; trust is enhanced by issuing receipts. Prodem's introduction of ATMs in Bolivia is a good example of a technology that meets these criteria (see box 7.1).

BOX 7.1 Prodem's ATMs and biometric technology respond to poor customers

In 2002, Prodem's private financial fund (FFP) in Bolivia began installing Smart Automatic Teller Machines (SATMs), which incorporate fingerprint readers to verify clients' identities rather than relying on Personal Identification Number (PIN) technology. The ATMs also use voice instructions in three languages and an easy-to-use graphic interface to allow illiterate clients to use them. The ATMs are used in conjunction with smart cards that contain the relevant client information, so transactions are immediately recorded on the card. The ATM updates data centrally only twice a day, which saves Prodem an estimated $800,000 per year in Internet charges. Today, Prodem has 52 ATMs, along with 40 POS devices at gas stations and supermarkets, where clients can use their smart cards to access funds 24 hours a day, seven days a week. Customers have found these user-friendly ATMs and POSs attractive, with nearly 50,000 smart card savings accounts by 2003 (out of a total of nearly 62,000 savers). The machines encouraged clients to save more often, whenever they have cash available, increasing deposits in regular savings accounts from $102,000 in 2000 to $19 million as of June 2005.

Sources: Whelan, "Automated Teller Machines," 2; www.prodemffp.com; www.sbef.gov.bo; Hernandez and Mugica, *What Works: Multilingual Smart ATMs for Microfinance*, 2; Miles, "Financial Intermediation and Integration of Regulated MFIs," 10; and interview with Eduardo Bazoberry, president and CEO, Prodem.

---

[4] These six criteria are outlined in Ivatury, "Harnessing Technology to Transform Financial Services for the Poor."

The sixth and final criterion is that technology solutions are physically accessible and affordable. Limited geographic distribution of transaction points reduces the value of a smart card to the customer. At the same time, extensive ATM and, to a lesser extent, POS networks can be expensive, requiring appropriate fees to recoup the investment. The right balance needs to be struck between extending a wide network of access points and controlling costs to customers (as well as costs to merchants that these customers frequent).[5]

Financial institutions accrue many potential benefits by deploying technology. Using a good information system, managers can make more informed decisions and produce reliable reports that follow recognized international and national standards. This transparency can also attract funders and provide clients with immediate information about their accounts, thus attracting more customers.

Perhaps the most important contribution of technology is lower operating costs. For instance, a recent study demonstrates that a typical ATM transaction costs nearly five times less than a teller transaction (see figure 7.2). These costs are based on data from the United States, and the actual costs would vary tremendously depending on the country context, the costs of labor relative to imported hardware and software, and other circumstances. The researchers tested the relative costs of tellers and ATMs in several emerging market countries (including Brazil, India, Kenya, Malaysia, Mexico, Nigeria, and South Africa), and with the exception of India, roughly the same relationship holds.[6] The comparison shows the potential of cost reduction through technology,

FIGURE 7.2 Illustrative Costs per Distribution Channel

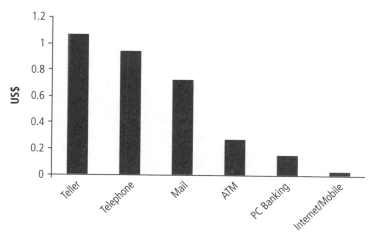

Sources: BAI.org, as quoted in Ketley, Davis, and Truen, "An Inter-country Survey of the Relative Costs of Bank Accounts: A Study for Finmark Trust," 19; and Ketley and Duminy, "Meeting the Challenge—The Impact of Changing Technology on MicroFinance Institutions."

[5.] Cracknell, *Electronic Banking for the Poor: Panacea, Potential and Pitfalls*, 3.
[6.] Ketley, Davis, and Truen, "An Inter-country Survey of the Relative Costs of Bank Accounts: A Study for Finmark Trust," 19–21; and interview with Richard Ketley, director, Genesis Analytics.

which is particularly important today as financial institutions face increasingly competitive markets.

Challenges. Despite the fact that the costs of technology are plummeting, and that financial institutions from Bolivia to India are using it, successful use of technology in microfinance is still the exception rather than the rule. Several challenges remain that inhibit the widespread adoption of technology to extend financial service delivery across vast distances and to millions of people quickly:

- **Consumer and staff literacy.** Illiterate and uneducated clients do not always trust technology. Staff members may also be reluctant or ill equipped to adopt new technologies. Efforts to educate them may be necessary.

- **Infrastructure.** Financial institutions in countries that lack strong communications and electric infrastructure may have a hard time implementing technology solutions that rely on Internet connectivity—or even electricity.

- **Policy environment.** As electronic banking expands, governments and regulators struggle to sort out the implications, for instance, of neighborhood shops taking deposits from the public without a formal license to do so. Conversely, governments can help expand access by issuing national identification systems (numerical- or biometric-based) or by distributing welfare payments, pensions, and salaries through electronic networks.

- **Capacity of financial service providers.** Financial institutions, especially MFIs, have limited capacity to absorb technology. Furthermore, financial service providers of all types tend to focus on their own needs, rather than developing a solution that really works for their clients.

- **Availability of suitable information systems.** Institutions should invest in advanced delivery technologies only if their baseline information systems are already sound. Yet, in many markets, these systems are not available or they are costly to develop.

When these challenges are overcome, the results can be explosive. Perhaps the case of Brazil is the most promising when it comes to using technology to "leapfrog" into more inclusive financial systems. Within the past few years, four banks have opened up 8 million new accounts by installing POS technology in around 27,000 banking correspondents—supermarkets, retailers, postal, and lottery outlets—with technology to deliver financial services.[7] Although it is not clear how poor these clients are, the banks involved have certainly brought new banking customers into the system. Also, some recent research indicates that nearly half of one bank's banking correspondents' clients earn less than $80 per month, even though they are not necessarily targeting poorer client groups. Over time, as Brazil's banks learn more about the financial service needs of poorer clients, they may begin to introduce more tailored, specialized microfinance products.[8]

[7.] Ivatury, Using Electronic Payments to Build Inclusive Financial Systems.
[8.] Interview with Gautam Ivatury, microfinance specialist, CGAP.

Leveraging Money Transfers

An estimated $126 billion or more is sent home per year by developing country immigrants working outside their country of origin.[9] More important for building inclusive financial systems, domestic transfers in many countries are likely to be even larger. The staggering growth of money transfers and the sheer amounts involved (larger than capital market flows and official development assistance for many countries) have attracted the attention of policymakers, including the G8, researchers, development agencies, and financial institutions. Poor and remote rural inhabitants are often the recipients of the funds—although other segments of society also receive them. Unfortunately, a relatively small proportion of these funds remain in the financial system, because many recipients pocket their money immediately and spend it. The challenge is to attract transfer recipients as banking clients. This would help poor recipients improve their money management and build their assets, as well as serve as a reliable source of funds and revenue for financial service providers.

The flow of money transfers today.[10] In terms of cross-border remittances, it is estimated that Latin America and the Caribbean receive more transfers than any other region, followed by South Asia and the Middle East and North Africa (see figure 7.3).[11] The top recipient countries include Mexico and India, and the top sending countries are the United States and Saudi Arabia.

Although most existing research focuses on transfers from developed to developing countries, migrants also transfer an enormous amount of money between and within developing countries. For instance, Chinese domestic migrants sent $45 billion in transfers in 2003. Domestic and regional transfers tend to be smaller and more numerous than north–south transfers, because domestic and regional migrants from developing countries appear to be poor-

FIGURE 7.3 Worldwide Flows of Worker Remittances by Region, 2002

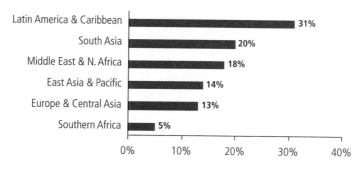

Source: Orozco, "Worker Remittances: An International Comparison," 3.

[9.] Ratha and Maimbo, "Remittances: An Economic Force in Many Countries."
[10.] This section draws on Isern and Deshpande, "Crafting a Money Transfers Strategy: Guidance for Pro-poor Financial Service Providers."
[11.] Orozco, "Worker Remittances: An International Comparison," 3.

er than immigrants to industrial countries. In this sense, harnessing domestic and regional money transfers will likely be even more important than cross-border remittances from an access perspective. Better solutions for regional and national money transfers need to be found. Even in the case of foreign transfers, the domestic transfer system is the "last mile" link connecting recipients who live in rural areas, for example, to the funds that arrive in the capital city.

Both formal and informal systems exist to transfer money (both internationally and within countries). Not surprisingly, most available information is about the formal methods. The market for person-to-person transfers is dominated by specialized money transfer companies like Western Union, MoneyGram, and Vigo Remittance Corporation. Other formal providers include commercial banks, post offices, foreign exchange bureaus, and credit unions. Different players dominate in different markets. For instance, 70 percent of remittances from the United States to Latin America go through money transfer companies, while banks play a more important role in transfers to countries like Turkey, India, and the Philippines. In China, the post office moves large amounts of money around the country.

Informal systems include all those cross-border and domestic transfers that do not involve legally registered or regulated entities. Estimates of funds channeled through friends, family, or other undocumented channels range from 40 to 100 percent of the amounts sent through formal mechanisms. The most common informal transfer system involves hand-carried cash. Some sophisticated systems have been developed in many countries that move large amounts of money informally. For example, informal channels are particularly active in Asia (especially India and China), the Middle East, and some African countries like Mali, Senegal, and the Sudan. Examples include *hundi* (South Asia), *fei-chen* (China), *padala* (Philippines), and *hawala* (Middle East). Many senders and receivers prefer informal mechanisms because they are fast, discreet, and involve little to no paperwork. They also are more accessible, especially for those without documentation in the sending country, and may seem more trustworthy because they are underpinned by personal relationships.

Challenges and opportunities. With so much money coursing through international and domestic money transfer systems, what is the problem? There are essentially three problems: costs, safety, and the lack of appropriate complementary savings products among financial service providers. These challenges relate to the larger problem of how to better incorporate these cash flows, and the poor and low-income people who receive them, into the financial system.

The costs of formal remittances and transfers have declined in recent years but remain high in many cases. For example, in 2002, the total costs of transferring $200 to Egypt or India through a money transfer company averaged nearly 14 percent. Interestingly, as shown in table 7.1, using banks to transfer funds tends to be cheaper than using money transfer companies—sometimes a great deal cheaper. This price tag differential helps explain why transfers to Latin America are so much more expensive than those to other countries in the

TABLE 7.1 Cost of Sending $200 to Selected Countries from Banks and Money Transfer Companies (MTCs)

Country	Bank	MTC
Philippines	8.0%	10.3%
India	6.0%	13.8%
Greece	6.8%	9.5%
Portugal	3.4%	12.3%
Turkey	3.1%	9.5%
Mean[a]	7.0%	12.0%

Source: Orozco, "Worker Remittances: An International Comparison," 10.
[a] Mean of total sample, including countries not shown in this table.

world, despite higher volumes. Most transfers in Latin America and the Caribbean still go through money transfer companies, although banks are starting to get more involved.[12] More competition in the remittance market, more effective payments systems that allow funds to flow more freely, and better consumer information about available options could help lower costs.[13]

Informal remittance and transfer systems might be cheaper still but pose risks of loss, delays, money laundering, financing of terrorism, and other dangers.[14] Many people have experienced loss because of theft or delays in transferring funds. Carrying money is risky in many countries. Agents can be unreliable, as when informal carriers dip into the remittance for car repairs or other expenses. Trust in informal arrangements seems to be declining in recent years.

Transitioning from informal mechanisms to working through financial service providers can reduce costs and improve security. But to successfully incorporate poor and low-income people into the financial system via transfers, an understanding of how recipients use these funds is required. A number of studies reveal that the majority of cross-border remittances are used for basic household consumption (around 80 percent). Investments in education, health, and better nutrition absorb another 5 to 10 percent. Other priorities include investments in land, housing, and livestock for an eventual return to the home country; social events; loan repayments; and savings. The link to savings is particularly relevant for building inclusive financial systems. Between 6 and 10 percent of cross-border remittances to Latin America are saved in banks or credit unions.[15]

Many financial service providers that already serve poor and low-income people have begun to see and seize the potential of international, regional, and domestic transfers as a way of attracting new clients. These institutions can

---

[12.] Orozco, "Workers Remittances: An International Comparison," 15, 16.
[13.] World Economic Outlook, "Globalization and External Imbalances."
[14.] See chapter 5 for a discussion of the impact of anti–money laundering measures on poor people's finance.
[15.] Intercooperation, "Remittances, the Money of the Migrants," 2.

often reach out more broadly to the community; offer lower-cost, secure services; and bundle remittance and transfer payments with other financial services valued by their customers.

One option for financial service providers of all types is to forge alliances with money transfer companies. Money transfer companies possess the know-how and systems to move money internationally and domestically, together with dense networks of service points in the originating countries. Financial institutions—especially those that cater to the poor—bring to the table their proximity to a large number of money transfer recipients. For example, the Kenya Post Office Savings Bank (KPOSB) has partnered with Western Union for 10 years. The system covers international and domestic transfers, linking more than 160,000 agent locations in more than 190 countries. KPOSB organizes regular marketing events with Kenyans living abroad in the United States.[16]

Banks can set up correspondent relationships with international banks in other countries or regions. To lower the end customer's cost on such bank-to-bank transfers, some financial institutions have taken to sending one or several days' transfers in a single bundle. Examples include FONKOZE in Haiti, City National Bank of New Jersey in the United States, Banco Solidario in Ecuador, and Spanish savings banks.[17]

Another mechanism is the global initiative that joins the World Council of Credit Unions (WOCCU) with MoneyGram, Travelex, and Vigo Remittance Corporation. WOCCU's International Remittance Network (IR*net*) allows savings and credit cooperative networks to distribute remittances among relatively poor and remote clients in developing countries. People can use IR*net* to send money from a credit union in the United States to credit unions and other partners throughout the western hemisphere, Australia, and some countries in Asia, Africa, and Europe. Participating credit unions can market other services to remittance customers.[18]

Technology offers another option for decreasing the costs of remittances and transfers, as well as linking these flows to other financial services for poor clients (see the earlier section "Optimizing Technology to Reduce Transaction Costs" for more on applications of advanced technology). Mobile phones are already being used for this purpose in countries like the Philippines, the United Arab Emirates, Mozambique, and South Africa. Also, card-based remittance services are gaining popularity, especially in Latin America, a region where plastic is widely used. For instance, Visa works with partner banks in Colombia, the Dominican Republic, Ecuador, El Salvador, Mexico, and Peru. Another example is a partnership between the microfinance network Opportunity International and MasterCard to develop a cobranded card called the Opportunity Card.[19]

[16.] www.postbank.co.ke; Kabbucho, Sander, and Mukwana, *Passing the Buck, Money Transfer Systems The Practice and Potential for Products in Kenya,* 12; and Sander, "Capturing a Market Share, Migrant Remittance Transfers and Commercialisation of Microfinance in Africa," 8.

[17.] Isern and Deshpande, "Crafting a Money Transfers Strategy: Guidance for Pro-Poor Financial Service Providers," 11.

[18.] Intercooperation, "Remittances, the Money of the Migrants," 2; www.woccu.org.

[19.] USAID/AMAP and DFID "Card-Based Remittance Services," 5.

The entry of new competitors in cross-border remittance and domestic transfers market, along with partnerships among different entities and the application of technology, could expand access to financial services among the unbanked. The impact of this trend on the lives of the poor depends on the ability of service providers to offer lower-cost, high-quality remittance and transfer services, along with other financial services demanded by poor and low-income people.

Reaching Farmers and Remote Rural Clients

Agricultural finance has a long history in developing countries. Unfortunately, earlier models of agricultural credit largely failed to offer permanent access to financial services.[20] And outside of densely populated areas in Asia, traditional microcredit has struggled to reach into rural areas. In most developing countries, policymakers recognize a large gap in the supply of financial services in rural areas. Additionally, three-quarters of the world's population living on less than $1 a day live in the countryside, a fact that fuels the urgency to find a solution to the conundrum of reaching remote rural areas with high-quality, sustainable financial services.

Financial services in rural areas—the terminology. There is a fair amount of confusion about the definitions of rural and agricultural finance, especially as they relate to poor people.[21] Rural finance refers to financial services offered and used in rural areas by people of all income levels. Agricultural finance is a subset of rural finance dedicated to financing agricultural activities, such as loans to buy fertilizer or for marketing crops, or insurance products designed to meet the specific needs of farmers and agricultural workers. Microfinance means financial services for poor and low-income people, and it encompasses the lower end of both rural and agricultural finance (see figure 7.4).

Three types of providers commonly serve rural and agriculturally based households with financial services. First, traditional agricultural lenders (often state-run agricultural or development banks, and sometimes financial cooperatives) offer loans that reflect the irregular cash-flow cycles and marketing relationships among farmers, but they often fall short in financial management and repayment performance. Second, MFIs, for their part, have made some inroads with their standard loan products, often reporting better repayment rates. But their tiny loans, with regular and frequent repayments, do not match the cash-flow patterns of most farm families (unless they have a diversified mix of income sources, for example, as seen in Bangladesh).

Third, the main source of finance for farming in most places is not a bank or a cooperative or an MFI. Rather, farmers rely on their own or families' resources, as well as on those with whom they have existing business relationships. These providers include input suppliers (for example, fertilizer ven-

---

[20] See chapter 5 for more on this.

[21] These definitions come from Pearce, "Financial Services for the Rural Poor."

FIGURE 7.4 Rural Microfinance Terminology

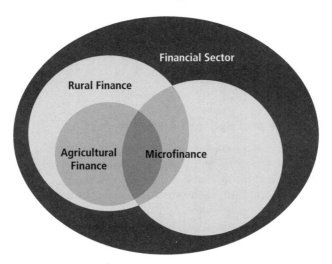

Source: Pearce, "Financial Services for the Rural Poor."

dors), traders, and processing companies. These more informal providers un-derstand farmers' financial needs and can offer funding appropriate to their cash-flow patterns. However, the true cost of this credit is not always transpar-ent—what is the "interest rate" on an exchange of fertilizer today for some pro-portion of the farmer's crop next harvest season?[22]

It is important to note that most farm families do not depend solely on agri-cultural income. Poor rural households tend to diversify their sources of in-come to survive. This means that agricultural credit may or may not be the main financial service that these households require. A safe place to store cash (for instance, after the harvest time), reliable transfer services to receive remit-tances from family members in the capital city or abroad; and different types of insurance may be just as critical to support the diverse strategies these house-holds employ to accumulate assets and minimize vulnerability.[23]

Challenges. Why is it so hard to serve rural areas sustainably? Rural areas present a number of specific challenges to financial service providers.[24]

- **Dispersed demand.** Low population density in many countries means that financial services are spread across long distances. This makes it harder for financial service providers to reach people cost effectively.

- **High information and transaction costs.** Poor infrastructure (roads, telecom-munications) and lack of client information (no personal identification or credit information) cause transactions costs to go up.

---

[22] Christen and Pearce, *Managing Risks and Designing Products for Agricultural Microfinance: Features of an Emerging Model,* 50.
[23] Evans and Ford, *A Technical Guide to Rural Finance,* 2.
[24] Pearce, "Financial Services for the Rural Poor."

- **Weak institutional capacity of rural finance providers.** The limited availability of educated and well-trained people in smaller rural communities makes staffing difficult and increases costs.

- **Seasonality** of many agricultural activities and long maturation periods for others. Because of the unevenness of farming income, demand for loans and credit varies across seasons and makes for a highly erratic and unpredictable business.

- **Risks linked specifically to farming.** Variable rainfall, pests and diseases, price fluctuations, and limited access to suppliers and markets are all risks in the business of farming. These risks can also hit many poor households at the same time, with a potentially devastating impact on the financial service provider. In low-income areas, these risks are increased.

- **Lack of usable collateral.** Ill-defined property and land-use rights, costly or lengthy registration procedures, and poorly functioning judicial systems in poor rural areas mean that reliable collateral is rarely available.

These challenges add up to a risky and high-cost operating environment for financial service providers. They are compounded by the fact that many households in a given area are affected by negative shocks at the same time. For example, bad weather will affect all farmers in an area, along with those who run nonfarm businesses but count on farmers as their main customers. At the same time, higher poverty levels in rural areas and the lack of assets as a cushion against shocks make rural dwellers even more vulnerable to what might seem like manageable crises for their urban counterparts.[25]

Overcoming constraints. A number of financial service providers have found innovative ways to address the many challenges, risks, and costs of offering permanent financial services to poor rural households, especially farm families. A recent review of 30 particularly promising approaches yielded the following 10 tips for successful lending to farming households.[26]

- **De-linking repayments from loan use.** Providers have dramatically increased repayment rates by taking the entire household into account, with a number of income-generating activities and financial strategies for coping with numerous obligations, when assessing capacity to repay. For example, Caja los Andes and Fondo Financiero Privado PRODEM of Bolivia and Financiera Calpiá of El Salvador exclude households that rely on one or two crops and who do not have any off-farm income.

- **Including character-based lending techniques** (such as group guarantees or non-traditional collateral) when selecting borrowers, setting loan terms, and enforcing repayment. Technical assessment of crop production and markets is not enough. Uganda's Centenary Rural Development Bank, for example,

---

[25.] Miller, *Twelve Key Challenges in Rural Finance,* 1, 2.
[26.] These features (and this subsection) come from Christen and Pearce, *Managing Risks and Designing Products for Agricultural Microfinance: Features of an Emerging Model.*

accepts nonagricultural guarantees, such as personal guarantors, land without titles, household items, and business equipment as loan collateral.

- **Providing savings mechanisms.** Many more farming households will save than will borrow if they are offered appropriate deposit accounts that help them save for lean times before harvests. Thailand's Bank for Agriculture and Agricultural Cooperatives (BAAC), for example, has evolved from an agricultural lending bank to a more diversified, self-reliant bank offering a range of deposit products. By 2003, BAAC had 5 million savings clients, among which 2.7 million had loans.[27]

- **Diversifying portfolio risk.** Successful institutions often lend to a variety of farming households, including clients engaged in more than one agricultural or non-agricultural activity, or those living in different geographic areas, thus protecting their loan portfolios against agricultural and natural risks. For instance, in the wake of *El Niño* and a plague in the late 1990s and early 2000s, Caja Rural San Martín, in Peru, improved its portfolio quality by diversifying its loans from mainly rice farmers to include a mix of client types, offering microenterprise, housing, and consumer loans in addition to agriculture loans.

- **Adjusting loan terms and conditions** to accommodate cyclical cash flows and bulky investments common in farming communities, while continuing to expect repayment, regardless of the success or failure of any individual productive activity. For example, the Small Farmer Cooperative Prithvinagar in Nepal lengthened the term of its agricultural loan and introduced a grace period and repayment terms to match expected cash flows from tea farming.

- **Including contractual arrangements** that combine technical support with the use of specific inputs to reduce price risk, enhance production quality, and help guarantee repayment, especially when the final quality or quantity of a particular crop is a core concern—for example, for agricultural traders and processors. An affiliate of the world's third-largest tractor maker— Mahindra Shubhlabh (MSSL)—in India helps farmers to access credit by acting as an agent for banks, recommending that the banks provide loans to farmers, and working with agribusiness buyers in a three-way arrangement with the bank, the buyer, and MSSL as the supplier of agricultural inputs.

- **Piggybacking financial service delivery on existing institutional infrastructure** or technology, such as ATMs, to reduce transaction costs for financial service providers and clients in remote communities. For example, the Georgian MFI Constanta works in temporary service centers, such as rented rooms in branches of local banks, to lower the costs of expanding into rural areas.

- **Lending to membership-based organizations** like farmers' associations to lower transaction costs (if the association can administer loans effectively).

[27.] Haberberger, "Creating an Enabling Environment for Microfinance—the Role of Governments: Experiences from Thailand."

Some of these organizations (for example, credit unions) can also be viable financial service providers themselves. The Union des Banques Populaires du Rwanda (UBPR), for example, finances coffee producer cooperatives by incorporating farmers into local *banques populaires*.[28]

- **Employing area-based index insurance,** which provides payouts linked to regional levels of rainfall, commodity prices, and the like, to protect against the risks of agricultural lending. Although successful examples are rare, the initial experience of the Tanzanian coffee cooperative (Kilimanjaro Native Cooperative Union or KNCU) is promising because it has successfully protected itself from price fluctuations, using financial instruments to guarantee a minimum coffee price for farmers.

- **Insulating credit decisions from political interference.** Even the best-designed and executed programs wither in the face of government moratoriums on loan repayment or other meddling. For example, the government debt pardon in Costa Rica in 1999 significantly lowered repayment rates for Financiera Trisan's credit card, which was issued to farmers to buy agrochemicals.

Box 7.2 illustrates a case of an institution in Madagascar that employed several of these successful features at the same time. Although numerous financial service providers have employed some combination of these features, it is not easily done. The multiple constraints are still so strong that the majority of people in rural areas remain excluded from formal financial services. As the three types of providers (traditional agricultural lenders, MFIs, and agribusiness partners) continue to learn from each other, new techniques will be found to incorporate ever larger numbers of the rural poor into the financial system.

BOX 7.2 CECAM in Madagascar offers a range of loans to farm families

In 1993, farmers from the Central Highlands of Madagascar created the Caisses d'Epargne et de Crédit Agricole Mutuels (CECAM), or Savings and Agricultural Credit Cooperative Societies. As of May 2003, the network had approximately 52,000 members. CECAM's five credit products are designed to recognize the diverse needs for financing among farm households. Farm loans finance cropping or breeding and the term structure appropriately matches the cash-flow cycle of agricultural households. The hire-purchase system helps small producers, artisans, or traders acquire farm implements, equipment, or other capital goods. Village community granary loans help farmers store produce in a communal warehouse after harvest time to wait for better prices. An emergency loan offers a good alternative to moneylenders in case of a problem. Trade loans to agricultural cooperatives help finance input supply as well as collection, storage, and joint marketing of members' products.

Source: Fraslin, *CECAM: A Cooperative Agricultural Financial Institution Providing Credit Adapted to Farmers' Demand in Madagascar,* 3, 4.

---

[28] Evans and Ford, *A Technical Guide to Rural Finance,* 9.

Measuring Social Performance

Today, many people think that social performance in microfinance should be measured. Following the logic that whatever is measured gets done, proponents of social performance measurement seek to balance the transparency of financial performance with the transparency of the "other bottom line" relevant for microfinance: meeting social goals.[29]

Governments and public-sector donors want to prove that taxpayer money spent on microfinance makes a difference in the lives of poor people. Assessing the social benefits of different kinds of development programs also helps decide how to best allocate public money. A growing group of private, socially responsible investors seeks a "double bottom line" in their investments—they are willing to forgo some financial return as long as the social return compensates for lower profits. Although this trade-off is far less acute than previously thought, better information on the social side of the equation gives these investors a higher level of comfort in making their investment decisions. Financial institutions themselves often see social performance as a critical element of their mission, and better management information on this dimension should help them better serve their clients. In 2005, a group of 30 leading microfinance networks, financial service providers, donors, and others made a formal commitment to assessing, reporting on, and improving management of their social performance and the organizations they support.[30]

At the same time, it should be recognized that much of the push for social performance standards comes from international public donors, social investors, and those who receive funding from them. As microfinance becomes increasingly integrated into the larger financial system and as private money gains influence, it remains to be seen whether monitoring social impact will continue to be a critical concern. In many contexts, financial institutions are discovering that very poor clients represent a good business opportunity—rather than approaching the market from a social perspective. What this means is that not all institutions need to measure social performance along the lines outlined in this section. It should be stressed that there is no one-size-fits-all solution when it comes to social performance.

Defining social performance. Leaders in the microfinance field have defined social performance as "the effective translation of an institution's social goals into practice (actions, corrective measures, outcome)."[31] There are currently no global standards or frameworks for social performance reporting in microfinance. In fact, academics, experts, investors, and financial institutions inter-

---

[29.] Social Performance Task Force in Microfinance, "What Is Social Performance?" www.microfinancegateway.org/resource_centers/socialperformance.

[30.] CGAP, "More than 30 Organizations Sign 'Social Performance' Pledge," 3.

[31.] Social Performance Task Force in Microfinance, "Promoting Social Performance in Microfinance: Toward a 'Double Bottom Line'." www.microfinancegateway.org/resource_centers/socialperformance.

ested in the issue are in the process of agreeing on methods for how to measure social performance. At least three performance levels are relevant:[32]

Aligning operations with mission. At the design level, the question is whether the financial institution has clearly defined its social mission, and whether its services and work methods are consistent with that social mission. For instance, if a financial institution's stated objective is to serve landless rural farm workers, then savings products should be easily accessible to their place of work when payday comes along. Another issue at this level is whether financial institutions use some sort of targeting mechanism to identify poor households. For instance, an institution might target those with thatched roofs (as opposed to tiled ones) in a particular region to ensure that they reach poor clients. The flip side of this question is whether there are mechanisms in place that effectively screen out the poor or those the financial service provider intends to reach (for example, insistence on collateral).[33]

A few international projects are currently under way to define and test indicators at this level, including the Social Performance Indicators Initiative, implemented by members of the Comité d'Echange, de Réflexion et d'Information sur les Systèmes d'Epargne-Crédit (CERISE) network in France.[34] The CGAP Poverty Audit Toolkit is another tool that can be used both by external parties such as funders and internally by management.[35]

Reaching the intended clients. At the next level, the big issue is whether a financial institution actually reaches those groups it intends to reach. It can be very difficult and costly to obtain reliable measurements on just how poor a person really is. People of all economic levels do not generally like to divulge information about their income, so asking direct questions is not likely to yield good results. To cope with this problem, some researchers have turned their inquiry to consumption levels as a proxy for income. Others have looked at other proxy indicators that cover a range of socioeconomic dimensions of poverty (for example, ownership of certain assets such as a television or housing conditions).

Given the complexity in measuring the poverty level of clients, many financial institutions report transaction sizes. The poorer the client, the smaller the loan or deposit account, it is argued. When expressed as a proportion of gross national income (GNI) per capita, a comparable, yet imperfect indicator is born. The *MicroBanking Bulletin,* a publication put out by the Microfinance In-

---

[32] See chapter 2 for more discussion of two of these levels' outputs (who is being reached?) and impact (how does access to financial services improve the lives of poor people?).

[33] The pros and cons of targeting are discussed in chapter 2.

[34] See, for instance, Zeller, Lapenu, and Greeley, "Social Performance Indicators Initiative"; and www.cerise-microfinance.org. The CERISE Network includes four French microfinance support organizations that work throughout the developing world: IRAM (Institut de Recherches et d'Applications des Méthodes de Développement, Paris), CIDR (Centre International de Développement et de Recherche, Autrêches), GRET (Groupe de Recherche et d'Echanges Technologiques, Paris), and CIRAD (Centre de Coopération Internationale en Recherche Agronomique pour le Développement, Montpellier).

[35] www.microfinancegateway.org/content/article/detail/14196.

formation eXchange (MIX), classifies those institutions whose average outstanding loan balance per borrower is less than 20 percent of per capita GNI as "low end"; because their loans are relatively small, they are assumed to be reaching poorer people.[36] Many experts question whether loan size really reflects the poverty level of clients—the size of the loan may be more a question of an MFI's policy or characteristics of clients (besides poverty) that make them demand smaller loans.

Beyond transaction size, there are two approaches to measuring the poverty level of clients—relative and absolute. Relative poverty measures compare a financial institution's clients with some other group with similar characteristics. For instance, the CGAP Poverty Assessment Tool (PAT) uses income proxy indicators (like footwear and clothing expenditure, frequency of meals, consumption of luxury foods, access to electricity, drinking water and sanitation, ownership of land, and other assets) to look at the poverty level of microfinance clients relative to those who live in the same villages or neighborhoods.[37] Absolute poverty measures compare clients with national or international poverty standards, like the national poverty line or consumption levels at less than $1–$2 a day. The U.S. Agency for International Development has a project to develop poverty measurement tools of this kind.[38]

Increasingly, financial institutions and networks are instituting social performance scorecards to track relative and absolute poverty levels of their clients. Recent research indicates that scoring models based on easily observable and obtainable client information is relatively reliable and may be cheaper than other methods of measuring client poverty.[39] The leading microfinance network, ACCIÓN International, measures the characteristics of clients that are selected for loans by their affiliate MFIs.[40] Box 7.3 profiles the experience of Prizma, a Bosnian MFI that uses a Poverty and Impact Scorecard.

Achieving impact. The third level of social performance is the most difficult to measure, yet it is the one that best reflects the idea of social returns: impact. Impact is about concrete improvements in the lives of poor clients as a result of their access to financial services.[41] A longstanding debate about the purpose of impact assessments and measurements revolves around "proving" impact versus "improving" the quality of financial services available to poor people. Typically, donors and other external funders want to prove the social and economic impact of microfinance. But rigorous studies that can truly isolate the impact of microfinance relative to many other variables are expensive and take years to complete.

In contrast, many MFIs and networks advocate user-friendly, simple methods that practitioners can employ to understand the impact of their services on clients. Many MFIs want to use these methods to help them understand and

---

[36] MicroBanking Bulletin, "Introduction to Peer Groups and Tables," 31, 32.
[37] CGAP, "Assessing the Relative Poverty of Microfinance Clients: A CGAP Operational Tool," 2.
[38] See chapter 2 for more discussion of this initiative.
[39] Schreiner, "Poverty Scorecard for Philippines," 1.
[40] Rhyne, "Maintaining the Bottom Line in Investor-Owned Microfinance Organizations," 15.
[41] See chapter 2 for a discussion of the impact of financial services on the lives of poor clients.

BOX 7.3 Prizma measures social performance

Prizma, an MFI in Bosnia, has developed a Poverty and Impact Scorecard to keep track of clients' household poverty levels based on a number of nonincome indicators. Prizma can compare its clients with national standards because four of the indicators it tracks (car ownership, female education, household size, and stereo CD ownership) are also collected in national household surveys. Furthermore, these indicators accurately reflect cultural values. For instance, music is extremely important to Bosnians, and they would go to great lengths to own a stereo—not having one is a good poverty indicator in that context.

The scorecard enables Prizma to understand different types of clients: new clients, long-term clients, and former clients. The scorecard helps Prizma measure changes in clients' well-being over time. Prizma includes selected indicators into its application paperwork to assess each client's poverty status at entry and every time they apply for a new loan. This information forms part of the regular reporting framework and helps management segment the market and think about their strategic positioning, as well as monitor impact and risks of certain types of clients. The scorecard is further used to calculate financial incentives for teams and individuals within the organization.

Sources: Schreiner, Matul, Pawlak, and Kline, "The Power of Prizma's Poverty Scorecard: Lessons for Microfinance"; Pawlak and Matul, "A Promising Approach to Social Performance Management"; and interview with Katarzyna Pawlak, deputy director and research manager, Microfinance Centre for CEE and the NIS.

manage their social performance. These methods may be less rigorous than the larger studies, but they offer valuable information on clients, allowing financial institutions to improve the design of their products.

In the end, the debate between proving and improving is likely to be resolved by recognizing the importance of larger, more rigorous impact studies (probably funded by donors) conducted on a periodic basis, as well as "lighter" versions that can be integrated into financial institutions' operations. Box 7.4 profiles initiatives that address the less rigorous yet more practical ways to measure impact.

The challenge of standardization. Coming up with standard ways to report financial performance has been relatively easy for the microfinance community. As outlined in chapter 4, these financial standards increasingly conform to accepted national and international accounting norms. It is less clear whether the same level of standardization can be expected for social performance because of the difficulty in finding relevant, reliable, and comparable measurements across countries. Each country's context is different. For instance, the kind of roofing materials used on a house might be a great proxy indicator of poverty in South Asia, but it could be totally irrelevant in South Africa. At the same time, forcing financial institutions to report on the same variables could actually distract them from their core business.[42] Many of the initiatives mentioned in

---

[42] Simanowitz, "Social Performance, Poverty and Organizational Learning: Institutionalizing Impact in Microfinance," 12.

BOX 7.4 Impact assessment initiatives

Several initiatives have focused on developing methodologies for user-friendly impact assessments that can be used by MFIs. One example is the "AIMS Tools," developed by a U.S. Agency for International Development project. This set of five tools that can be used by financial institutions to gather client information useful for impact assessment and market research. Worldwide testing has shown that these tools provide valuable information on client satisfaction, empowerment, and impact.[a]

The Imp-Act project, funded by the Ford Foundation, has also supported the application of a number of user-friendly methods to assess impact in more than 30 MFIs, with positive results. In addition, the project conducted studies on the cost-effectiveness of social performance measurement and management at four organizations: Organización de Desarrollo Empresarial Femenino (ODEF) in Honduras, Small Enterprise Foundation (SEF) in South Africa, FINRURAL in Bolivia, and Prizma in Bosnia Herzegovina. The studies confirmed that using social performance measurements for management purposes

pays for itself through improved financial and social performance, by retaining good clients longer and introducing more client-responsive products. For instance, ODEF improved retention of repeat clients by 12 percent between 2002 and 2003, and expanded its portfolio by about one-third through the introduction of individual loans.[b]

Finally, CGAP and the Ford Foundation are working with 35 financial institutions in a range of countries to develop and test simple proxy indicators that mirror the Millennium Development Goal targets on income, health, and education. This Social Indicators Project will track the social performance of MFIs by monitoring changes in client social and economic well-being without attempting to attribute causality. The project will look at (1) whether MFIs are reaching the very poor, (2) whether client households are increasing incomes and gaining assets, (3) whether greater numbers of children are going to school, (4) whether health conditions are improving, and (5) whether women are becoming more empowered.[c]

[a] www.usaidmicro.org/componen/aims/activities/tools.asp; and Simanowitz, "A Review of Impact Assessment Tools," 12.

[b] www.ids.ac.uk/impact.

[c] From CGAP, CGAP Investment Committee Proposal, Developing Social Indicators for Financial Institutions: Monitoring Progress on the MDGs.

this chapter are trying to address the standardization problem. In addition, a group of six leading microfinance banks in Asia, Africa, and Latin America has begun to tackle these challenges through a partnership with the Dutch Triodos Bank and the Global Reporting Initiative (GRI). They plan to use GRI Guidelines to disclose the social and environmental impact of their activities.[43]

Another approach would be to hold financial institutions accountable to their own missions and objectives, rather than insist on accountability to universal standards. This approach might fit better with the idea that a diverse range of financial service providers are needed to meet the massive demand of those currently unserved. Diverse institutions will likely have different but complementary social missions. For instance, some financial service providers may not

---

[43.] www.globalreporting.org/news/updates/article.asp?ArticleID=379.

have an explicit social mandate, but nonetheless find serving poorer clients with quality financial services an interesting business proposition. Many of the issues outlined in this chapter will likely be irrelevant for these providers.

For those shareholders and funders who do prioritize social performance, one proposal is to devise a social auditing system that verifies financial institutions' systems and reports against their own defined benchmarks.[44] In the end, probably the best way for shareholders and funders to hold financial institutions accountable for their social performance is by insisting that managers stick to a "double bottom line."[45] As long as those calling the shots (and reaping the financial benefits) care about maintaining a focus on social goals, such as reaching very poor or remote rural households or increasing the incomes of their clients, then the promise of social performance will most likely be realized.

Protecting Poor Consumers[46]

In many countries there is concern about the impact of over-indebtedness, high interest rates, and abusive lending practices on poor borrowers. But so far there has been relatively little exploration of how consumer protection might apply to financial services for the poor. This section focuses on the credit side, although consumer protection is also relevant for deposit services.

Consumer protection defined. Consumer protection encompasses all the means necessary to safeguard the interests of consumers (in the case of microfinance, usually poor borrowers in developing countries) and educate them about their rights and help them make wise, educated decisions. Typical consumer protection measures include disclosure requirements, rules and prohibitions related to lending practices, mechanisms for handling complaints or disputes, and consumer education (see figure 7.5).

Disclosure requirements. The basis for many consumer protection measures is adequate disclosure of lending terms and conditions. Disclosure, or "truth-in-lending," laws exist in many countries. They typically require lenders to clearly state interest rates and loan terms in contracts and other public documents.

Comparable and widely available information on true loan costs allows borrowers to comparison shop for loans. It can also stimulate price competition that reduces costs and interest rates. Disclosure, however, is a complex challenge, because the variable nature of loan terms, installments, and fee structures make comparisons particularly tricky for microcredit.

Rules and prohibitions on lending practices. These laws, regulations, and norms restrict certain types of lending practices. They may apply to any stage of the borrowing cycle, but tend to focus on loan origination and collection, the stages in

---

[44] Ibid, 12.

[45] Rhyne, "Maintaining the Bottom Line in Investor-Owned Microfinance Organizations," 17.

[46] Except when otherwise noted, this section draws exclusively from Porteous and Helms, "Protecting Microfinance Borrowers."

FIGURE 7.5 The Elements of Consumer Protection

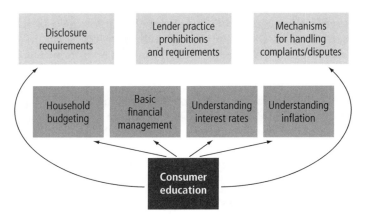

Source: Based on Porteous and Helms, "Protecting Microfinance Borrowers."

which consumers are most vulnerable. Rules may limit the pressure that lenders can apply on potential borrowers to take a loan and prohibit collection techniques that are viewed as unduly coercive or otherwise inappropriate. In addition to sanctions applied directly by the government, consumers may be given the right to private redress for violations of these rules. For instance, when a consumer lender in South Africa engages in certain prohibited lending practices, any affected borrower has the right to treat the loan contract as invalid, thus avoiding the legal obligation of repayment.

Consumer protection rules often try to protect consumers from exorbitant fees and interest rates. Some governments try to control this risk though usury laws that set interest rate ceilings. Usury limits are controversial. It may be politically impossible to set the limit high enough to make room for the abnormally heavy administrative costs involved in making and collecting tiny loans. The result can be to reduce poor people's access to loans, because viable service providers will not enter or stay in the microloan business if interest rates are set too low to allow them to cover their costs.[47]

Mechanisms for handling complaints and disputes. Individual lenders may employ staff to handle customer complaints, and industry bodies may establish dedicated offices or agencies to resolve issues that consumers cannot solve directly with financial institutions. In South Africa, the Micro Finance Regulatory Council (MFRC) has set up a toll-free call center to connect consumers with complaints officers who investigate complaints and alleged abuses.[48] This kind of complaint-driven enforcement is an inexpensive way to enforce rules, but many cases and patterns of abuse go unreported or unnoticed.

[47.] For more detail, see chapter 5 and Helms and Reille, "Interest Rate Ceilings and Microfinance."
[48.] The Micro Finance Regulatory Council Web site is www.mfrc.co.za.

Consumer education. Especially in industrial countries, promoting consumer education is usually considered a vital strategy that underpins all the other elements of consumer protection. To be effective, consumer protection measures, such as disclosure requirements, lender practice rules, and complaint mechanisms, require consumers to be educated about products and rights. Consumer education teaches clients how to acquire the appropriate information about lending and savings options so they can make wise decisions.

Most consumer education programs are offered by nongovernmental organizations (NGOs) and financed by philanthropic foundations. For example, the Citigroup Foundation is stepping up its activity in this area by funding NGOs around the world with close to $10 million annually.[49] In Uganda, the Association of Microfinance Institutions of Uganda (AMFIU), the Uganda Consumer Protection Association (UCPA), and the Financial Sector Deepening Project Uganda (FSDU) jointly launched a consumer education initiative. The aim of the initiative is to educate microfinance clients (or prospective clients) about their rights, such as redress, dignified treatment, transparent information, legal appeal, protection from overly aggressive marketing, abusive collection procedures, and so on. Consumers are also taught about their responsibilities, such as repaying loans.[50]

Enforcement issues. Whereas many people would agree on consumer protection measures in principle, they may disagree strongly on the preferred enforcement method. In general, there are two distinct approaches:

- **Industry self-regulation:** Institutions within an industry form an association that subscribes to a voluntary code of conduct, agree on mechanisms of surveillance and monitoring for adherence to the code, and decide on consequences of violating the code, for example, expulsion from the association.

- **Government agency enforcement:** A state regulatory body, such as a consumer protection agency, is authorized to enforce the relevant law.

Self-regulation is often more flexible and pragmatic than government agency enforcement. In the case of microfinance, it is less likely to result in excessive measures that reduce access to financial services and more likely to promote expanded access over time. However, one major drawback is that once an institution is expelled from the association for nonadherence, the association has no further authority over it. That institution may continue its abusive practices without risk of retribution. Additionally, an association of lenders may have some incentive not to adopt certain rules that may be good for the consumer but highly inconvenient for the lenders.

The Pro-Consumer Pledge adopted in late 2004 by ACCIÓN International and MicroFinance Network (MFN) member institutions is an example of self-regulation. MFN's active working group on proconsumer policies developed the pledge and now seeks to document best practice as members implement it.[51]

[49.] For more information, visit the Citigroup Foundation Web site, www.citigroup.com/citigroup/corporate/foundation.

[50.] Musinguzi, "Micro-Finance See Training as Key."

[51.] For more information, visit the Microfinance Network Web site at www.mfnetwork.org.

Similarly, the network SEEP has recently documented experiences in self-regulation as it applies to consumer protection in microfinance.[52]

In contrast to self-regulation, state enforcement of consumer protection laws can become cumbersome and bureaucratic. Substantial human and financial resources are required to monitor compliance and run effective complaint investigation operations. Because of their mandate, regulators may pursue consumer protection goals single-mindedly, possibly at the expense of expanding access to those who presently lack services. However, state regulation has some advantages. It is less likely to be distorted by the interest of the lenders; it has more powerful enforcement tools; and it applies to all institutions, regardless of whether they are members of an industry association.

Each of these two approaches offers its own advantages and disadvantages, and neither is a one-size-fits-all solution. But when state enforcement is seen as a complete replacement for self-regulation, the balance tends to tip toward over-enforcement. The result may be to discourage competition and ultimately limit access to services for poor people. In the end, some combination of the two approaches may be in order.

Toward the future. Consumer protection in microfinance is a challenge that is here to stay. In countries where political pressure to implement new protection measures is strong, regulators and policymakers should carefully consider the full impact such measures may have, both immediately and over time. Even in countries where consumer abuse is not yet a problem, promoting consumer education could reduce, if not completely eliminate, future pressure to overregulate. Financial institutions should consider adhering to voluntary pledges or codes that promote effective consumer protection and a consumer-oriented culture.

Conclusion

The five issues complement and cut across the bigger picture challenges at the client, micro, meso, macro, and funder levels already discussed in this book. Taken together, these cross-cutting issues offer insight about how to tackle the core frontier challenges: achieving massive scale, reaching poorer and more remote clients, and reducing costs (see table 7.2).

Of course, these issues are also interlinked. For instance, rural finance and remittances both require the use of technology to achieve scale, reach poorer and more remote clients, and reduce costs. Consumer literacy is critical for the acceptance of technological solutions among poor clients. Technology can play an important role in tracking social performance. Social performance and consumer protection are, in many ways, two sides of the same coin: social performance is about financial institutions having better information about clients, and consumer protection is about clients having better information about financial institutions.

[52.] McAllister, "Trust through Transparency."

TABLE 7.2 How Cross-Cutting Issues Relate to Core Frontier Challenges

	Optimizing Technology	Leveraging Remittances and Other Transfers	Reaching Farmers and Remote Clients	Measuring Social Performance	Protecting Poor Consumers
Achieving scale	Applying technology to extend the reach of financial services	Leveraging remittances to reach more people	Improving quality and efficiency of rural finance will extend services	Attracting more capital and deposits through transparent reporting on financial and social performance	Increasing understanding of financial options among more people through consumer education
Reaching poorer and more remote clients	Harnessing technology to make it financially feasible to reach people in very remote areas	Helping poor and rural households to manage remittances and cross-sell with other needed financial services	Solving the problem of offering financial services in rural areas	Offering financial institutions the intelligence they need to serve poor clients better	Informing poor people about how best to use financial services to help them overcome their reluctance to enter the world of "banking"
Reducing costs	Reducing costs is the main purpose of applying advanced technology to microfinance	Reducing the costs of remittances and transfers by working through banks relative to money transfer companies	Reaching poor and remote clients sustainably is only possible when costs and risks are brought down	Applying social performance information to make services more client-responsive and reduce transactions costs for clients	Promoting competition, the most powerful driver of efficiency, is possible only if consumers are protected and informed

The pace of change in these cross-cutting issues (as in the rest of microfinance) means that every day new opportunities arise to expand the frontier of finance. The sooner these issues are addressed by the international development community, governments, and—most important—financial service providers themselves, the sooner the dream of truly inclusive financial systems will become a reality.

Chapter 8
Conclusion

Microfinance is a powerful instrument against poverty. Access to financial services can help poor and low-income clients increase and stabilize their incomes, build assets, and invest in their own future. And advances over the past 30 years have shown that microfinance has the potential to reach large numbers of poor people more effectively than ever thought possible. This potential means that within our lifetime poor and low-income people throughout the developing world can enjoy permanent access to the financial services they need. These financial services, in turn, expand clients' options for solving a range of financial problems—and enable poor people to climb the first rung on the ladder out of poverty on their own terms.

In fact, when international and domestic funders, governments, and financial service providers commit themselves to the vision of inclusive financial systems, the results are spectacular. Consider the example of Cambodia. Less than 15 years ago, there could not have been a more hostile environment for microfinance. Twenty years of civil unrest destroyed the financial system. At one point, even money itself was abolished. Today, Cambodia has 17 banks (foreign and domestic, private and government-owned), including a globally recognized microfinance bank, the Association of Cambodian Local Economic Development Agencies (ACLEDA) Bank. What began as small, isolated donor-dependent initiatives has evolved into a financial system of profitable, regulated institutions serving nearly 400,000 poor clients.[1]

Despite the significant advances and success stories like this one in Cambodia, the goal of reaching the majority of the world's population still excluded from financial services remains elusive. Looking to the future, the people and organizations that dedicate themselves to extending the frontiers of finance will have to face some tough questions: Will microfinance reach its full potential? Will financial systems become truly inclusive? Will there be access for all? This book has argued that the answer to these questions can be "yes," as long

---

[1.] Flaming, Duflos, Latortue, Nayar, and Roth, "Country Level Effectiveness and Accountability Review: Cambodia," 3.

as a number of interlocking challenges highlighted throughout this book are addressed.

Historically, MFIs have offered mainly credit to a relatively narrow range of microentrepreneurs whose income hovers around their countries' poverty lines. But poor and low-income **clients** of all kinds need more than short-term working capital loans to fuel their businesses. Just like everyone else, they require a range of financial services (savings, money transfers, insurance, and indeed credit of all kinds) that are convenient, flexible, and reasonably priced. At the same time, microfinance, particularly microcredit, is not always the answer. It cannot solve all of poverty's ills and is certainly not a substitute for investments in basic services like health and education.

A better understanding of clients' needs is critical, but it is not sufficient. Client demand will be met only when this understanding is translated into high-quality, affordable, and convenient financial services offered by a range of **providers** (the micro level). Financial service providers come in all shapes and sizes—from informal moneylenders and neighborhood savings clubs to commercial banks and everything in between. To reach large numbers of poor clients on a permanent basis, these financial service providers must cover their costs of doing business. In fact, according to available data, although they are a relatively small proportion of the total number of institutions, those financial institutions that are sustainable reach the majority of clients served (at least among privately owned financial institutions). Moreover, sustainability ensures that poor clients have permanent access to services. It is now well established that the trade-off between reaching poor people and financial viability is less stark than once assumed.

No single type of financial service provider can meet the diverse needs of all those who lack access. Most poor and low-income—and even middle-class— people in developing countries use some form of informal finance. However, informal providers are often insecure, offer a limited range of financial services, and cannot easily touch the lives of more than a few people in their immediate community. Larger, more formal financial institutions have extensive distribution networks, a broader range of clients, and the capacity to tap into domestic funding markets and invest in advanced technology solutions that might lower the cost of services to poor clients. But they do not necessarily have the mission or the systems to reach very poor or remote clients. In an inclusive financial system, these different providers jostle and compete for poor clients' business—right there in the urban neighborhoods and remote villages where these clients live.

If retail-level financial service providers are the building blocks on which the rest of the financial system can be built, then the cement that holds those blocks together is the **financial infrastructure** (the meso level). This infrastructure consists of the systems that allow for electronic payments and service providers such as auditors, raters, consulting services, information and point-of-sale technology vendors, specialized technical support, and professional associations. The significance and impact of the meso level is perhaps the least well understood by the microfinance community. What is clear, however, is that better financial infrastructure and more service providers will be required than are currently available in most places. Increasingly, mainstream financial infrastructure and technical service providers will take on this task, rather than those specialized in microfinance. Instead of seeing microfinance as a marginal, unprofitable niche market for their services, technical service providers will increasingly pursue this line of business as an attractive option for expansion.

Payments systems in many countries are inadequate because they do not allow poor clients to move money in a secure, cost-effective, and reasonably priced manner. By taking advantage of advances in communications, many countries could use technology (such as mobile phones) to resolve this problem for hundreds of millions of people. Accurate, standardized, and comparable information on financial performance is vital to integrate microfinance into the larger financial system. Bank supervisors and regulators, donors, investors, and, more important, the actual clients of microfinance need this information to adequately assess risk and returns. The bad news is that many of these financial service providers do not conform to reporting standards. The good news is that specialized MFIs, banks, and international bodies are beginning to converge around these standards.

At all levels of the financial system, technical skills are weak—a key constraint to extending access to financial services. It is therefore critically important to ensure a reliable supply of high-quality consultants, trainers, and academics to provide education opportunities to build the skills of existing and future employees of financial institutions as well as relevant government officials. Networks and associations can help financial service providers improve their transparency on performance, build up technical and managerial skills, negotiate with service providers and funders, and advocate for policy changes that make access to financial services possible. In tomorrow's inclusive financial systems, budding professionals will see financial services for the poor as a prestigious and exciting career opportunity—and attempt to attain the right skills to take advantage of it.

Financial service providers as well as the financial infrastructure are affected by policy decisions taken by developing country governments. In fact, the **role of government** in building inclusive financial systems—the macro level—has been a matter of controversy over the past several years. Microfinance experts have consistently discouraged governments from directly providing microfinance, and many have expressed skepticism about the need for regulating microfinance in all contexts. Governments, for their part, have not always agreed with this advice. Today, it is well understood that government has a positive role to play.

The government's most constructive role is to foster an environment that allows a diverse set of financial service providers to flourish and compete. Specifically, governments are most helpful when they maintain macroeconomic stability, liberalize interest rates, and refrain from distorting the market with unsustainable subsidized, high-delinquency loan programs. Governments can also adjust banking sector regulations and supervision to facilitate microfinance, while also protecting poor people's deposits. Possibly, governments could play a useful promotional role by offering fiscal incentives or requiring financial institutions to serve poor or low-income people—although not enough is known about these kinds of policies to foresee their ultimate impact in developing countries.

One thing is certain: governments are under constant pressure to use microfinance as a quick fix for distributing money to various population groups. Over time, governments would ideally perceive that the poor are not only bankable, but also legitimate clients of the financial system, as opposed to recipients of subsidized charity.

Building financial systems will not happen automatically: progress at all levels requires money and, more important, technical support. A growing maze of **international and domestic funders** offers a range of support that can fuel increased access to financial services. But for that to happen, funders need to identify and act on their relative strengths—instead of undermining one another and getting in each other's way. Effective international donor subsidies stimulate or complement private capital, rather than compete with it. More commercially minded international investors have recently grown in importance in microfinance and will continue to do so. The many funds that have cropped up in recent years signal that international investors are beginning to see the value of microfinance—although so far most of the money still comes from public sources and is not strictly profit-maximizing.

In an ideal world, microfinance would be funded mainly from domestic sources such as public deposits, bank loans, bond issues, and equity investment. These domestic funding sources are beginning to emerge in some countries. Regulated financial institutions are finding lower-cost ways to mobilize deposits from large numbers of poor people. Recent experiments in tapping domestic capital markets through bond issues in Latin America and Kenya reinforce this tendency. Although international sources are still needed to complement these domestic funds in many markets, integration into domestic funding markets holds the best promise for large-scale access to financial services among those currently excluded.

In the end, the myriad interlinked problems at all levels of the financial system add up to three core challenges that define the frontier of finance: scaling up to extend access to billions more people; reaching poorer and more remote clients; and reducing costs. A few additional cross-cutting issues pose particularly stubborn dilemmas and represent enormous opportunities. These issues include optimizing technology, leveraging money transfers and cross-border remittances, reaching farmers and remote rural clients, measuring social performance, and protecting poor consumers.

The rapid progress in addressing these core challenges reflects the highly dynamic nature of microfinance. In fact, as the field has moved from microcredit to microfinance to inclusive financial systems, it has changed and evolved so quickly it is hardly recognizable from the scene encountered even just 5 or 10 years ago. In many countries, poor and low-income clients are already being integrated into their financial systems:

- In India and Brazil—both enormous potential markets—commercial banks are experimenting with microfinance. They are forging alliances with agents as wide-ranging as supermarket chains, lottery outlets, and gas stations (Brazil) and with such local entrepreneurs as franchise owners and community-based MFIs (India). While relatively young yet, these experiments promise to reach large numbers of poor clients very quickly.

- More traditional microfinance markets like Bolivia, Bangladesh, and Uganda are becoming more competitive, spurring financial service providers to innovate by making their products more client-friendly (Bangladesh), broadening the range of services they can offer through transformation from nongovernmental organizations to licensed intermediaries (Bolivia, Uganda), and introducing cost-saving technological advances such as intelligent automatic teller machines that allow illiterate people to more easily access basic banking services (Bolivia).

- Countries as varied as South Africa, the Philippines, and Kenya are introducing mobile phone banking that would allow poor clients to deposit funds, repay loans, pay bills, and transfer funds to relatives without necessarily having to leave their villages or open up formal bank accounts.

- Mainstream credit bureaus in countries as disparate as Bosnia, Peru, and Haiti have integrated microcredit borrowers into their databases.

- Donors and investors show an increasing commitment to making a difference with their funds by adhering to "what works" and expanding poor and low-income people's access to financial services.

These and other examples help light the path for others to follow. If it can happen in these widely varying countries, then it can happen anywhere. Working together, financial service providers, governments, and the international development community can transform the dream of truly inclusive financial systems into a reality. And inclusive financial systems are the only way to ensure access for all.

Afterword

In March 2005, I went to access my email account at a makeshift Internet café in a small town called San Pablo La Laguna in the Philippines. Next to me sat a boy, barefoot, probably about nine years old, surfing the Internet. It struck me that this is what we mean by *access*.

This experience prompted me to do a little research on the origins of the Internet. When I was about nine years old, the ARPANET was born. Few people remember the ARPANET, but it was the embryo of today's Internet, with four hosts and limited scope. Through a process of continuous innovation, in the early 1990s the World Wide Web emerged. Growth was exponential, and the number of hosts jumped from 1 to 2 million between 1992 and 1993 alone. Today, the Internet offers multiple services that many take for granted (such as Web access, email, and file transfer protocols), with more than 140 Internet service providers and nearly 1 billion users—more than double the number of just five years ago.[1] The service has become more accessible, cheaper, and less cumbersome.

Financial systems have gone through a similar trajectory. Twenty-five or 30 years ago, microcredit was born (the ARPANET phase). There were relatively few "hosts" in a few key countries like Bangladesh, Indonesia, and Bolivia. In 2005, the equivalent of the World Wide Web has just been invented—the groundwork has been laid with a critical mass of financial service providers that have the know-how to serve poor and low-income clients on a viable, permanent basis. The numbers of poor people served are growing every day. The challenge ahead is to achieve the radical expansion of Internet proportions.

Even though inclusive financial systems might seem like an impossible goal today, the same could have been said of the Internet 25 years ago. We never would have dreamed that poor neighborhood kids in a small town like San Pablo La Laguna could hit the Internet café and surf the net. What this shows is that change can happen quickly. Within one generation we could live in a world where everyone who needs financial services has access to them. And this access will in turn contribute in some small way to a world where poverty is indeed history.

[1.] www.internetworldstats.com/stats.htm.

Recommended Reading and Web Sites

General

Christen, Robert P., Richard Rosenberg, and Veena Jayadeva. "Financial Institutions with a 'Double Bottom Line': Implications for the Future of Microfinance." CGAP Occasional Paper, no. 8. Washington, D.C.: CGAP, July 2004.

Consultative Group to Assist the Poor (CGAP). *Key Principles of Microfinance*. Available at www.cgap.org.

Consultative Group to Assist the Poor (CGAP) Web site, www.cgap.org.

Littlefield, Elizabeth, and Richard Rosenberg. "Microfinance and the Poor: Breaking Down the Walls between Microfinance and Formal Finance." *Finance & Development* 41, no. 2, 38–40, June 2004.

Microfinance Gateway Web site, www.microfinancegateway.org.

Robinson, Marguerite. *The Microfinance Revolution*. Vol. 1, *Sustainable Finance for the Poor*. Washington, D.C.: World Bank, 2001.

Clients

Littlefield, Elizabeth, Jonathan Morduch, and Syed Hashemi. "Is Microfinance an Effective Strategy to Reach the Millennium Development Goals?" CGAP Focus Note, no. 24. Washington, D.C.: CGAP, January 2004.

Rutherford, Stuart. *The Poor and Their Money*. New Delhi: Oxford University Press, 2000.

Sebstad, Jennifer, and Monique Cohen. *Microfinance, Risk Management, and Poverty*. Washington, D.C.: U.S. Agency for International Development, 2000.

Micro-Level: Financial Service Providers

Branch, Brian, and Janette Klaehn. "Striking the Balance in Microfinance: A Practical Guide to Mobilizing Savings." Washington, D.C.: World Council of Credit Unions, 2002.

Financial Sector Team. *Banking the Underserved: New Opportunities for Commercial Banks*. London: Department for International Development, 2005.

Harper, Malcom, and Sukhwinder Singh Arora. *Small Customers, Big Market: Commercial Banks in Microfinance*. London, United Kingdom: ITDG Publishing, 2005.

Ledgerwood, Joanna. *Microfinance Handbook*. Washington, D.C.: The World Bank, 1998.

Meso-Level: Financial Infrastructure and Technical Services

Isern, Jennifer, and Tamara Cook. *What Is a Network? The Diversity of Networks in Microfinance Today.* Washington, D.C.: CGAP, July 2004.

MicroBanking Bulletin Web site, www.mixmbb.org.

MIX Market Web site, www.mixmarket.org. Small Enterprise Education and Promotion (SEEP) Network. "The 7 Cs for Improving Technical Service Delivery to Microfinance Institutions: A Practical Guide for Microfinance Institutions, Technical Service Providers, and Donors." Washington, D.C.: SEEP, 2003.

Macro-Level: Role of Government

Caprio, Gerard, and Patrick Honohan. "Finance for Growth." A World Bank Policy Research Report. Washington, D.C.: World Bank, 2001.

Christen, Robert Peck, Timothy R. Lyman, and Richard Rosenberg. *Guiding Principles on Regulation and Supervision of Microfinance.* CGAP Consensus Guidelines. Washington, D.C.: CGAP, 2003.

Duflos, Eric, and Kathryn Imboden. "The Role of Governments in Microfinance." CGAP Donor Brief, no. 19. Washington, D.C.: CGAP, June 2004.

Helms, Brigit, and Xavier Reille. "Interest Rate Ceilings and Microfinance." CGAP Occasional Paper, no. 9. Washington, D.C.: CGAP, September 2004.

Isern, Jennifer, David Porteous, Raul Hernandez-Coss, and Chinyere Egwuagu. "AML/CFT Regulation: What Are the Implications for Financial Service Providers That Serve Poor People." CGAP Focus Note, no. 29. Washington, D.C.: CGAP, July 2005.

Levy, Fred. "Apex Institutions in Microfinance." CGAP Occasional Paper, no. 6. Washington, D.C.: CGAP, January 2002.

Peachey, Steven, and Alan Roe. "Access to Finance." A study for the World Savings Banks Institute, October 2004.

Funders

Consultative Group to Assist the Poor (CGAP). *Building Inclusive Financial Systems—Donor Guidelines on Good Practice in Microfinance.* Washington, D.C.: CGAP, 2004.

de Sousa-Shields, Marc, and Cheryl Frankiewicz. *Financing Microfinance Institutions: The Context for Transitions to Private Capital.* Micro Report, no. 8. Accelerated Microenterprise Advancement Project. Washington, D.C.: U.S. Agency for International Development, 2004.

Duflos, Eric, Brigit Helms, Alexia Latortue, and Hannah Siedek. *Global Results: Analysis and Lessons.* CGAP Aid Effectiveness Initiative. Washington, D.C.: CGAP, April 2004.

Featherston, Scott, Elizabeth Littlefield, and Patricia Mwangi. "Foreign Exchange Risk in Microfinance: What Is It and How Can It Be Managed?" CGAP Focus Note, no. 31. Washington, D.C.: CGAP, January 2006.

Ivatury, Gautam, and Julie Abrams. "The Market for Microfinance Foreign Investment: Opportunities and Challenges." CGAP Focus Note, no. 30. Washington, D.C.: CGAP, August 2005.

Cross-Cutting Challenges

Christen, Robert, and Douglas Pearce. *Managing Risks and Designing Products for Agricultural Microfinance: Features of an Emerging Model.* CGAP Occasional Paper, no. 11. Washington, D.C.: CGAP, August 2005.

Cracknell, David. *Electronic Banking for the Poor: Panacea, Potential and Pitfalls,* Nairobi: MicroSave-Africa, 2004.

Imp-Act Programme. "Social Performance Management in Microfinance: Guidelines." Brighton: Institute of Development Studies, 2005.

Isern, Jennifer, and Rani Deshpande. "Crafting a Money Transfers Strategy: Guidance for Pro-poor Financial Service Provider." CGAP Occasional Paper, no. 10. Washington, D.C.: CGAP, March 2005.

Ivatury, Gautam. *Using Electronic Payments to Build Inclusive Financial Systems.* Washington, D.C.: CGAP, forthcoming.

McAllister, Patrick. "Trust through Transparency." Washington, D.C.: Small Enterprise Education and Promotion Network, 2003.

Microfinance Gateway Web site. "Social Performance Resource Center." www.microfinancegateway.org/resource_centers/socialperformance.

Orozco, Manuel. "Worker Remittances: An International Comparison." Inter-American Dialogue Project commissioned by the Multilateral Investment Fund of the Inter-American Development Bank, February 2003. Available at http://www.iadb.org/mif/v2/files/28feb1.pdf.

Porteous, David, and Brigit Helms. "Protecting Microfinance Borrowers." CGAP Focus Note, no. 27. Washington, D.C.: CGAP, May 2005.

Rhyne, Elisabeth. "Maintaining the Bottom Line in Investor-Owned Microfinance Organizations." *MicroBanking Bulletin,* Issue no. 11, May 2005.

Zeller, Manfred, Cécile Lapenu, and Martin Greeley. "Social Performance Indicators Initiative: Final Report," 2003. Available at http://www.cerise-microfinance.org/publication/pdf/impact/SPI-summary.pdf.

References

Anft, Michael. "A New Way to Curb Poverty." *Chronicle of Philanthropy,* April 15, 2004.

Apgar, William C., and Mark Duda. *The Twenty-Fifth Anniversary of the Community Reinvestment Act: Past Accomplishments and Future Regulatory Challenges.* New York: Federal Reserve Board of New York Policy Review, 2003.

Appui au Développement Autonome. An internal unpublished survey conducted under the auspices of the multidonor Rating Fund that covered six microfinance specialized rating agencies: PlanetRating, M-CRIL, MicroRate, Microfinanza, CRISIL, and ACCION International, 2004.

Asian Development Bank. *The Role of Central Banks in Microfinance in Asia and the Pacific.* Vol. 1. Overview. Washington, D.C.: Asian Development Bank, 2000.

Association of Financial Entities Specialized in Microfinance. *Regulatory Framework That Governs the Operation of the Microfinance in Bolivia.* La Paz: ASOFIN, 2003.

Bank for International Settlements—Committee on Payment and Settlement Systems. *Core Principles for Systemically Important Payment Systems.* Basel: Bank for International Settlements, 2001.

Barry, Nancy. Welcome Remarks for the Federación Latinoamericana de Bancos-Women's World Banking Seminar on Microfinance as a New Banking Opportunity. Cartagena, Colombia, September 8–9, 2004.

Beck, Thorsten, Asli Demirguc-Kunt, and Ross Levine. "Finance, Inequality and Poverty." World Bank Policy Research Working Paper no.3338. Washington D.C.: World Bank, 2004.

Benston, George. "The Community Reinvestment Act—Looking for Discrimination That Is Not There." Cato Policy Analysis, no. 354. Washington, D.C.: CATO Institute, 1999. http://www.cato.org/pubs/pas/pa-354es.html.

Boon, Hans. *Worldwide Landscape of Postal Financial Services (Middle East and North African Region), The Role of Postal Networks in Expanding Access to Financial Services.* Amsterdam, Unpublished paper, June 2004.

Brown, Warren. "Building the Homes of the Poor, One Brick at a Time: Housing Improvement Lending at Mibanco." *InSight,* no. 4. Washington, D.C.: ACCION International, 2003.

Campos Bolaño, Pilar. *El Ahorro Popular en México: Acumulando Activos para Superar la Pobreza.* México: Centro de Investigación para el Desarrollo, 2005.

Caprio, Gerard, and Patrick Honohan. "Finance for Growth." A World Bank Policy Research Report. Washington, D.C.: World Bank, 2001.

Cavazos, R., J. Abrams, and A. Miles. *Foreign Exchange Risk Management in Microfinance.* New York: Women's World Banking, 2004.

Chao-Beroff, Rene, Thi Hanh Houmard Cao, Jean Pierre Vandenbroucke, Muli Musinga, Edith Tiaro, and Leonard Mutesasira. *A Comparative Analysis of Member-based Microfinance Institutions in East and West Africa.* Nairobi: MicroSave, 2000.

Charitonenko, Stephanie. *Commercialization of Microfinance, The Philippines.* Manila, Philippines: Asian Development Bank, 2003.

Chatterji, Subhrendu. *The Domestic Architecture of Financial Sectors in Developing Countries.* Background note to a presentation at the Overseas Development Institute. The Consulting Base, March 2001. www.theconsultingbase.com.

Christen, Robert Peck, and Douglas Pearce. *Managing Risks and Designing Products for Agricultural Microfinance: Features of an Emerging Model.* CGAP Occasional Paper, no. 11. Washington, D.C.: CGAP, August 2005.

Christen, Robert Peck, and Richard Rosenberg. "The Rush to Regulate: Legal Frameworks for Microfinance." CGAP Occasional Paper, no. 4. Washington, D.C.: CGAP, 2000.

Christen, Robert Peck, Richard Rosenberg, and Veena Jayadeva. "Financial Institutions with a 'Double Bottom Line': Implications for the Future of Microfinance." CGAP Occasional Paper, no. 8. Washington, D.C.: CGAP, July 2004.

Christen, Robert Peck, Timothy R. Lyman, and Richard Rosenberg. *Guiding Principles on Regulation and Supervision of Microfinance.* CGAP Consensus Guidelines. Washington, D.C.: CGAP, 2003.

Churchill, Craig. *Microinsurance Products,* presentation for the Kreditanstalt für Wiederaufbau Microinsurance Meeting, Frankfurt, Germany, October 21, 2004.

Clark, Heather. "Credit Components." CGAP Donor Brief, no. 10. Washington, D.C.: CGAP, February 2003.

Coates, David, and Leesa Wilson Shrader. "Turning an NGO into a Bank." *Microfinance in CEE and the NIS,* Issue no. 1/2003, Poland, 2003.

Cohen, Monique. "The Impact of Microfinance." CGAP Donor Brief, no. 13. Washington, D.C.: CGAP, July 2003.

Comptroller of the Currency Administrator of National Banks. "Community Developments—Individual Development Account: An Asset Building Product for Lower-Income Consumers." *Community Development Insights,* February 2005.

Conger, Lucy. "To Market, To Market," *Enterprise Americas Magazine,* Autumn edition. New York: Inter-American Development Bank, September 2003.

Consultative Group to Assist the Poor. "Apex Institutions in Microfinance." CGAP Donor Brief, no. 5. Washington, D.C.: CGAP, 2002.

———. "Assessing the Relative Poverty of Microfinance Clients: A CGAP Operational Tool." http://www.cgap.org/docs/TechnicalTool 05 overview.pdf.

———. *Building Inclusive Financial Systems—Donor Guidelines on Good Practice in Microfinance.* Washington, D.C.: CGAP, 2004.

———. CGAP Investment Committee Proposal, Project: Developing Social Indicators for Financial Institutions: Monitoring Progress on the MDGs. Unpublished document. Washington, D.C.: CGAP, May 2005.

———. CGAP IT Innovations Series. www.cgap.org.

———. Charter Reporting, 2004. www.cgap.org.

———. "Commercial Banks in Microfinance: New Actors in the Microfinance World." CGAP Focus Note, no. 12. Washington, D.C.: CGAP, July 1998.

———. *Key Principles of Microfinance.* Accessed August 2005. www.cgap.org.

————. "Microfinance and Risk Management: A Client Perspective." CGAP Focus Note, no. 17. Washington, D.C.: CGAP, May 2000.

————. "Microfinance Donor Projects: 12 Questions about Sound Practice." CGAP Donor Brief, no. 1. Washington, D.C.: CGAP, 2002.

————. "More Than 30 Organizations Sign 'Social Performance' Pledge." *Portfolio.* Issue no. 3. Washington, D.C.: CGAP, August 2005.

————. "Point of Sale for Microfinance: A CGAP Presentation." http://www. microfinancegateway.org/content/article/detail/19053.

————. *Pro-poor Innovation Challenge.* www.cgap.org.

————. *Review of Commercial Bank and Other Formal Financial Institution (FFI) Participation in Microfinance.* Washington, D.C.: CGAP, 2004.

————. Survey on Information Infrastructure in Microfinance. Unpublished study. Washington, D.C.: CGAP, 2003.

CGAP and Central Bank for West Africa. *Determining the Outreach of Senegalese MFIs.* Washington, D.C.: CGAP, September 2004.

Cracknell, David. *Electronic Banking for the Poor: Panacea, Potential and Pitfalls.* Nairobi: MicroSave-Africa, 2004.

Credit and Development Forum. "Microfinance Statistics." Vol. 16. Dhaka: Credit and Development Forum, 2003.

Cunningham, Gord. "Microfinance: Flavour of the Month or Practical Development Alternative?" Presented at the Yukon Economic Forum: "Ideas Summit," Coady International Institute, St. Francis Xavier University, March 25, 2000.

Daley-Harris, Sam. *State of the Microcredit Summit Campaign Report 2004.* http://www. microcreditsummit.org.

Department of Trade and Industry. *The Effect of Interest Rate Controls in Other Countries.* London: DTI, 2004.

de Sousa-Shields, Marc, and Cheryl Frankiewicz. "Financing Microfinance Institutions: The Context for Transitions to Private Capital." Micro Report, no. 8. Accelerated Microenterprise Advancement Project. Washington, D.C.: U.S. Agency for International Development, 2004.

DFID Financial Sector Team. *Banking the Underserved: New Opportunities for Commercial Banks.* London: Department for International Development, 2005.

————. *The Importance of Financial Sector Development for Growth and Poverty Reduction.* Policy Division Working Paper. London: Policy Division, Department for International Development, August 2004.

Diaz Ortega, Enrique. CGAP Rating Fund Project Evaluation. Unpublished document. Washington, D.C.: CGAP, April 2004.

Dileo, Paul. "Building a Reliable MFI Funding Base: Donor Flexibility Shows Results." CGAP Case Study in Good Practice, no. 5. Washington, D.C.: CGAP, September 2003.

Dressen, Robert, Jay Dyer, and Zan Northrup. "Turning Around State-Owned Banks in Underserved Markets." *Small Enterprise Development,* vol. 13, no. 4, 58–67.

Duflo, Esther, William Gale, Jeffrey Liebman, Peter Orszag, and Emmanuel Saez. "Savings Incentives for Low- and Middle-Income Families: Evidence from a Field Experiment with H&R Block." The retirement security project. Washington, D.C.: Outreach & Business Development group, H&R Block, 2005.

Duflos, Eric, Brigit Helms, Alexia Latortue, and Hannah Siedek. *Global Results: Analysis and Lessons.* CGAP Aid Effectiveness Initiative. Washington, D.C.: CGAP, April 2004.

Duursma, Marjan. *Community-Based Microfinance Models in East Africa.* SNV-Tanzania, Hivos and FACET (Financial Assistance, Consultancy, Entrepreneurship and Training), 2004.

Ellis, Karen. "DFID Supports the FinScope Survey in Five Countries in Southern Africa: Collecting Better Data on Access to Financial Services." *Microfinance Matters,* Issue no. 11. New York: UNCDF Microfinance, April 2005.

El Qorchi, Mohammed, Samuel Munzele Maimbo, and John F. Wilson. "Informal Funds Transfer Systems: An Analysis of the Informal Hawala System." IMF Occasional Paper, no. 222. Washington, D.C.: International Monetary Fund, 2003.

Espinosa, Rodrigo. "Supervision and Regulation of Microfinance Industry in Ecuador. Case Study—Paving the Way Forward for Rural Finance: An International Conference on Best Practices." University of Wisconsin-Madison: Broadening Access and Strengthening Input Market Systems (BASIS) Collaborative Research Support Program, 2003.

Evans, Anna Cora, and Catherine Ford. *A Technical Guide to Rural Finance,* World Council of Credit Unions, 2003. https://www.woccu.org/pubs/technical_guides.php.

Featherson, Scott, Elizabeth Littlefield, and Patricia Mwangi. "Foreign Exchange Risk in Microfinance: What Is It and How Can It Be Managed?" CGAP Focus Note, no. 31. Washington, D.C.: CGAP, 2006.

Feltner, Tom. "A Global Survey of Community Reinvestment Laws: The Obligation of the Private Sector to Serve the Underserved in Several Countries." *Woodstock Institute International Alert,* Vol. 1. Chicago, IL: Woodstock Institute, 2004.

Fernando, Maheshan. "Managing Foreign Exchange Risk: The Search for an Innovation to Lower Costs to Poor People. United Nations Capital Development Fund. *Microfinance Matters,* Issue no. 12. New York: UNCDF Microfinance, May 2005.

Fernando, Nimal. *Do Governments in Asia Have a Role in Development of Sustainable Microfinance Services?* Manila: Asian Development Bank, 2003. http://www.adb.org/Documents/ Slideshows/Microfinance/Fernando_paper.pdf.

———. *Micro Success Story? Transforming of Nongovernment Institutions into Regulated Financial Institutions.* Manila: Asian Development Bank, June 2004. Reproduced with permission from the Asian Development Bank. For more information on development in Asia and the Pacific, see www.adb.org.

Flaming, Mark, Eric Duflos, Alexia Latortue, Nina Nayar, and Jimmy Roth. "Country Level Effectiveness and Accountability Review: Cambodia." Country-Level Effectiveness Assessment Report (CLEAR). Washington, D.C.: CGAP, 2005.

Fraslin, Jean-Hervé. *CECAM: A Cooperative Agricultural Financial Institution Providing Credit Adapted to Farmers' Demand in Madagascar,* University of Wisconsin-Madison: BASIS Collaborative Research Support Program, 2004.

Freedman. Paul L. "Designing Loan Guarantees to Spur Growth in Developing Countries." USAID Paper. Washington, D.C.: U.S. Agency for International Development, 2004.

German Agency for Technical Cooperation. "The Challenge of Sustainable Outreach— How Can Public Banks Contribute to Outreach in Rural Areas? Five Case Studies from Asia." Eschborn, Germany: Deutsche Gesellschaft fuer Technische Zusammenarbeit, 2003.

———. "Microfinance Associations (MFAs)—Their Role in Developing the Microfinance Sector." Eschborn, Germany: Deutsche Gesellschaft fuer Technische Zusammenarbeit, April 2003.

Gibbons, David, and Jennifer Meehan. "Financing Microfinance for Poverty Reduction." Draft paper commissioned by the Microcredit Summit Campaign. Malaysia: CASHPOR Financial and Technical Services, 2002.

Gonzalez-Vega, Claudio. "Microfinance Apex Mechanisms: Review of the Evidence and Policy Recommendations." Report prepared for the CGAP–Ohio State University Research Project on Apex Mechanisms. Ohio State University, 1998.

Gonzalez-Vega, Claudio, and Villafani Ibarnegaray. *Las Microfinanzas en el Desarrollo del Sistema Financiero de Bolivia.* La Paz: Proyecto Premier, 2004. http//aede.ose.edu/ programs/ruralfinance/bolicia/htm/.

Goodman, Patrick. *International Investment Funds—Mobilizing Investors towards Microfinance.* Luxembourg: Appui au Developpement Autonome, 2003.

Haberberger, Marie Louise. "Creating an Enabling Environment for Microfinance— The Role of Governments Experiences from Thailand." Document prepared for High-Level Policy Conference on Microfinance in India, New Delhi, May 3–5, 2005.

Haider, Elinor. "Credit Bureaus: Leveraging Information for the Benefit of Microenterprises." *Microenterprise Development Review,* vol. 2, no. 2. Washington, D.C.: Inter-American Development Bank, 2000.

Hannig, Alfred, and Gabriela Braun. *Transforming NGOs: Becoming a Deposit-Taking Financial Intermediary.* Eschborn, Germany: German Agency for Technical Cooperation, forthcoming.

Harper, Malcom, and Sukhwinder Singh Arora. *Small Customers, Big Market: Commercial Banks in Microfinance.* London: ITDG Publishing, and New Delhi: TERI, 2005.

Hashemi, Syed. "Linking Microfinance and Safety Net Programs to Include the Poorest: The Case of IGVGD in Bangladesh." CGAP Focus Note, no. 21. Washington, D.C.: CGAP, May 2001.

Helms, Brigit, and Alexia Latortue. *Elements of Donor Effectiveness in Microfinance: Policy Implications.* CGAP Aid Effectiveness Initiative. Washington, D.C.: CGAP, April 2004.

Helms, Brigit, and Xavier Reille. "Interest Rate Ceilings and Microfinance: The Story So Far." CGAP Occasional Paper, no. 9. Washington, D.C.: CGAP, September 2004.

Hernandez, Roberto, and Yerina Mugica. *What Works: Multilingual Smart ATMs for Microfinance.* Washington, D.C.: World Resources Institute, 2003. Reprinted courtesy of the World Resources Institute Digital Dividends Project, www.digitaldividend.org. Other What Works case studies are available.

Herrera, Carlos, and Bernardo Miranda. "COLUMNA, Guatemala, Good and Bad Practices Case Study," no. 5. CGAP Working Group on Microinsurance. Washington, D.C.: CGAP, 2004.

Hirschland, Madeline. *Savings Services for the Poor: An Operational Guide.* Bloomfield: Kumarian Press, forthcoming.

Hollis, Aidan. *Women and Microcredit in History: Gender in the Irish Loan Funds.* In Gail Campbell, Beverly Lemire, and Ruth Pearson, eds., *Women and Credit: Researching the Past, Refiguring the Future,* pp. 73–89. Oxford: Berg Press, 2002.

Honohan, Patrick. "Financial Development, Growth and Poverty: How Close Are the Links?" In Charles Goodhart, ed., *Financial Development and Economic Growth: Explaining the Links.* London: Palgrave, 2004.

ICICI Bank. *ICICI Bank's Microfinance Strategy: A Big Bank Thinks Small,* September 2003. http://www.microfinancegateway.org/content/article/detail/13446.

Inter-American Development Bank. *Unlocking Credit—The Quest for Deep and Stable Bank Lending.* Washington, D.C.: IADB, 2004.

Intercooperation, SDC's Backstopping Mandate Finance. "Remittances, the Money of the Migrants." Berne: Swiss Agency for Development and Cooperation (SDC/DSC), May 2004.

Isern, Jennifer, and Tamara Cook. *What Is a Network? The Diversity of Networks in Microfinance Today.* CGAP Focus Note, no. 26. Washington, D.C.: CGAP, July 2004.

Isern, Jennifer, and Rani Deshpande. "Crafting a Money Transfers Strategy: Guidance for Pro-poor Financial Service Provider." CGAP Occasional Paper, no. 10. Washington, D.C.: CGAP, March 2005.

Isern, Jennifer, David Porteous, Raul Hernandez-Coss, and Chinyere Egwuagu. "AML/CFT Regulation: What Are the Implications for Financial Service Providers That Serve Poor People." CGAP Focus Note, no. 29. Washington, D.C.: CGAP, July 2005.

Ivatury, Gautam. "Harnessing Technology to Transform Financial Services for the Poor." *Intermediate Technology Publications,* vol. 15, no. 4, December 2004.

——. *Using Electronic Payments to Build Inclusive Financial Systems.* Washington, D.C.: CGAP, forthcoming.

Ivatury, Gautam, and Julie Abrams. "The Market for Microfinance Foreign Investment: Opportunities and Challenges." CGAP Focus Note, no. 30. Washington, D.C.: CGAP, 2005.

Ivatury, Gautam, and Xavier Reille. "Foreign Investment in Microfinance: Debt and Equity from Quasi-Commercial Investors." CGAP Focus Note, no. 25. Washington, D.C.: CGAP, 2004.

Jansson, Tor. *Financing Microfinance—Exploring the Funding Side of Microfinance Institutions.* Washington, D.C.: Inter-American Development Bank, 2003.

Jaquand, Marc. "Finding a Role for Public Donors in the Privatized World of Microfinance." *Microfinance Matters,* Issue no. 8. New York: UNCDF Microfinance, January 2005.

Jazayeri, Ahmad. *Financial Services Association (FSA): Concept and Some Lessons Learnt.* Ahmad Jazayeri, 2000.

Johnson, Susan, Markku Malkamaki, and Kuria Wanjau. *Tackling the "Frontiers" of Microfinance Provision in Kenya: The Role of Decentralized Services.* Draft, December 2004.

Kabbucho, Kamau, Cerstin Sander, and Peter Mukwana. *Passing the Buck, Money Transfer Systems: The Practice and Potential for Products in Kenya.* Nairobi: MicroSave-Africa, 2003.

Kamewe, Hugues. "Reinventing Postal Savings Institutions in Africa: A New Role as Large-scale Microfinance Providers." *Microfinance Matters,* Issue no. 11. New York: UNCDF Microfinance, April 2005.

Ketley, Richard, and Ben Duminy. "Meeting the Challenge—The Impact of Changing Technology on MicroFinance Institutions." MicroSave Briefing Note, no. 21. Nairobi: MicroSave, 2003.

Ketley, Richard, Ben Davis, and Sarah Truen. "An Inter-country Survey of the Relative Costs of Bank Accounts: A Study for Finmark Trust." Unpublished manuscript, 2005.

Latortue, Alexia. "Microinsurance: A Risk Management Strategy." CGAP Donor Brief, no. 16. Washington, D.C.: CGAP, July 2003.

Ledgerwood, Joanna. *Microfinance Handbook.* Washington, D.C.: World Bank, 1998.

Levine, Ross. "Finance and Growth: Theory and Evidence." In Philippe Aghion and Steven Durlauf, eds., *Handbook of Economic Growth.* The Netherlands: Elsevier Science, forthcoming.

Levy, Fred. "Apex Institutions in Microfinance." CGAP Occasional Paper, no. 6. Washington, D.C.: CGAP, January 2002.

Lhériau, Laurent. "Précis de Réglementation de la Microfinance." Paris: Agence Française de Développement, 2005.

Littlefield, Elizabeth, and Richard Rosenberg. "Microfinance and the Poor: Breaking Down the Walls between Microfinance and Formal Finance." *Finance & Development* 41, no. 2, 38–40, June 2004.

Littlefield, Elizabeth, Jonathan Morduch, and Syed Hashemi. *Is Microfinance an Effective Strategy to Reach the Millennium Development Goals?* CGAP Focus Note, no. 24. Washington, D.C.: CGAP, January 2004.

Llanto, Gilberto M. *Micro Finance and Rural Finance Options in the Philippines.* World Bank Report, parts I and II. Draft, October 2004.

Macharia, Gerald. "Faulu Kenya Issues KES 500 Million (US$7 Million) Bond to Assist Poor People: A Journey to the Capital Markets." *Microfinance Matters,* Issue no. 11. New York: UNCDF Microfinance, April 2005.

Mahajan, Vijay, and Bharti Gupta Ramola. "Financial Services for the Rural Poor and Women in India: Access and Sustainability," *Journal of International Development* 8, no. 2, 1996.

Maimbo, Samuel Munzele. *The Money Exchange Dealers of Kabul—A Study of the Hawala System in Afghanistan.* Washington, D.C.: World Bank, 2003.

Maimbo, Samuel Munzele, and Dilip Ratha. *Remittances: Development Impact and Future Prospects.* Washington, D.C.: World Bank, 2005.

Marulanda, Beatriz, and Maria Otero. *The Profile of Microfinance in Latin America in 10 Years: Vision and Characteristics.* Boston: ACCION International, 2005.

McAllister, Patrick. "Trust through Transparency." Washington, D.C.: Small Enterprise Education and Promotion Network, 2003.

Mexican Banking Association. Annual Report April 2003–March 2004. http://www.abm.com.mx/.

MicroBanking Bulletin. "Introduction to the Peer Groups and Tables." *MicroBanking Bulletin,* Issue no. 10, March 2005.

Microfinance Gateway. "Q&A with Elisabeth Rhyne: ACCION and Microfinance Network's Pro-consumer Pledge." Washington, D.C.: Microfinance Gateway, 2004.

Microfinance Information eXchange (MIX). "Benchmarking Microfinance in Eastern Europe and Central Asia." www.mixmarket.org.

Miehlbradt, Alexandra O., and Mary McVay. *BDS Primer.* For the Small Enterprise Development Programme of the International Labour Organization. Geneva: International Labour Organization, September 2003.

Miles, Ann. "Financial Intermediation and Integration of Regulated MFIs." *MicroBanking Bulletin,* Issue no. 11, May 2005.

Miller, Calvin. *Twelve Key Challenges in Rural Finance,* FAO, 2004. http://www.seepnetwork.org/content/library/detail/2062.

Miller, Hillary. "The Paradox of Savings Mobilization in Microfinance: Why Microfinance Institutions in Bolivia Have Virtually Ignored Savings." Washington, D.C.: Development Alternatives, Inc., and U.S. Agency for International Development, 2003.

Miller, Jared. *The Role of Performance Information in Deepening Microfinance Markets.* Presentation at the VII Foro Interamericano de la Microempresa. Cartagena, Colombia, September 2004.

Miller, Mark. "Political Economy of Directed Credit." Research Internship Paper, no. 14. New Delhi: Centre for Civil Society, 2002.

Miranda, Aida L. "Philippines: Telecommunications and Broadcasting Market Brief." http://strategis.ic.gc.ca/epic/internet/inimr-ri.nsf/en/gr115033e.html.

Musinguzi, Bamuturaki. "Micro-Finance See Training as Key." *The Monitor* (Kampala), February 22, 2005.

Ndii, David. *Role and Development of Microfinance and Savings and Credit Cooperatives in Africa.* African Stock Exchanges Association Conference, Nairobi, 2004.

Norell, Dan, Georgia Emory-Smith, and Till Bruett. "How Do International Networks Manage Grants, Investments, and Loans to Their Partners and Affiliates?" SEEP Focus Note, no. 1. Washington, D.C.: Small Enterprise Education and Promotion Network, 2003.

Odell, Malcolm J. *Moving Mountains: Appreciative Planning and Action and Women's Empowerment in Nepal.* Appreciative Inquiry Practitioner, August 2004.

Orozco, Manuel. *The Remittance Marketplace: Prices, Policy, and Financial Institutions.* Washington, D.C.: Pew Hispanic Center, Annenburg School for Communication, University of Southern California, 2004.

———. "Worker Remittances: An International Comparison." Inter-American Dialogue Project commissioned by the Multilateral Investment Fund of the Inter-American Development Bank, February 2003. http://www.iadb.org/mif/v2/files/28feb1.pdf.

Ouattara, K. "Implementation of the PARMEC Law for Regulation of Microfinance." Washington, D.C.: World Bank, 2004.

Oxford Analytica. "South Africa: Banking the 'unbanked' proves viable," June 14, 2005, and "Africa: Low banking penetration constrains growth," July 15, 2005.

Pawlak, Katarzyna, and Michal Matul. "A Promising Approach to Social Performance Management." http://www.microfinancegateway.org/section/resourcecenters/impactassessment/practitioner/mfc/.

Peachey, Steven, and Alan Roe. "Access to Finance." A study for the World Savings Banks Institute, October 2004.

Pearce, Douglas. "Financial Services for the Rural Poor." CGAP Donor Brief, no. 15, Washington, D.C.: CGAP, October 2003.

Pearce, Douglas, and Myka Reinsch. *Caisses Villageoises d'Epargne et de Crédit Autogérées.* Niono, Mali, unpublished paper.

Porteous, David. "Cooperative Banking in Context." Presentation on FINMARK Trust. South Africa, 2003. www.finmarktrust.org.za/documents/2003/APRIL/TCIconf_April03.ppt.

Porteous, David, and Brigit Helms. "Protecting Microfinance Borrowers." CGAP Focus Note, no. 27. Washington, D.C.: CGAP, May 2005.

Portocarrero Maisch, Felipe, and Alvaro Tarazona Soria. *Cómo deberían financiarse las IMFs.* Lima: Inter-American Development Bank, 2004.

Prakash, L. B., Anuradha Pillai, Syed Hashemi, and Jennifer Isern. *Self-help Groups in India: Value for Money?* Washington, D.C.: CGAP, forthcoming.

Pytkovska, Justyna. *Overview of the Microfinance Industry in the ECE Region in 2003.* Poland: Microfinance Centre, 2004.

Ratha, Dilip. "Workers' Remittances: An Important and Stable Source of External Development Finance." Chapter 7 in *Global Development Finance 2003.* Washington, D.C.: World Bank, 2003.

Ratha, Dilip, and Samuel Munzele Maimbo. "Remittances: An Economic Force in Many Countries." Washington, D.C.: World Bank, Internal Web site, August 4, 2005.

Rating Fund. Rating Fund Statistics. Microfinance Rating and Assessment Fund. www.ratingfund.org.

Reille, Xavier, and Gautam Ivatury. *IT Innovations for Microfinance.* Presentation for the workshop "Innovative Technologies for Microfinance in Latin America," Costa Rica, October, 2003. Washington, D.C.: CGAP, 2003.

Rhyne, Elizabeth. *Mainstreaming Microfinance: How Lending to the Poor Began, Grew, and Came of Age in Bolivia.* Bloomfield: Kumarian Press, 2001.

———. "Maintaining the Bottom Line in Investor-Owned Microfinance Organizations," *MicroBanking Bulletin,* Issue no.11, May 2005.

———. "Perspectives from the Council of Microfinance Equity Funds," *Small Enterprise Development,* vol. 16, no. 1, March 2005.

Robinson, Marguerite. "The Future of Commercial Microfinance Industry in Asia," *Finance for the Poor,* vol. 6, no. 2. Manila: Asian Development Bank, June 2005. Reproduced with permission from the Asian Development Bank. For more information on development in Asia and the Pacific, see www.adb.org.

———. *The Microfinance Revolution.* Vol. 1, *Sustainable Finance for the Poor.* Washington, D.C.: World Bank, 2001.

———. *The Microfinance Revolution.* Vol. 2, *Lessons from Indonesia.* Washington, D.C.: World Bank, 2002.

———. "Why the Bank Rakyat Indonesia Has the World's Largest Sustainable Microbanking System." Paper presented at BRI International Seminar, Bali, Indonesia, December 1, 2004 (updated April 2005).

Robinson, Marguerite, and Graham Wright. "Mobilizing Savings." MicroSave Briefing Note, no. 3. Nairobi: MicroSave, 2001.

Rutherford, Stuart. *The Poor and Their Money.* New Delhi: Oxford University Press, 2000. Reprinted from *The Poor and Their Money* by Stuart Rutherford with the permission of the Oxford University Press India, New Delhi.

Ruthven, Orlanda. *Money Mosaics: Financial Choice and Strategy in a West Delhi Squatter Settlement.* United Kingdom: Institute for Development Policy and Management, University of Manchester, 2001.

Safavian, Mehnaz S., Douglas H. Gram, Claudio Gonzalez-Vega, and Dennis Whelan. *The State of Microfinance Activity and Regulation in Russia.* FINCA International-Ohio State University Project commissioned by United States Agency for International Development, 1999.

Sander, Cerstin. "Capturing a Market Share, Migrant Remittance Transfers & Commercialisation of Microfinance in Africa," 2003. http://www.bannock.co.uk/PDF/CapturingMarketShareFull.pdf.

———. *Passing the Buck in East Africa, The Money Transfer Practice and Potential for Services in Kenya, Tanzania, and Uganda.* Nairobi: MicroSave-Africa, 2004.

Schonberger, Steven N., and Robert Peck Christen. "A Multilateral Donor Triumph over Disbursement Pressure." CGAP Focus Note, no. 23. Washington, D.C.: CGAP, 2001.

Schreiner, Mark. "Poverty Scorecard for the Philippines." Report to the Grameen Foundation, mark@microfinance.com, 2005.

Schreiner, Mark, Michal Matul, Ewa Pawlak, and Sean Kline. "The Power of Prizma's Poverty Scorecard: Lessons for Microfinance," 2005. http://www.microfinance.com/English/Papers/Scoring_Poverty_in_BiH_Long.pdf.

Sebstad, Jennifer, and Monique Cohen. *Microfinance, Risk Management, and Poverty.* Washington, D.C.: U.S. Agency for International Development, 2000.

Sharma, Alok Kumar. "Assessment of Rural Poverty in India." New Delhi: United Nations Economic and Social Commission for Asia and the Pacific, 1997. http://www.unescap.org/rural/doc/beijing_march97/india.PDF.

Simanowitz, Anton. "A Review of Impact Assessment Tools," *Guidelines,* no. 2, 2001. www.ids.ac.uk.

———. "Social Performance, Poverty and Organizational Learning: Institutionalizing Impact in Microfinance," 2003. http://www.enterprise-impact.org.uk/pdf/Simanowitz.pdf.

Sizwekazi, Jekwa. "Banks, DTI nuke it out." *Southafrican Sunday Times,* March 24, 2005.

Skully, Michael. *The Development of the Pawnshop Industry in East Asia.* The Netherlands: Mansholt Graduate School of Social Sciences, 1994.

Small Enterprise Education and Promotion Network. *Global Directory of Regional and Country-level Microfinance Networks.* Washington, D.C.: SEEP Network, 2004.

Social Performance Task Force in Microfinance. "Promoting Social Performance in Microfinance: Toward a 'Double Bottom Line.'" www.microfinancegateway.org/resource_centers/socialperformance.

———. "What Is Social Performance?" www.microfinancegateway.org/resource_centers/socialperformance.

South Africa Info Reporter. "Mzansi: SA banking spreads its net," August 2005. www.southafrica.info/public_services/citizens/consumer_services/mzansi.htm.

Srivastava, Pradeep, and Priya Basu. *Scaling-up Access to Finance for India's Rural Poor.* Washington, D.C.: World Bank, 2004.

Steel, William F., and David O. Andah. *Rural and Micro Finance Regulation in Ghana: Implications for Development and Performance of the Industry.* International Conference on Ghana at the Half Century, 2004.

Stephens, Blaine. Data Brief 1:1. The MIX (Microfinance Information eXchange), 2004. www.themix.org.

Trigo Loubiere, Jacques, Patricia Lee Devaney, and Elizabeth Rhyne. "Supervising and Regulating Microfinance in the Context of Financial Sector Liberalization—Lessons from Bolivia, Colombia and Mexico." Report to the Tinker Foundation. ACCION International, 2004.

United Nations Capital Development Fund. "Challenges and Prospects in the Mobilization of Domestic Resources through Microfinancial Intermediation." *Microfinance Matters,* Issue no. 3. New York: UNCDF Microfinance, May–June 2004.

University of California and Food and Agriculture Organization Office for Latin America. *Credit Bureaus and the Rural Microfinance Sector: Peru, Guatemala, and Bolivia.* University of Wisconsin-Madison: BASIS Collaborative Research Support Program, December 2003.

U.S. Agency for International Development/Accelerated Microenterprise Advancement Project and Department for International Development. "Card-Based Remittance Services." *MIGRANT Remittances,* vol. 2, no. 1, 2005.

Wenner, Mark, D. *Lessons Learned in Rural Finance, The Experience of the Inter-American Development Bank.* Washington, D.C.: Inter-American Development Bank, 2002.

Whelan, Steve. "Automated Teller Machines," CGAP IT Innovation Series. www.cgap.org.

World Bank. "Microfinance in India: Issues, Constraints, and Potential for Sustainable Growth." Report no. 22531-IN. Finance and Private Sector Development Unit, South Asia Region. Washington, D.C.: World Bank, 2001.

———. "Mexico's Oportunidades Programme." Case study presented at the Shanghai Poverty Conference, 2004. http://www.worldbank.org/wbi/reducingpoverty/case-Mexico-OPORTUNIDADES.html.

World Council of Credit Unions. *A Technical Guide to Remittances: The Credit Union Experience.* www.woccu.org/development/remittances/index.php.

World Economic Outlook. "Globalization and External Imbalances," April 2005. http://www.imf.org/external/pubs/ft/weo/2005/01/pdf/chapter2.pdf.

Wright, Graham A. N. *Beyond Basic Credit and Savings: Developing New Financial Service Products for the Poor.* MicroSave-Africa, 1997.

———. *Understanding and Assessing the Demand for Microfinance.* MicroSave, prepared for Expanding Access to Microfinance: Challenges and Actors, Paris, June 20, 2005.

Wright, Graham A. N., and Aleke Dondo. "Are You Poor Enough?" Client Selection by MicroFinance Institutions. Nairobi: MicroSave-Africa, 2000.

Wright, Graham A. N., and Leonard Mutesasira. *The Relative Risks to the Savings of Poor People.* Nairobi: MicroSave, 2001.

Xinhua News Agency. "France guarantees first microfinance bond issue in Africa," April 7, 2005.

Young, Robin. "Credit Bureaus in Latin America: Expanding Financial and Other Services to the Base of the Pyramid." *Microfinance Matters,* Issue no. 12. New York: UNCDF Microfinance, May 2005.

Zeller, Manfred. "Promoting Institutional Innovation in Microfinance: Replicating Best Practices Is Not Enough," *D+C Development and Cooperation,* no. 1, January/February 2001.

Zeller, Manfred, Cécile Lapenu, and Martin Greeley. "Social Performance Indicators Initiative (SPI): Final Report," 2003. http://www.cerise-microfinance.org/publication/pdf/impact/SPI-summary.pdf.

Interviews

Mostaq Ahmmed, director, training, and technical support, PlaNet Finance, April 2005.

Leslie Barcus, president, The Microfinance Management Institute, Microfinance Management Institute (MFMI), March 2005.

Eduardo Bazoberry, president and CEO, Prodem, July 2005.

Renée Chao-Béroff, research director, Centre International de Développement et de Recherche, April 2005.

Robert Peck Christen, president of the Boulder Institute of Microfinance Training for Sustainable Development, April and May 2005.

Mark Crawford, chief financial officer, Opportunity Bank, Montenegro, April 2005.

Tiphaine Crenn, microfinance analyst, CGAP, April 2005.

Robert Dressen, group vice president, Economics, Business, and Finance, Development Alternatives, Inc., March 2005.

Equity Bank internal management report, 2004.

Cesar Fernández Fernández, marketing director, Mibanco, January 2005.

Clara Fosu, business development manager, GHAMFIN, March 31, 2005.

Adrian Gonzalez, research analyst, CGAP/The MIX, July 2005.

Syed Hashemi, senior microfinance specialist, CGAP, February 2005.

Senada Havic, general manager, Long-Range Company, Bosnia and Herzegovina, March 25, 2005.

Julio C. Herbas Gutierrez, manager, Banco Solidario, S.A., April 2004.

Alfonso Higueras, commercial manager, Infocom, April 2005.

Iftekhar Hossain, consultant, February 2005.

Jennifer Isern, lead microfinance specialist, CGAP, July 2005.

Gautam Ivatury, microfinance specialist, CGAP, July 2005

Richard Ketley, director, Genesis Analytics, September 2005.

Carlos Labarthe, co-executive director, Compartamos, April 2005.

Michael McCord, microinsurance expert, February 2005.

Cheryl Neas, manager, Policy, National Community Capital Association, April 2005.

Katarzyna Pawlak, deputy director and research manager, Microfinance Centre for Central and Eastern Europe the Newly Independent States, June 2005.

Gonzalo Paz, consultant, March 2005.

Juan Carlos P. Peñafiel S., chief, Emigrant Products, Banco Solidario, January 2005.

Marguerite Robinson, independent consultant, May 2005.

Thomas Schuppius, program advisor, German Agency for Technical Cooperation/Sida Financial Systems Development Programme, Bank of Uganda, March 2005.

Enrique Soruco, general manager, Fondo Financiero Privado para el Fomento a Iniciativas Economicas, Bolivia, April 2005.

Web sites

ACCION International, www.accion.org, April and July 2005.

Banco Solidario, www.banco-solidario.com, January 2005.

Bankakademie International, www.international.bankakademie.de, June 2005.

BANKSCOPE, www.bankscope.bvdep.com, July 2005.

CARE USA, www.careusa.org, May 2005.

Cellular Online, www.cellular.co.za, June 2005.

Citigroup Foundation, www.citigroup.com/citigroup/corporate/foundation, June 2005.

Comité d'Echange, de Réflexion et d'Information sur les Systèmes d'Epargne-Crédit (CERISE), www.cerise-microfinance.org, June 2005.

Consultative Group to Assist the Poor, www.cgap.org, July 2005.

FINCA International, www.villagebanking.org, May 2005.

Finextra, www.finextra.com, June 2005.

Fondo Financiero Privado, www.ffpfie.com, April 2005.

Fondo Financiero Privado PRODEM, www.prodemffp.com, July 2005.

Global Development Research Center, www.gdrc.org/icm/finca/finca-1.html, May 2005.

ICICI Bank, www.icicbank.com, June 2005.

Institute of Development Studies, www.ids.ac.uk/impact/, June 2005.

Internet World Stats, www.internetworldstats.com/stats.htm, July 2005.

Kenya Post Office Savings Bank, www.postbank.co.ke, July 2005.

Micro Finance Regulatory Council, www.mfrc.co.za.

MicroBanking Bulletin, www.mixmbb.org, July 2005.

Microenterprise Access to Banking Services, www.rbapmabs.org, April 2005.

Microfinance Gateway, www.microfinancegateway.org, February, March, and June 2005.

Microfinance Information eXchange, www.themix.org, April 2005.

MicroFinance Network, www.mfnetwork.org, June 2005.

MIX Market, www.mixmarket.org, March–July 2005.

National Bank for Agriculture and Rural Development, www.nabard.org, April 2005.

Opportunity International, www.opportunity.org, April 2005.

Self-Employed Women's Association Bank, www.sewabank.org, July 2005.

Share Microfin Limited, www.sharemicrofin.com, March 2005.

Southern New Hampshire University, www.snhu.edu, June 2005.

Superintendencia de Bancos, República de Panamá, General Resolution No. 3-2000, www.superbancos.gob.pa.

Superintendencia de Bancos y Entidades Financieras Bolivia, www.sbef.gov.bo, July 2005.

USAID Microenterprise Development, www.usaidmicro.org/componen/aims/activities/tools.asp, June 2005.

World Council of Credit Unions, Inc., www.woccu.org, July 2005.

Index

A

Accident insurance, 28
ACCION International, 3, 4, 52, 108, 130, 135
Accumulating savings and credit associations, 39–40
ACEP. *See* Agence de Credit pour l'Entreprise Privée
ACLEDA. *See* Association of Cambodian Local Economic Development Agencies
Afghanistan
  payments systems, 63
Africa
  Banking Association South Africa, 72
  cell phone-based banking services, 55
  Faulu Kenya, 107–108
  financial cooperatives, 42
  Financial Sector Charter, 90
  financial service associations, 41
  Micro Finance Regulatory Council, 134
  microfinance characteristics, 10, 12
  specialized microfinance regulation and supervision, 88
Ag Bank. *See* Agricultural Bank of Mongolia
Agence de Credit pour l'Entreprise Privée, 43
Agribusiness lenders, 38
Agricultural Bank of Mongolia, 50
Agricultural finance
  agricultural banks, 49–50
  agricultural credit, 4
  agricultural insurance, 28
  challenges for financial service providers, 124–125
  farmers' cooperatives, 3, 4
  strategies for providing financial services, 125–127
  types of providers, 123–124
Aid effectiveness, 98

AIG, 28, 51
AIMS Tools, 132
AlSol. *See* Alternativa Solidaria
Alternativa Solidaria, 48
AML regulations. *See* Anti-money laundering regulations
Anti-money laundering regulations, 81
Apex Bank, 26
Apex funds, 79–80, 96
Argidius, 94
ARPANET, 145
ASCAs. *See* Accumulating savings and credit associations
Asia
  credit unions, 42
  microfinance characteristics, 8, 11
Asian Development Bank, 94–95
Association of Cambodian Local Economic Development Agencies, 105, 106, 139
Associations, 60, 71–73
ATMs. *See* Automatic teller machines
Automatic teller machines, 115–117

B

BAAC. *See* Bank for Agriculture and Agricultural Cooperatives
Banco do Nordeste, 78
Banco Solidario, 52
BancoSol, 52, 85, 107, 108
Bangladesh
  Delta Life, 51
  education patterns, 31
  lottery ROSCAs, 39
  microfinance clients, 19, 21
  pension savings accounts, 25

Bangladesh Rural Advancement Committee
Income Generation for Vulnerable Groups
Development, 30, 32
Bank for Agriculture and Agricultural
Cooperatives, 126
Bank Kredit Desas, 87
Bank of International Settlements, 81
Bank Rakayat Indonesia, 4, 24–25, 31, 50, 78,
82
Bankakademie International, 70
Banking Association South Africa, 72
Banking sector regulation, 85–89
Banking Superintendency, 88
BASIX, 97
Benchmarking, 64
Bilateral donors, 94
Biometrics, 115–116
BKDs. *See* Bank Kredit Desas
Blacklists, 67
BN. *See* Banco do Nordeste
Bolivia
access to second-tier funding, 80
ATM technology, 116
BancoSol, 52, 85, 107, 108
Fondo Financiero Privado para el Fomento
a Iniciativas Económicas, 46
health status of microfinance clients, 31
microfinance clients, 21
Private Financial Funds, 51
specialized microfinance regulation and
supervision, 88
Bosnia
Long Range Company, 67
Prizma, 131
BPRs. *See* People's Credit Banks
BRAC. *See* Bangladesh Rural Advancement
Committee
Brazil
Banco do Nordeste, 78
Caixa Economica, 55
financial services franchises, 13
BRI. *See* Bank Rakayat Indonesia
Building Inclusive Financial Systems:
Donor Guidelines on Good Practice in
Microfinance, 96–97
BURO, Tangail, 19
Business associations, 60, 71–73

C

Caisses d'Epargne et de Crédit Agricole
Mutuels, 127
Caisses Villageoises d'Épargne et de Crédit
Autogérées, 41
Caixa Bank, 13
Caixa Economica, 55
Calmeadow Foundation, 52

Cambodia
Association of Cambodian Local Economic
Development Agencies, 105, 106, 139
Capitec, 55
CARD Bank, 47
CARE International, 48
CECAM. *See* Caisses d'Épargne et de Crédit
Agricole Mutuels
Cell phone-based banking services, 55
Center for Institutional Reform and the Infor-
mal Sector, 43
Central Asia
credit unions, 42
microfinance characteristics, 11
Central Bank, 63, 88
Centrales Privadas de Información de Riesgos,
69
Centre International de Développement et de
Recherche, 41–42
CEPIRS. *See* Centrales Privadas de Información
de Riesgos
CERISE. *See* Comité d'Echange, de Réflexion
et d'Information sur les Systèmes d'É-
pargne-Crédit
CFT. *See* Combating the financing of terrorism
CGAP. *See* Consultative Group to Assist the
Poor
Children
impact of financial services access, 31
Chit funds, 39
CIDR. *See* Centre International de
Développement et de Recherche
Client targeting, 21
Clients of financial systems, 13–14. *See also*
Poor and low-income clients
CMS. *See* Cooperative and Mutual Solutions
Collateral
nontraditional forms, 23
Collective clubs, 39–40
Colombia
La Equidad, 51
microfinance clients, 19
microfinance committee, 72
Women's World Banking, 107
COLUMNA, 28
Combating the financing of terrorism, 81
Comité d'Echange, de Réflexion et
d'Information sur les Systèmes
d'Épargne-Crédit, 129
Commercial banks, 50–55
Commercialization, 45–47
Community banks, 50–51
Community development funds, 96
Community Reinvestment Act, 90
Compartamos, 51–52, 107
Complaints, 134

Computerization levels, 65
Consultative Group to Assist the Poor
    CGAP Skills for Microfinance Managers, 70
    key principles of microfinance, xi–xii
    Poverty Assessment Tool, 20, 43, 130
    Poverty Audit Toolkit, 129
    Pro-Poor Innovation Challenge, 48
    purpose of, 1
    web site, 1n
Consumer Credit bill, 72
Consumer education, 135
Consumer protection, 133–136
Cooperative and Mutual Solutions, 43
Counterterrorism regulation, 81
CRA. *See* Community Reinvestment Act
CRECER. *See* Credito con Educación Rural
Credit
    credit lines, 96
    government involvement in credit delivery,
        76–80
    for poor and low-income clients, 23–24
Credit bureaus, 67–68, 69
Credit components, 96
Credit life insurance, 27–28
Credit scoring, 115
Credit unions, 42
CreditAmigo, 78
Credito con Educación Rural, 31
CVECAs. *See* Caisses Villageoises d'Épargne et
    de Crédit Autogérées

D
Delta Life, 51
Deposit collectors, 38
Destitute households, 20, 21, 30
Development banks, 49–50
Development Credit Authority, 108
Direct credit delivery, 76–79
Disclosure laws, 133
Domestic funding markets, 104–109

E
East Africa
    accident insurance, 28
Eastern Europe
    microfinance characteristics, 11
Ecuador
    Banco Solidario, 52
Education
    impact of financial services access, 31
EFTs. *See* Electronic fund transfers
Electronic fund transfers, 62
Emergency needs, 22
Endowment policies, 28
Equity Bank, 22–23
Esusu, 39

Europe
    microfinance characteristics, 11
European Commission, 95
External audits, 64, 65–66
Extreme poor households, 18, 20, 21

F
FAMA. *See* Fundación para el Apoyo a la
    Microempresa
Farmers' cooperatives, 3, 4. *See also*
    Agricultural finance
Faulu Kenya, 107–108
FENACOAC. *See* National Federation of
    Credit Unions, Guatemala
FENAGIE-PECHE, 43
FFP-FIE. *See* Fondo Financiero Privado para el
    Fomento a Iniciativas
    Económicas
FFPs. *See* Private financial funds
FIE. *See* Fomento a Iniciativas Económicas
Financial cooperatives, 42–44
Financial infrastructure, 59–60
Financial service associations, 41
Financial service providers
    macro, 14, 75–92
    meso, 14, 59–74
    micro, 14, 35–57
Financial services
    impact on poor and low-income clients,
        29–32
Financial systems framework. *See* Inclusive
    financial systems framework
Financial transparency, 59–60, 62–68
FINCA. *See* Foundation for International
    Community Assistance
Foccas, 31
Fomento a Iniciativas Económicas, 46
Fondo Financiero Privado para el Fomento a
    Iniciativas Económicas, 46
Ford Foundation, 94, 97, 132
Foreign exchange risk, 103
Formal financial service providers, 35–36,
    49–55
Forward contracts, 103
Foundation for International Community As-
    sistance, 48, 51
Foundations, 94
Freedom from Hunger, 30
FSAs. *See* Financial service associations
Fundación Mario Santo Domingo, 19
Fundación para el Apoyo a la Micro-
    empresa, 62
Funding options
    aid effectiveness, 98
    alternative funding instruments, 110–111
    domestic funding markets, 104–109

guaranteed loans, 108
international donor agencies, 94–99
international investors, 99–103
motivating factors for seeking foreign
     investment, 105
types of funders, 93–94

G
G8. *See* Group of Eight
Georgia
     ProCredit Bank, 52
GHAMFIN. *See* Ghanaian Microfinance
     Institutions Network
Ghana
     Freedom from Hunger, 30
     money transfers, 26
     poverty outreach, 43
     rural and community banks, 50–51
Ghanaian Microfinance Institutions Network,
     72
Global Reporting Initiative, 132
Government-owned banks, 49–50
Government payments, 90–91
Governments
     involvement in credit delivery, 76–80
     policy environment, 80–89
     proactive government promotion, 89–91
     role in financial systems, 75–76
Grameen Bank, 3, 4, 24, 25, 31
GRI. *See* Global Reporting Initiative
Group-based joint liability, 23
Group of Eight, 13, 75
Guaranteed loans, 108
Guatemala
     savings life insurance, 28

H
Hawala system, 63
Health insurance, 29
Health status
     impact of financial services access, 31
Herzegovina
     Long Range Company, 67
High-risk groups, 47
Home improvement loans, 24

I
ICICI Bank, 13, 53–54
IDAs. *See* Individual Development Accounts
IFAD. *See* International Fund for
     Agricultural Development
IFIs. *See* International financial institutions
IGVGD. *See* Income Generation for Vulnerable
     Groups Development
IJM. *See* International Justice Mission
Imp-Act project, 132

Inclusive financial systems framework
     challenges for, 113–138
     clients, 13–14
     macro, 14, 75–92
     meso, 14, 59–74
     micro, 14, 35–57
Income Generation for Vulnerable Groups
     Development, 30, 32
India
     ICICI Bank, 13, 53–54
     Integrated Rural Development Programme,
        77
     Mahindra Shubhlabh, 126
     Self-Employed Women's Association Bank,
        3, 4, 31, 51
     self-help groups, 40–41
     Share, 51–52
     Society for Helping Awakening Rural Poor
        through Education, 30
Indirect credit delivery, 79–80
Individual Development Accounts, 91
Individual informal providers, 37–38
Indonesia
     Bank Rakayat Indonesia, 4, 24–25, 31, 50,
        78, 82
     impact of financial services, 30, 31
     macroeconomic crisis, 82
     People's Credit Banks, 2
Inflation, 81–82
Informal financial service providers, 35–36,
     37–40
Information infrastructure, 62–68
Information systems, 64, 65, 115
Initial-investment ASCAs, 39
Input suppliers, 37–38
Insurance. *See* Microinsurance
Integrated Rural Development Programme, 77
Inter-American Development Bank, 94–95
Interest rate ceilings, 82–85
Internal controls, 64
International donor agencies, 94–99
International financial institutions, 99–101
International Fund for Agricultural Develop-
     ment, 94
International investors, 99–103
International Justice Mission, 48
International Remittance Network, 122
Internet banking, 115
Internet kiosks, 13, 53
Investment opportunity financing, 22
IRDP. *See* Integrated Rural Development Pro-
     gramme
IRIS. *See* Center for Institutional Reform and
     the Informal Sector
Irish Loan Fund, 2, 3
IRnet. *See* International Remittance
     Network

K

Kenya
  Equity Bank, 22–23
  microfinance clients, 19
  Savings and Credit Societies, 42
Kenya Post Office Savings Bank, 122
Kibati, 39
KMB Bank, 52
KPOSB. *See* Kenya Post Office Savings Bank
Kreditni Biro, 67

L

La Equidad, 51
Latin America
  macroeconomic crisis, 82
  microfinance characteristics, 9
Latin America Bridge Fund, 108
LCRF. *See* Local Currency Risk Fund
Liberalized interest rates, 82–85
Life-cycle events, 22
Life insurance, 27–28
Loan repayments, 23–24
Loans
  by institutional type, 37
Local Currency Risk Fund, 102
Long Range Company, 67
Lottery kiosks, 55
Lottery ROSCAs, 39
Low-income clients. *See* Poor and
      low-income clients
LRC. *See* Long Range Company

M

Macro financial systems
  government involvement in credit
      delivery, 76–80
  overview, 14
  policy environment, 80–89
  proactive government promotion, 89–91
  role of government, 75–76
Macroeconomic stability, 81–82
Madagascar
  CECAM, 127
Magstripe cards, 115
Mahindra Shubhlabh, 126
Mali
  microfinance association, 72
Management information systems, 64
Mata Masu Dubara, 48
Matching deposits, 91
MDI law, 88
Member-based financial service providers,
      35–36, 40–44
Merry-go-rounds, 19, 39
Meso financial systems
  associations, 60, 71–73

information infrastructure, 62–68
infrastructure, 59–60
networks, 60, 71–73
overview, 14
payments systems, 61–62, 63
technical support services, 59–60
training, 68–70
transparency, 59–60, 62–68
Mexican Bankers Association, 72
Mexico
  Alternativa Solidaria, 48
  Compartamos, 51–52, 107
  savings patterns, 26
MFIs. *See* Microfinance institutions
MFMI. *See* Microfinance Management
      Institute
MFN. *See* MicroFinance Network
MFRC. *See* Micro Finance Regulatory Council
Mibanco, 24, 107
Micasa, 24
Micro Finance Regulatory Council, 72, 134
Micro financial systems
  commercial bank involvement in services
      for the poor, 54
  formal financial institutions, 49–56
  informal providers, 37–40
  member-based organizations, 40–44
  nongovernmental organizations, 44–49
  overview, 14
  relative profitability, 53
  strengths and weaknesses of, 57
  types of, 35–37
  unconventional distribution channels, 55
MicroBanking Bulletin, 129–130
Microcredit
  development of, 3
  impact on poor and low-income clients,
      29–32
Microcredit Summit, 20, 45
Microenterprise credit, 22–24
Microenterprise Development Institute, 70
Microfinance
  accounts by region, 6
  in Asia, 8
  in Central Asia, 11
  challenges for, 5, 113–138
  characteristics of clients, 18–21
  combined loans and savings accounts, 7
  defined, 1
  in Eastern Europe, 11
  features of, 17
  goals for, 139–144
  history of, 2–5
  impact of, 31–33
  inclusive financial systems framework, 13–15
  key principles of, xi–xii

in Latin America, 9
in Middle East, 12
in North Africa, 12
in sub-Saharan Africa, 10
Microfinance-deposit-taking institutions, 88
Microfinance Information eXchange, 72,
    129–130, v
Microfinance institutions
    interest payments to, 4
    loans by institutional type, 36–37
Microfinance Management Institute, 70
MicroFinance Network, 135
Microfinance Training Institute, 70
Microinsurance
    for poor and low-income clients, 27–29
    providers, 51
Middle East
    microfinance characteristics, 12
Millennium Development Goals, 31
MIS. See Management information systems
Mission drift, 46–47
MIX. See Microfinance Information eXchange
MIX Market, 45, 47
Mixmonitor, 72
MMDs, 48
Mobile phone messaging, 115–116
Moderate poor households, 18, 20, 21
Money exchange dealers, 63
Money laundering, 81
Money transfers
    alliances between financial service providers
        and money transfer
        companies, 122
    costs of, 120–123
    flow of, 119–120
    informal systems, 120–121
    for poor and low-income clients, 26–27
    safety of, 121
Moneylenders, 37–38
Mongolia
    Ag Bank, 50
MSSL. See Mahindra Shubhlabh
Multilateral development banks/organiza-
    tions, 94

N

NABARD. See National Bank for
    Agriculture and Rural Development
National Bank for Agriculture and
    Rural Development, 41
National Federation of Credit Unions,
    Guatemala, 28
National Microfinance Bank, 50
NBFIs. See Nonbank financial institutions
Nepal
    microfinance clients, 20

Pact's WORTH model, 48
Women's Empowerment Program, 31
Network connections, 115
Networks, 60, 71–73
NGOs. See Nongovernmental organizations
Nicaragua
    Fundación para el Apoyo a la
        Microempresa, 62
    impact of interest rate ceilings, 84–85
Niger
    CARE's MMD project, 48
Nirdhan Uttan Bank Ltd., 20
NMB. See National Microfinance Bank
Nonbank financial institutions, 36, 50–55
Nongovernmental organizations, 35–36, 44–49
North Africa
    microfinance characteristics, 12

O

OBM. See Opportunity Bank Montenegro
Oikocredit, 102
Open Society Institute, 94
Opportunity Bank Montenegro, 46
Opportunity Card, 122
OSI. See Open Society Institute

P

Pact, 48
Pali Karma Sahayak Foundation, 80
PAME-CAS. See Programme d'Appui aux
    Mutuelles d'Épargne et de Crédit au
    Sénégal
PARMEC Law, 88
PAT. See Poverty Assessment Tool
Pawn shops, 3
Pawnbrokers, 37–38
Payments systems, 61–62, 63
PDAs. See Personal digital assistants
Pension savings accounts, 25
People's Credit Banks, 2
Performance measurement, 64
Performance standards, 64
Personal accident insurance, 28
Personal digital assistants, 115
Peru
    credit bureaus, 69
    home improvement loan, 24
    Mibanco, 107
    poverty outreach, 43
Philippines
    CARD Bank, 47
    initial-investment ASCAs, 39
    microfinance clients, 21
    rural and community banks, 51
PKSF. See Pali Karma Sahayak Foundation
PlaNet University, 70

Policy environment, 80–89
Poor and low-income clients
    characteristics of microfinance clients,
        18–21
    consumer protection, 133–136
    credit, 23–24
    events requiring extra money, 22
    features of microfinance, 17
    impact of financial services, 29–32
    loan repayments, 23–24
    microinsurance, 27–29
    money transfers, 26–27
    savings, 24–26
    services required, 22–23
    targeting, 21
    use of financial services, 22–29
Pope Leon X, 3
POS devices, 115
Post Office Card Accounts, 91
Postal banks, 49–50
Poverty and Impact Scorecard, 131
Poverty Assessment Tool, 20, 43, 130
Poverty Audit Toolkit, 129
Poverty levels, 18, 20
Priority sector lending, 89–90
Private commercial banks, 50–55
Private financial funds, 46, 51, 88, 116
Prizma, 131
Pro-Consumer Pledge, 135
Pro-Poor Innovation Challenge, 48
Proactive government promotion, 89–91
Processors, 37–38
ProCredit Bank, 52, 107
Prodem, 52, 116
Programme d'Appui aux Mutuelles d'Épargne
    et de Crédit au Sénégal, 43
Property insurance, 28
Providers. See Financial service providers
Prudential regulation, 85–86

R
Raiffeisen, Friedrich Wilhelm, 3
Rating Fund, 66–67
Ratings, 64, 66–67
Real-time gross settlement systems, 62
Registries, 67–68
Regulatory incentives, 90
Remittances
    defined, 26
Revolving funds, 96
Risk protection, 27–29
ROSCAs. See Rotating savings and
    credit associations
Rotating savings and credit associations, 39–40
RTGS. See Real-time gross settlement
    systems

Rural banks, 50–51
Rural finance
    challenges for financial service providers,
        124–125
    strategies for providing financial services,
        125–127
    types of providers, 123–124
Russia
    KMB Bank, 52
Rutherford, Stuart, 22
Rwanda
    savings patterns, 25

S
SACCOs. See Savings and Credit Societies
SATMs. See Smart automatic teller machines
Savings
    for poor and low-income clients, 24–26
    savings accounts by institutional type, 37
Savings and Agricultural Credit Cooperative
    Societies, 127
Savings and credit cooperatives, 42
Savings and Credit Societies, 42
Savings banks, 49–50
Savings collectors, 37–38
Savings life insurance, 28
Second-tier funding, 79–80, 96
SEEP. See Small Enterprise Education and
    Promotion Network
Self-Employed Women's Association Bank, 3,
    4, 31, 51
Self-help groups, 40–41
Self-Managed Village Savings and Credit
    Banks, 41
Senegal
    poverty outreach, 43
Service providers. See Financial service
    providers
SEWA. See Self-Employed Women's Association
    Bank
SHARE. See Society for Helping Awakening
    Rural Poor through Education
Share, 51–52
SHGs. See Self-help groups
Small Enterprise Education and Promotion
    Network, 71, 136
Smart automatic teller machines, 116
Smart cards, 115
Social performance, 128–133
Social Performance Indicators Initiative, 129
Society for Helping Awakening Rural Poor
    through Education, 30
South Africa
    Banking Association South Africa, 72
    Capitec, 55
    Financial Sector Charter, 90

Micro Finance Regulatory Council, 134
Special Life Plan, 28
State Bank of India, 41
Sub-Saharan Africa
microfinance characteristics, 10
Supervisory bodies, 64
Supervisory practices, 85–89
Support services, 59–60
Sustainability, 45, 56
Swaps, 103
Swift, Jonathan, 3

T
Tandas, 26, 39
Tanzania
National Microfinance Bank, 50
UMASIDA, 51
Targeting, 21
Technical support services, 59–60
Technical training services, 68–70
Technology-enabled services, 114–118
Technology map, 114
Term life insurance, 28
Terrorism funding, 81
Thailand
Bank for Agriculture and Agricultural
Cooperatives, 126
The Poor and Their Money, 22
Traders, 37–38
Training services, 68–70
Transaction cost reduction, 114–118
Transformation, 46
Transparency, 59–60, 62–68
Triodos Bank, 102, 132
Truth-in-lending laws, 133

U
Uganda
education patterns, 31
health status of microfinance clients, 31
microfinance clients, 21
payments systems, 63
savings patterns, 25
specialized microfinance regulation and supervision, 88
Ukraine
ProCredit Bank, 107
UMASIDA, 51

UNDP. *See* United Nations Development
Program
Unit Desas, 78
United Kingdom
universal banking services, 90–91
United Nations Development Program, 94
United States
Community Reinvestment Act, 90
Individual Development Accounts, 91
Universal banking services, 91
University of Maryland
Center for Institutional Reform and the
Informal Sector, 43
U.S. Agency for International Development,
21, 108, 132
USAID. *See* U.S. Agency for International
Development

V
Vulnerable non-poor households, 18, 20, 21

W
Web sites, 147–149, 162
West Africa
financial cooperatives, 42
specialized microfinance regulation and
supervision, 88
Western Union, 122
WOCCU. *See* World Council of Credit Unions
Women
credit for entrepreneurs, 3, 4
impact of financial services access, 31
Women on the Move program, 48
Women's Empowerment Program, 31
Women's World Banking, 107
World Bank, 94–95
World Council of Credit Unions, 122
WORTH model, 48
WWB. *See* Women's World Banking

Y
Yunus, Muhammad, 4

Z
Zurich International, 48